ISLANDS of MAINE

By Bill Caldwell

Collector's Special
Limited, Numbered
First Edition

by Bill Caldwell

ENJOYING MAINE   (1977)

MAINE MAGIC   (1979)

First edition June, 1981.
Second edition November, 1981. Printed in the United States of America
Fourth Printing, 1988, by the Knowlton & McLeary Co.,
Farmington, Maine 04938

Published by Guy Gannett Publishing Co.,
Portland, Maine, 04101

Library of Congress Catalog Card #81-81541

ISBN #0-930096-17-7

ISLANDS of MAINE
Where America really began

By Bill Caldwell

Guy Gannett Publishing Co.

Portland, Maine

ACKNOWLEDGEMENTS

For their expert assistance and patient courtesy in helping me gather historical material for this book, I'd like to express thanks to: The Maine State Archives, Samuel Silsby, Director; the Maine State Library Research staff; the Maine State Museum, Paul Rivaud, director; the Maine Historical Society; to town historical societies along the coast of Maine, especially to the Skidompha Library, Damariscotta; the Maine State Island Registry; the Marine Coast Heritage Trust; the Maine Maritime Museum at Bath; the Pierpont Morgan Library of New York.

I am particularly grateful to Spencer Apollonio, Commissioner of Marine Resources for his expert guidance on the chapters concerning the early fisheries and the men and boats of those days; to Mr. J. W. P. Frost of Eliot for checking the facts in the Isles of Shoals chapter; to Dr. Alta Ashley of Monhegan for her advice and help on the Monhegan chapter; to Mr. Robert Drake of Vinalhaven for his advice on the Fox Islands chapter; to Maine State archaeologist Bruce J. Bourke for his expert comment on the Early Indians and archaeological history in Chapter one; to Mr. Robert Snowman for copy reading the manuscript and proofs; to Mrs. Wroth Orrick for typing and indexing; to photographers Don Johnson and Tom Jones for their photos made from Steer Clear while on newspaper assignments with me; and most important of all to Barbara Caldwell for her help, advice and patience from start to finish.

Damariscotta

1980-1981

*In celebration of the Maine islands
and Maine island people who have given
safe anchorage to Steer Clear and much
happiness to all those who have sailed
in her.*

Front Cover painting:

*West Point, Prout's Neck
By Winslow Homer, 1900*

*Courtesy Sterling and Francine Clark
Art Institute, Williamstown, Mass.*

Back cover photos by:

Paul Knaul, Dover-Foxcroft, Maine

Cover design by:

Stewart Vreeland Agency, Yarmouth, Maine

Contents

1.

Island Beginnings:
Ice Age To Indians

Here among the islands of Maine is where America really began.

Long before there was a colony at Jamestown, long before the Pilgrims set foot on Plymouth, white men from England and Europe were sailing among the islands of Maine, exploring for a new route to Cathay, drawing charts of unmapped worlds, catching fish in quantities which astounded them, going ashore to cut timber for ships' stoves, filling water barrels from cold island streams, building work places and rough shelters on these island shores. These islands of Maine are the roots from which America grew.

For a full hundred years before the Mayflower raised a landfall in the New World, explorers and then fishermen from England, France, Spain, Portugal were familiar with Maine's islands. By the early 1600s as many as 300 foreign fishing vessels were working the waters off the Province of Maine. Maine seafood had a bigger share of the market in Europe in the early 1600s than it has today.

That brave and celebrated band of Pilgrims which steered its way toward religious freedom in 1620 was not sailing through uncharted waters, however often the history books say it. The way to North America, fraught with all the sea's perils though it was, had already been well charted.

Those charts, made by Cabot in 1497, by Verrazano in 1524, by Gomez in 1525, by Walker in 1580, by Gosnold in 1602, by Pring in 1603, by Champlain in 1604, by Weymouth in 1605, by Smith in 1614, all led to Maine. Maine had been their landfall and their discovery.

The constant traffic between Maine, England and Europe in small boats without instruments 400 years ago is almost incredible today. After the explorers came the treasure hunters, and after them, the commercial fishing boats. It was that everlastingly powerful magnet of money — fish — which made these waters the target of so much action, long before the dream of colonies or religious freedom spurred the famed founding fathers to Jamestown or Pilgrims to Pilgrim Rock. Small wonder therefore that the first white settlements of the roughest kind were begun in Maine by fishermen, drying and salting their catch on Maine islands; that the first European attempt at a colony was made downeast at St. Croix (or Douchet) Island in 1604; that Weymouth celebrated the first Protestant church service in George's Harbor in Muscongus Bay in 1605; that the first full-fledged attempt at establishing an English colony in North America was in Maine, the Popham colony of 1607.*

From the Isles of Shoals to beyond Mount Desert, the coast of Maine had been a busy, much frequented focus of exploration, fishing and fur trade, long before the Mayflower came to Plymouth. So well established were the outposts on Maine islands that when the Plymouth colony was on the brink of starvation in 1621, settlers came to Maine for food, and were freely given it by established settlers in fishing centers on Damariscove and Monhegan islands.

But the islands of Maine are far more than the historic roots where our nation really began, far more than unique and lovely jewels of the North American coast. These islands are special havens where man's spirit is renewed, where a human is dwarfed by nature and timelessness, and yet finds happy unison, instead of rivalry, with the universe.

Stand on a Maine island alone and feel the awesome glory of rock, soil, sky, sea. On a peacock day in summer, these islands, more than most places on earth, can give world-stained mankind the healing balm of natural peace. But the power of

---

* In 1585, the Lost Colony at Roanoke began. But within a year, it failed. Most of the 108 colonists, sponsored by Sir Walter Raleigh and led by Ralph Lane, were evacuated by Sir Francis Drake. The 15 men who stayed soon vanished, leaving no trail and no roots upon which America would grow.

the restless sea around you is immense: 200 billion tons of water move in and out of the downeast bays every day. In a storm, the force of gales and power of seas which beats upon the islands are terrifying. The only solace is the knowledge that millions of storms have done their worst and the rugged islands have survived.

Stand on a Maine island, surrounded by ocean, and you are actually standing atop a mountain, which many millions of years ago was part of the mainland continent.

On a Maine island, you are halfway between the equator and the north pole. You are 300 miles closer to Europe than any other part of the United States. You are south of London, south of Paris, on the same latitude as Madrid, Spain. When each new day dawns over America, here is where the sun's first rays strike. Dawn comes to the islands of Maine while darkness still hangs over most of the United States.

Beneath the ocean around your island there were once forests and open country where giant mastodons roamed. The great bays of Maine — Casco, Muscongus, Penobscot, Blue Hill, Frenchman's and Machias — were once sweeping valleys.

Then came the Ice Ages. Beginning about one million years ago, at four different times, all Maine was covered with ice thousands of feet thick, weighing many tons per acre. Four times these massive ice sheets advanced and retreated. Maine then looked much like the coast of Antarctica does today.

Only the final Ice Age has left a record still decipherable on our land. That last Ice Age began about 40,000 years ago. The ice rose thousands of feet higher than Cadillac mountain and towered above the Camden Hills. The final great but gradual meltdown began about 13,000 years ago. As the ice melted, the ocean rose and the land was drowned. The one-time valleys filled with ocean waters and became the great bays of Maine. The waters flooded as far up as Bingham on the Kennebec and Millinocket on the Penobscot. As the land drowned, only the highest hills and mountains still reached above the level of the flooding sea. These are the islands of Maine. Stand on an island, and you are standing on a mountain top.

As those massive glaciers moved, they tore the land asunder, ripped the ancient granite mountains, gashed the valleys. The result is the ragged coast, the deep bays, and the heavenly islands of Maine today. The glaciers scoured away all rem-

nants of previous human habitation. We know nothing, because we can find no traces at all of the people who lived here
before the meltdown of the last Ice Age.

After that last Ice Age, the first known people, the Paleo
Indians, came to the coast of Maine. They were a wandering,
stone age people, a race which moved vast distances, from
northern Mexico, up through the United States and into Canada, hunting the now extinct giant bisons, giant beavers, giant
sloths, mammoths and mastodons. A few traces of their presence here have been found and carbon-dated as being about
11,000 years old. Those traces are mostly the large, sharp
stone tips of spears, hollowed out so that long shafts could
be inserted into them for hunting the huge stone-age animals.

"The uniformity of their spear tips is almost unnerving,"
said state archaeologist Bruce J. Bourque. "There is little dis-
cernible difference between a spear tip made by the Paleo
Indians in Mexico and those found in Maine, except in the
kind of stone used."

The Paleos lived, roamed, hunted in Maine for 2,000 years,
or about five times longer than white men have been here.

As the climate warmed during those first 2,000 years after
the last Ice Age, the giant animals they hunted gradually
moved away and the Paleo people vanished 9,500 years ago.
There is a mystery about what people, if any, came to Maine
after the Paleos left. Archaeologists have found no traces of
human presence for the 2,000-year period after the Paleos
vanished.

The next archaeological finds are traces of the Early Archaic Indians, who were here about 8,000 years ago. Their
spear tips were smaller, indicating perhaps that the animals
they hunted were smaller, and that the giant beavers, bison
and mammoths once hunted by the Paleos had become extinct
due to the warming climate.

After the Early Archaic Indians, came the most fascinating
of all Maine's early people, the Red Paint people, who flourished here some 4,000 years ago. Archaeologists have given
them the name Red Paint people because of the ochre, stained
red and sometimes yellow, which they put into their graves.
Close to fifty large gravesites of the Red Paint people have
been found in Maine, often with scores of small, individual
graves in each burying ground. In every grave there was

red "paint," actually clay stained red with iron oxide. Scientists think the Red Paint people traveled regularly to Mount Katahdin to mine the red clay they revered so much, which abounds there. They surmise the red clay was put into each grave either to preserve the bodies or because it had a religious meaning. Maybe it was simply a decorative tradition of a skilled and artistic people.

Among those hunting stones and skinning knives found in the gravesites, archaeologists have also found many strangely large gouging chisels. These outsize chisels, say archaeologists, were probably used to make large dug-out canoes from tree trunks, canoes strong enough to use in the choppy ocean. Further indication that the Red Paint people were the first sea-going fishermen in Maine has been found near a Red Paint village on North Haven island. Diggers there uncovered skeletons of many codfish and swordfish. The swordfish skeletons indicate that the big fish could not have been caught in water less than 1,000 feet deep. To get out into water that deep would have required massive canoes gouged from large tree trunks. These Red Paint people, say archaeologists who have examined their well-made tools, were technically the most advanced race to inhabit Maine until the white men came 4,000 years later.

Few bones, skulls or skeletons of the Red Paint people have ever been found. The acidity of Maine soil apparently dissolved and disintegrated their skeletons as well as the bones of all earlier inhabitants. The earliest human skeletons found in Maine date back about 3,500 years, to the Susquehannas, successors to the Red Paint people. Almost complete skeletons of the Susquehannas were found in 1973 during a routine dig in sites of much later Indian villages. The name Susquehanna comes only from the fact that traces of this tribe were first found in the Susquehanna Valley, Pennsylvania. There is no known link between the Susquehannas and present-day Indian tribes in Maine.

After the Susquehannas disappeared, there is another thousand-year gap in the archaeological history of Maine's early inhabitants. About 2,500 years ago, shortly before the time of Christ, the Ceramic Group of Indians arrived here. The odd name derives from the fact that these were apparently the first people in Maine to make ceramics, or at least leave behind traces of their work in clay.

These Ceramic people were the first Maine inhabitants to to form year-round communities. They lived mostly inland, were farmers and planters of corn. But they also made birch bark canoes, in which most of the settlement would come down rivers in the summertime and camp on the islands. There they used canoes to fish and hunt seals. They would skin the seals, dry the hides for later use. They'd dry the fish too, for winter food. They were apparently a social people. For on various islands and along riverbanks, they left behind huge heaps of various shells. Near where I live by the Damariscotta River, there is a mammoth pile of ancient oyster shells which measures 45 million cubic feet, the greatest assembly of its kind on the entire earth. The supposition is that on their annual migrations up and down river according to the seasons, the Indians from scattered settlements would enjoy a huge reunion. Families from scattered settlements would meet for days of feasting at the same spot for thousands of years. Perhaps because oysters always grew in massive quantities in the same places, different races of Indians came to the same place to feast on them. The oyster shell heaps at Damariscotta are 31 feet deep in places. There are three distinct layers of shells, each separated by a thick layer of mold, indicating that 300 years or more passed between the ending of one layer of shells and the beginning of the next layer. Scientists say it takes about a hundred years for one inch of vegetable mold to accumulate. The most recent or top layer of mold over these oyster heaps is three and a half inches thick, which may indicate that this top layer began to form about the time the Wawenock Indians began to leave the Damariscotta region in the 1600s. In the second stratum of oyster shells traces of "red paint" (iron oxide) have been found, indicating the Red Paint people may have feasted on this same river bank 4,000 years ago. Below is another layer of mold, and then still a third layer of ancient oyster shells.

By the time white men set foot on the Maine islands, two principal Indian nations lived in Maine. Down east were the Micmacs, fierce and aggressive. In the rest of Maine were the Abnakis, a more peaceful nation, made up of many tribes, each of which kept mostly to its own territory. The tribes which lived closest to the coast were the Passamaquoddy and Penobscots and Wawenocks. These were the tribes the first white explorers and settlers met.

The records written by those early voyagers refer to the tribes as aborigines, savages, natives, as well as Indians. The words had different and nobler connotations then than they do now.

To get a better perspective on the kind of people these Indians were, I quote from detailed descriptions by the first white man who wrote about them.

Captain George Weymouth in his voyage of 1605 met very often with Indians on the islands. James Rosier, the journalist aboard Weymouth's vessel, reported:

"Their canoes are made without any iron, of the bark of a birch tree, strengthened within with ribs and hoops of oak, in so good fashion and with such ingenuous arts, that they are able to bear seven or eight persons, far exceeding any in the Indies."

The famed Old Town canoe, made in Maine today, and considered one of the best-designed canoes in the world, is patterned precisely after the Indian canoes about which Rosier wrote 375 years ago.

These Indians also made far larger, stronger canoes, capable of holding many more people at sea on a whale hunt. Rosier described the amazing feat of killing a whale from these canoes:

"One skill in special is their manner of killing the Whale, which they call Powdawe; they say how he bloweth up water and that he is 12 fathoms (72 feet) long and that they go in company with their King with a multitude of boats and strike him with a bone made in the shape of a harpoon iron, fastened to a rope, which they make great and strong from the bark of trees; with such rope and bone, they wear out the Whale; and when he is worn, then all their boats come about him, and as he riseth above the water, with their arrows they shoot him to death; when they have killed him and dragged him to shore, they call all their chief lordes together and sing a song of joy; divide the spoil and give to every man a share, which pieces they hang about their houses in profusion; and when they boil them, blow off the fat, put in their peaze and maize and eat."

The Indians must have been alarmed by the sight of strange vessels, disembarking strange white-skinned and bearded men on their islands. A natural reaction might have been to immediately fight them off.

But most of the first contacts were friendly. Rosier describes one:

"They gave us of their tobacco, which was excellent, as good as any we ever took, strong and of sweet taste ... They filled their pipes, which were made of the short claw of a lobster, which will hold ten of our pipes full. ... They signed to us that the leaf would grow a yard high with a leaf as broad as both their hands. . . . They likewise showed me a great piece of fish, whereof I tasted, and it was fat like porpoise; and another kind much like salmon."

The Indians who greeted the early explorers and later the English fishermen made fishing lines which greatly impressed the civilized professionals from across the Atlantic.

"Their fishing lines are so even, soft and smooth, they look more like silk than hemp, and are more cunningly wrought and of stronger material than the English lines."

These Indians left the islands before the storms of November came, and returned to their permanent settlements upriver, taking back seal hides and dried fish. One precious item they carried on all travels was fire. They placed a piece of smouldering punk between two halves of a large clamshell, and further protected its glow by enclosing it all in wet clay, leaving one hole for the air to get through and keep the punk burning. They also had fire strikers of flint and iron pyrites.

At their upriver settlements, the Indians planted corn and worked their gardens with hoes made from clamshells and stone-tipped sticks. They had a written language, made up of symbolic drawings. They recorded all important records with these symbols on the inside of birch bark, which served them well as a strong, durable paper.

The early Indian settlements were no slap-dash, haphazard collection of wigwams. Captain John Smith, in his voyages along the Maine coast in 1614, refers with admiration to the orderly plan of the Indian settlement at Norridgewock, near the Kennebec River close to where Skowhegan stands today.

A Jesuit priest described Norridgewock: "The cottages were distributed with an order very much like the houses in cities . . . although built of poles and bark, they were elegant and convenient." Each Indian settlement contained a council house 30 or 40 feet long. The wigwams were shaped like large beaver houses rather than in the tent shape of the prairie Indians. Each had a stove of stones, floors covered with colored and woven rushes, and the sides of the wigwams were decorated with ornaments and furs. A protective well-built wall of thick brush 12 or 15 feet high, enclosed each Indian settlement. Each settlement was locally governed by a head man and an advisory council. They were in turn, governed by the Bashaba or Great Chief.

Weymouth describes the dress and appearance of Headmen and Chiefs he met in 1605:

"They had newly painted their faces very deep, some all black, some red, with stripes of excellent blue over their upper lips, nose and chin. One of them wore a kind of coronet about his head, made very cunningly of a substance like stiff hair colored red. Others wore white feathered skins around their heads, jewels in their ears, and bracelets of little white round bone, fastened together with a leather string. They possess very good dyes, which they carry with them in bladders."

Another early explorer wrote that the Indian mothers "fashioned from corn husks queer little dolls for their children. These dolls were about six inches in length with long hair made from cornsilk."

The arts of the Indians swiftly declined after a generation of exposure to white traders. They soon lost the skill and the need to make graceful pottery, when for a few animal skins, which the Indians could get in a morning, they could obtain an indestructible brass kettle or iron axe from a white man. Knives and hatchets from Europe became their weapons, and later they got firearms. The only arts which lasted were those which English and European craftsmen could not match: the snowshoe, the moccasin, the birch bark canoe, the woven baskets.

In less than a hundred years, the first friendliness between whites and Indians had largely disappeared, replaced by warfare, scalpings, burnings. But these were never large-scale Indian attacks. In all of Maine in the 17th century there were probably fewer than 3,000 Indians, perhaps a third of whom were scattered along the entire coast. The biggest attacks on white settlements were probably made by fewer than one or two hundred Indians, often by far fewer. But the Indians took back most of Maine in the 1670s, except for a few holdouts in York County.

Sickness, brought over from England and Europe, killed more Indians than did warfare. The tribes weakened, diminished in numbers and abilities; many sided with the French and moved away to Canada. Today the Indians in Maine have dwindled to a thousand or so, concentrated on two reservations at Penobscot and Pleasant Point. These Indians in the 1970s sued for their lost lands and after eight years won a settlement. Their lawsuit had asked for the return of almost two-thirds of the state of Maine. They finally received $81.5 million and some 350,000 acres, the most land ever involved in settlement of an Indian land claim. The 500 Indians of the Penobscot nation who live on the reservation at Penobscot invested their $40.3 million. In the first quarter of 1981, they received $700,000 in interest. By June 1981, the landless tribe of Penobscot assumed title to some 150,000 acres of land.

Newest figures recently released by the Census Bureau indicate that as many as 4,000 Indians are now living in Maine. This is almost four times as many as reported in the previous census. The increase may be due to several facts: a better effort by census takers to count minorities; a greater pride in Indian blood, which leads to more people with some Indian blood to claim Indian nationality; and the advent of the new wealth to Maine's Indian tribes.

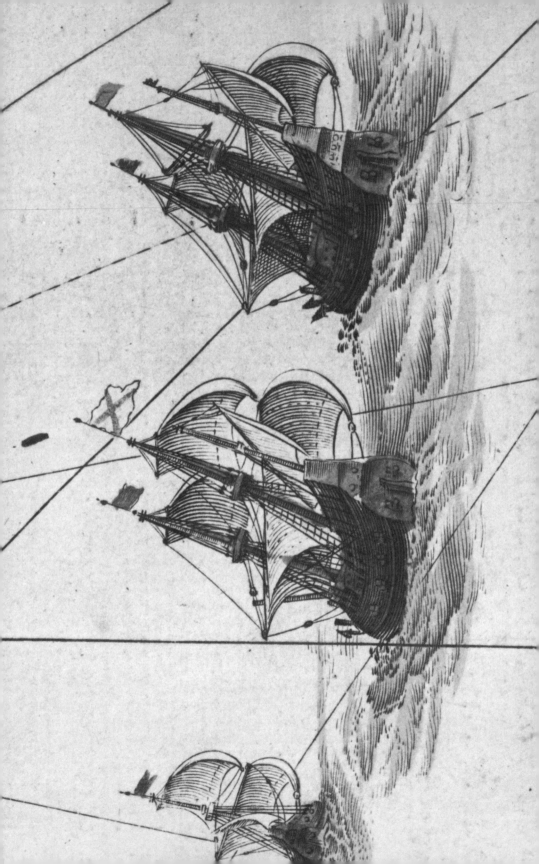

2.

Treasure Hunters:
The First Explorers Of Maine

There is a sweet hour in the days of summer, around four o'clock in the afternoon, when a cruising boat drops anchor in an island cove and prepares to spend the night. Behind are the adventures and the chores of a day's cruise; and now a peace comes with the tranquillity and stillness of evening.

Your anchor is down. The children, their mother and dog have rowed ashore, and are racing along the empty island beach, exploring, shouting, swimming, gathering driftwood for a picnic fire at the tidemark.

Now is the time to sit alone on the forward deck and let the visions creep in; to feel a mystic brotherhood across 1,000 years of history with the early voyagers to these islands of Maine.

The Vikings were probably the first white men to land on the islands of North America. They came in 1000 A.D., before William the Conqueror set invading foot on the shore of England. They came not from their homeland in distant Scandinavia, but from closer by, their outpost in Greenland, barely 400 miles from North America. They came not for territory, but for timber. Few trees grew in Greenland. They needed wood to build boats and houses. They came not in the romantic Viking ships of picture-story books, with high prows in the shape of dragons and sea monsters, with 20 men manning long-sweep oars and a helmeted Viking in breastplate on the bow, brandishing a sword as he leaped ashore.

Instead, the simpler truth is the first Vikings came in 54-foot sailing boats, 15 feet in the beam, clinker built of stout oak fastened with iron rivets. These boats had space for 30 people plus cargo holds for timber, and a pen for several head of cattle. We know this because several such vessels carbon dated to 1,000 A.D. were unearthed in 1969 in a Danish fjord. These Viking ships left us the name "starboard." On the right hand side of their stern was a steering board; and 1,000 years later we still call the right-hand side of our vessels "starboard."

The first Viking leader to explore North American shores was Leif Ericson, son of Eric the Red. They were tough men, both. Eric the Red had been banished from his homeland for killing a girl in a drunken brawl. With a band of followers, he sailed west, in exile, and discovered "Greenland." He gave it that enticing but misleading name to attract settlers. About 15 years after Eric the Red settled in Greenland, his teen-age son, Leif, sailed back to Norway. There he met King Olaf Tryggvason, was converted to Christianity and sailed back to Greenland.

One night at dinner a fellow-Norseman, Biarni Herilfson, captain of a trading ship, told young Leif Ericson that when he had been blown off course on his way to Greenland he had sighted another country. It was level and heavily wooded, far to the west of Greenland. But he had not landed there. The mention of woods excited Leif Ericson. Timber for boats and houses was lacking in Greenland. He assembled a crew, chartered Biarni's boat and sailed west. Leif Ericson and his 35 men found Newfoundland and took delight in the climate, warmer than Greenland. He marveled at the salmon-filled waters and his men harvested the wild berries from which they made wine. Remembering that his father, Eric the Red, had chosen the name Greenland to attract more settlers, Leif Ericson called his discovery "Vinland the Good," believing that mention of vines might entice thirsty wine drinkers to settle there.

In 1960, two Norwegian archaeologists located a spot in Newfoundland, L'Anse aux Meadows, which some believe is where Leif Ericson and his crew briefly settled. Sites of two great houses, similar to the Norse houses in Greenland, were excavated. The bigger one measured 70 feet long by 55 feet wide, had floors of clay, walls of turf and roofs of timber covered with sod, in true Nordic style.

One incident in the saga is too colorful to omit. When native Indians attacked the Viking settlement, a woman saved the day. Freydis, half sister to Leif, bared her breasts, slapped them with a sword and screamed like a fiend. She so alarmed the Indian attackers that they fled. So says the saga.

A different version of Leif Ericson's voyage also exists in legend. It says that he was repelled by the incessant fogs and raiding Indians of Newfoundland and sailed on to the south. Here he found what he was looking for; bigger stands of trees on Maine islands, together with rich fishing grounds. In this version, the Vikings encamped at Monhegan and Manana Islands and chiseled early Norse inscriptions on the rocks by the water springs. The same or later groups of Vikings supposedly sailed on to Pemaquid, the nearest mainland to the west. Some archaeologists claim that a recently uncovered, deeply buried piece of roadway at Pemaquid was built by these Vikings. Three more runic stones, at first claimed to be of Viking origin, were found at Phippsburg, a little west of Pemaquid. Later tests proved that these, like the Nordic inscriptions at Manana Island, were probably not authentic.

One sure bit of evidence that the Vikings were here 400 years before Christopher Columbus "discovered" North America, is a Viking coin of the 11th century, made of 25 percent silver and 75 percent copper, found in Blue Hill in Penobscot Bay in 1968. This has been authenticated through tests by Dr. Kolbjorn Skaare, coin expert at the University of Oslo. This Norse penny, dating to the reign of King Olaf Kyrre, 1067-1093, is the oldest European artifact ever found in the United States. How it got to Blue Hill Bay in Maine remains a mystery. No one knows whether the Vikings brought it there; or whether they had given it in trading with Indians in Newfoundland, and the Indians had carried it home to their ancient village near Blue Hill.

Some historians say that Viking boats continued making trips among the Maine islands for 200 years after Leif Ericson. If they did, these white-skinned, bearded strangers made strangely little impression. They are not mentioned in the legends and the myths of the Abnaki Indians, who were on these islands and this coast long before the Vikings came and long after they left. Maybe the Vikings voyaged among the Maine islands. Maybe they didn't.

There is no question that Italians were the first sailors to chart the islands of Maine. These ship captains were mercenaries who hired out to the kings and queens of England, France and Spain; the rulers who were hungry to seize the rich spice lands and gold and silver mines of the Orient. After the Ottoman Turks seized Constantinople, they slammed shut the gateway east to the East Indies and legendary Cathay. European rulers were determined to find a new way to reach those treasures of the orient through the "back door," by crossing the Atlantic and discovering a North American passage to the Pacific.

That is how an Italian from Venice, Giovanni Caboto, became the first man to claim Maine for England. John Cabot (he changed his name after moving to Bristol, England) hired out to Henry VII of England in 1497. Financed by the king, he sailed west in the track of the Vikings. His ship was only 50 tons, and was manned by a crew of only 17 men. Cabot made his landfall in Nova Scotia, then coasted down to Maine. His written reports to the king vividly describe the dark forests and the treacherous reefs and ledges which guarded the new country. King Henry, his mind filled with dreams of riches from China, was not excited by this mundane news. He abandoned the Cabot voyage of exploration in disappointment. But Cabot's written reports to the King of England became of vast future importance. The Cabot reports became the basis of England's claims to New England.

Twenty-five years later, in May, 1524, another Italian master mariner from Tuscany, Giovanni da Verrazano, (whose name now graces the spectacular bridge near Manhattan, the island he discovered) explored the Maine islands.

Verrazano was a well-seasoned expert when he hired out to the King of France. He had previously sailed to Carthage, Damascus, the Levant; was a friend of Magellan and a thoroughly experienced voyager. At age 38, he sailed to America from France in La Dauphine, a ship built for the French navy in 1519 and named in honor of Francois, heir to the throne of France. This ship was 100 tons, twice the size of John Cabot's. It carried a crew of 50, three times the number of Cabot's crew, and was loaded with provisions for eight months.

Verrazano made his destination clear in the will he wrote just before departure. His intent was to reach the east coast of Asia, and to find a new route to Cathay.

La Dauphine sailed January 17, 1524. Heavy storms during late February, forced Verrazano to alter course to the westward. On March 1 he made a landfall at Cape Fear in North Carolina. Along the Outer Banks of Carolina, Verrazano found an isthmus and thought that from his lookout he could see the Pacific Ocean, the sea which flows around the shores of India and China. He turned north, hoping to discover a passage through to the Pacific, so he could steer for the shores of Cathay. His mapmaker brother, Girolamo, drew his charts of North America that way. Consequently, for the next 100 years, maps of North America were circulated showing a narrow strait, something like the Panama Canal, through a pinched waist of North Carolina, with the Pacific Ocean on the other side.

All that March, blessed with fantastic luck and good weather, Verrazano sailed north, somehow missing the reefs and ledges around Hatteras which have sunk over 600 ships. On April 17 he sailed into New York Bay. He and his men were the first Europeans to sight what is now Manhattan, Staten Island and Brooklyn Heights.

From there, he sailed on again, heading east to Block Island. It reminded him of the Island of Rhodes, "filled with trees, full of hills, well peopled." With foul weather approaching, he took shelter and anchored in Narragansett Bay. That night Verrazano named a future state of the Union. He called Block Island, "Rhode Island." Piloted by friendly Wampanoag Indians in their canoes, La Dauphine sailed to deep shelter, and its crew spent two weeks in friendly visits with the tribe. This may account in part for the Indians' friendliness to the Pilgrims 100 years later.

By May 6, 1524, La Dauphine was under sail across Massachusetts Bay heading for the coast of Maine at Casco Bay. But here the Abnaki, though they looked like the Wampanoag Indians, were hostile. Verrazano described them as "being of such crudity and evil manners . . . that we could not converse with them even with signs." When the French crew came ashore in Casco Bay to trade, they were shot at with arrows and driven away. La Dauphine continued east. Finally, at an island described by Verrazano as at latitude 43 degrees, 40 minutes north, unfriendly Indians let down a basket from a high cliff and grudgingly traded a few items. The only places that tally with Verrazano's log are Seguin Island or Bald Head, at the tip of Cape Small, at the eastern entrance to Casco Bay. The behavior that most enraged the Frenchmen was the way the Indians liked to show their disdain: "by exhibiting bare buttocks and laughing immoderately at us." On their map, the Verrazano brothers called this part of Maine "The Land of Bad People"; and sailed on, heading east among the islands.

"In the space of 50 leagues, we counted some 32 islands, lying all near the land, being small and pleasant to the view, high, and having many turnings and windings among them, making many fair harbors and channels as they do in the gulf of Venice and Dalmatia," wrote Verrazano.

As we cruise today among these same islands, I like to think of this Italian-born captain, with a French crew, writing in his log for King Francois I of France, about his first sightings of the islands of Maine. That May of 1524, some 457 spring-times ago, were shadbushes in bright white bloom? Were porpoises playing? Were the wildflowers of May and the first green buds of summer bursting? When La Dauphine dropped anchor, did the crew row ashore and find mussels among the seaweed clinging to the island ledges? Did they dig fat clams at the low tide mark, or find lobsters under rocks close to shore? Were the small white clouds of spring scudding in a Maine blue sky? And where they walked on the land behind the shore, did those sailors revel too in the smell of spruce and sweet fern? Did they watch the gulls soar, and laugh at the quick-legged shore birds racing ahead of the wavelets as they hurriedly dug their sandy meals?

The three biggest, most beautiful Maine islands Verrazano saw, he named after the most beautiful princesses in the court of the king of France — the teen-age daughters of Catherine, Queen of Navarre. The islands were Monhegan, Isle au Haut and Mount Desert, still the greatest island landmarks on the coast.

On the Verrazano map another name appears, a name which soon would send a generation of treasure hunters to search the Maine coast. The name was "Oranbega," which in the Abnaki Indian language means a stretch of quiet water between two rapids. It describes the Penobscot River. It is the only Indian name on the Verrazano map. Soon after the map was in circulation in Europe, the name became altered to Norumbega, and was used to describe a larger region, a region supposedly filled with gold, silver, precious gems and containing a fabled city of enormous wealth.

Downeast fogs may have plagued Verrazano before he completed his island cruise, for he missed recording the Bay of Fundy and Nova Scotia and put into land which he plotted at 50 degrees latitude, presumably Funk Island, Newfoundland.

"Having spent all our naval stores and victuals, and having discovered 700 leagues (a league is equivalent to three miles) of new country, we topped off with water and wood and decided to return to France," wrote Verrazano.

La Dauphine made a fast passage on her return, and anchored in Dieppe two weeks later, on July 8, 1524. Verrazano reported personally to King Francis and was promised four more ships for a second voyage, which he never got. The bankers refused to invest more money in explorations of North America. However, Verrazano made two more transatlantic voyages. In 1526, he sailed to Brazil. And in 1528, he sailed to Florida, thence to the Bahamas and on to Guadeloupe. There, at age 42, he rowed ashore with his brother to meet the natives gathered on the beach, waving to them. Giovanni da Verrazano waded ashore. That proved to be a fateful decision. The Carib natives were cannibals. They killed the great sailor right on the beach, cut up and then ate his still quivering body. "To so miserable an end came this valiant gentleman," wrote Ramusio, chronicler and mapmaker of such voyages.

The next explorer-navigator was a Spaniard, Estaban Gomez, who was driven by dreams of finding gold and silver in Maine to match the treasures found earlier by Spain in Mexico and Peru. Empty-handed and disappointed by Maine, he sailed hastily away. But this sailor left his mark, which lasts until today. For Gomez and his crew chose to give names to Maine's bays and islands. When his boat put ashore at a lovely island far downeast he christened it Campo Bello. When he sailed through the bay with the highest tides in the world, he christened it Bahia Profundo, deep bay, the Bay of Fundy. And when sailing further west, he came upon another vast bay shaped like a helmet, he named it Bahia de Casco, Casco Bay.

Almost 50 years passed before the next treasure hunter sailed to the Maine islands from Europe. This time, 1597, it was a Portuguese, Simon Ferdinando, who hired out to England. He too found nothing here to line his pockets, and left. The magnet which brought these and other treasure-hunters to Maine was the fabled land of Norumbega, which supposedly was up the Penobscot River. Norumbega was the Wildcat oil or Klondike of its day. Norumbega was the dream of riches in profusion; the city where little children played with diamonds and pearls for toys; where cooking pots were made from silver, and the temples were of filigree gold; where the roofs of homes were gold leafed; where every woman and every man wore rubies and brilliant emeralds; where great palaces shone with silver walls and sparkled with "pyllars of cristol," and the gardens bloomed with everlasting artificial flowers with stems made from precious metals and blooms of priceless jewels.

It is easy to smile today at such wild and foolish dreams. But those were the days when the royal courts of Europe glowed with dreams of riches on distant continents. It was the age of exploration, discovery and wealth to be taken for the asking by men of courage who would dare to sail to far Cathay, the rich Indies, the Levant.

To minds and imaginations already ripe for such an adventure, the tales of Norumbega were believable. The powerful and the greedy were ready to listen spellbound to the greatest liar of his time, David Ingram.

Ingram was a member of an expedition to Mexico in 1568, led by the freebooting pirate Sir John Hawkins. Cast ashore in Mexico, David Ingram and two others started on one of the longest, most unlikely walks in American history. Ingram claimed he walked from Mexico to Maine. Finally he met a French vessel trading on the St. John River, and took passage home to Europe. Once home, David Ingram wrote a highly spiced adventure story of his journey. In his lively book he gave a lavish account of the incredible wealth of the city he had found: Norumbega. That glittering city became the pot of gold at the end of the rainbow in the new, undiscovered world of Maine.

Ingram was by no means the first traveler to bring home romantic tales of the New World. The Norumbega legend had been born earlier, with the inclusion of Oranbega on the map drawn in 1529 by Girolamo Verrazano. Then in 1539, the fabled wealth of Norumbega was played up in Ramusio's "Voyagos," a widely read book. When, in 1580, Sir Humphrey Gilbert, a highly respected figure in England, financed the voyage of John Walker, Gilbert hoped they'd find the fabled city and make him rich. Walker sailed into Penobscot Bay, where Norumbega was said to be. He planted the flag of Queen Elizabeth on shores near Camden, and claimed this region to be Norumbega. In his reports to Sir Humphrey,* seeking to please his sponsor, Walker sang not only the praises of Penobscot Islands, but also claimed to have seen mountains of silver. Indeed, Walker, and many after him, probably mistook the mica and quartz glinting from the island ledges, shining from Mt. Battie, to be silver.

Then, as today, men are apt to see what they dream of seeing.

The dream had substance enough to send brave and foolhardy men in small boats across the Atlantic. Even when dozens returned empty handed, the dream persisted. More men, hungry for easy fortunes, came to strike it rich in Maine. Such quests continued, as men after them have crossed mountains to hunt for California gold, and others have braved harsh lands, the Arctic, the North Sea, to hunt for oil.

But as the dream of easy fortune finally faded, more level headed voyagers found in the Maine islands a more reliable although much more mundane source of wealth: Fish.

Fish proved to be the real silver mines of Maine.

---

* Sir Humphrey Gilbert himself led four vessels in June 1583 to Newfoundland. He found 30 fishing vessels there and claimed possession in the name of Queen Elizabeth. On his return trip to England in September, aboard the tiny pinnace Squirrel, Sir Humphrey was lost at sea.

3.

Fish:
The Silver Mines Of Maine

The first roots of the United States are not in the soil of the mainland, but in the fishing grounds off the coast of Maine. Fishermen began this nation in rough, temporary settlements on the Maine islands, spreading down the coast from Newfoundland to the Isles of Shoals, off Kittery. Fish, in size and numbers not found in European waters, provided not only a reliable, steady food supply, but the first "cash crop" to the men who began this nation. America's earliest trading centers were fishing ports; and those were on the islands, stretching from St. Croix and Mt. Desert on through Monhegan, Damariscove, Richmond to the Isles of Shoals.

It was the pursuit of money more than the search for religious freedom which built the first rough trading posts and settlements. Yet the church had a finger in it. In Catholic Europe, the church calendar decreed more than 160 meatless — or fish-eating — days a year. Even in Protestant England, an Act of Parliament declared Wednesdays and Saturdays were meatless or fish-eating days. That was the law of the land. It was this demand for fish in Europe and in England which caused the seafaring rush to exploit the real silver mines of Maine — Fish.

For the early fishermen, Europe was a long sail home.

Fish caught by the English vessels had to be dried and preserved on shore for that trip to market. This led to the first rough settlements on the Maine islands.

Settlements also required boat-building and repairing. The first boat made by white men in North America was built on the banks of the Kennebec, near Popham, in 1607, the pinnace named Virginia. The need for timber led to the beginnings of lumbering in Maine. The English navy also urgently needed tall, strong trees for the masts of its new vessels. Cutting trees for these masts created the first big market for what has long been one of Maine's biggest industries — the lumber business.

For almost 400 years, the growth of fishing, boat building and lumbering went hand in hand. Boat-building and lumbering became the hallmark skills of Maine. Maine has led the world in building many different kinds of boats for many different uses: Boats to carry massive masts, for the lumbering trade; boats for the ice trade, the lime trade, the granite trade, each of which played great roles in Maine's development. Maine's shipyards built the fastest clipper ships for the wheat trade to England, Europe, Australia; which in turn brought expansion into world markets and prosperity to American agriculture. Then Maine boatyards again adapted their skills to a changing market and created huge four-, five- and six-masted schooners, the money-making ships which hauled larger cargoes with less sail and fewer in their crews than the fast, beautiful, pointed clipper ships.

These skills, born in the building of fish boats, were applied 170 years later in defending our fledgling young nation. Boatyards at Kittery built the first warships for the U.S. Navy at the time of the Revolution. From these yards on Badger's Island at Kittery came Kearsage and Ranger, skippered by John Paul Jones. Developing on from there, Maine contributed the first "ironsides" man o' war, the fastest and best of the World War II destroyers, submarines, sub chasers, on through to today's guided missile frigates at Bath Iron Works, the only yard in the nation regularly able to deliver warships ahead of schedule and under budget.

But fish and fishermen, almost 500 years ago, began it all on these Maine islands.

It was the abundance of fish, and the money that fishing earned, which lured hundreds of fishing boats across 3,000 miles of ocean to the uncharted but rich fishing grounds off the Maine islands.

Ship captains since Cabot and Gilbert wrote glowingly about the plentiful fishing here. Capt. John Smith, a man who had voyaged to most of the known world, wrote that he had never seen such good fishing anywhere as he did in Maine.

In his book "Description of New England," published in 1616, he wrote:

"In March, April, May and halfe June, heere is Cod in abundance; in May, June, July and August, Mullet and Sturgion, whoes Roes do make Caviare and Puttargo. Herring, if any desire them; I have taken many out of the bellies of Cod; but the Savages compare their store in the sea to the haires of their heads, so surely there are an incredible Abundance on this Coast. In the end of August, September, October and November, you have Cod againe; Hake you may have when the Cod fails in summer, if you will fish the night, which is better than Cod. Now each hundred fish you take here (in Maine) is as good as two or three hundred in Newfoundland."

Another who shouted the praises of fishing here was Thomas Morton, who wrote in 1632 in his book "New England Canaan":

"This Coast aboundeth with such multitudes of Codd that the inhabitants of New England doe dung their ground with Codd; and it is a commodity better than the golden mines of the Spanish Indies; for without dried Codd the Spaniard, Portugal and Italian would not be able to vittel a ship for the Sea."

And so by the hundreds, the early fishing boats came to the "silver mines of Maine." Money — the demand of the market-place in the early 1600s — was what caused men to risk their lives and ships in the rough, cold, foggy waters of fishing grounds, 3,000 miles from home. The market was assured in fish-eating Catholic Europe.

Fish-eating was so ingrained a habit that consumption was higher even than the law demanded. For example, according to the ship's stores stocked by Frobisher for his North American voyage of 1578, the crew ate fish 14 days a month. By comparison today, the average American eats only 12 pounds of fish in an entire year.

Europe's demand for fish from New England has not changed through the centuries. In 1975, just as in 1475, 500 years before, foreign fishing fleets were reaping the sea harvest off our shores.

In the 1400s, ships from the Hanseatic League were working as a cartel-combine. Banded together in a self-protective association, merchants and bankers from 60 cities in the Germanic states tried to monopolize foreign trade. They financed fishing trips to the fishing banks off Maine where Vikings had fished before them. As the grip of the Hanseatic League was weakened, a few tough sailors from Cornwall and Devon began fishing off Maine in the 1480s. By the 1580s, a fishing boom was in full swing. Captains of fishing boats from England, Spain, Italy, Portugal, France, had heard the news of huge catches along the banks of the Gulf of Maine. They flocked here. By the 1600s, 300 fishing boats from Europe were off our coast. This was where the fish and the money were.

The fishing world hasn't changed much in all these centuries.

Leap ahead in time to a day in late June, 1975, and join me aboard a Coast Guard plane on a surveillance mission over Georges Bank. The account of what we saw on that flight is taken from my column in the Maine Sunday Telegram, July 6, 1975.

Aboard Surveillance Flight — Two signs show they are Soviets: The hammer-and-sickle emblem on their smokestacks, and the Russian letters of the alphabet which precede the identification numerals amidships.

Lt. Jim Holland, U.S. Coast Guard pilot, banks our 22-year-old Grumman amphibian into a turn, so we can fly back to circle, inspect, identify each vessel in the Russian fishing fleet, 200 feet below our wings. We are 70 miles off the U.S. coast, over Georges Bank.

It is an eerie feeling to see so many huge Russian fishing ships so close to American shores. It is an infuriating feeling to see them harvesting enormous catches of fish in traditionally American fishing grounds — and to recall the American draggers left behind in Portland and Port Clyde, in New Bedford and Gloucester. These Americans can't afford to leave port. "The price for fish is too low or the catch is too small," they say.

But below our surveillance plane are the Soviets, the Bulgarians, the Poles, the East Germans, and others. They have millions of dollars worth of fishing vessels manned by up to 17,000 fishermen, working just off our shores. They catch and process millions of tons, here on the spot; load them onto refrigerator ships which head home to Russia. The fleet stays here and keeps on fishing, fishing, fishing. They will be here six months before going home for overhaul, after steaming over 30,000 miles.

In one day of flying surveillance over only one area of Georges Bank, we have seen 90 ships. But only one ship has been an American.

Behind the copilot sits Charles L. Philbrook, eyeballing each ship through special binoculars. Philbrook has 20 years experience in this surveillance business, tracking and identifying foreign fishing fleets off our shores. His card reads: "Senior Resident Agent" of the Law Enforcement Division of the National Marine Fisheries.

Herring by the millions come to spawn on Georges Bank during July and August. Then, says Philbrook, there are usually 250 or more foreign vessels on the northern edge of Georges Bank.

"Fly over, and you'll see the crew waist-deep in herring on the decks, filling up the holds below."

The West German stern trawlers are 300 feet or more of extremely modern and efficient fishing machinery. "Last year 15 such vessels took 29,000 metric tons in 75 days' work," says Philbrook, shaking his head.

For the record, in 1972 the foreign catch of finfish totaled 925,000 metric tons compared to a U.S. catch of only 175,000. In 1973, the comparison was 990,000 metric tons for foreign fleets and under 200,000 for United States ships.

The sea below is so calm that Soviet fishermen, who work the night through purse seining, are rowing skiffs, visiting each others' ships, 75 miles out in the Atlantic. Out here, water depths in the Georges Bank shallow to 40 feet in places, then at the edges plunge to 1,000 or more feet.

These big foreign fleets are run with the discipline of a navy task force. There is a fleet commander in over-all charge, and under him are nine group commands, going down to skippers of individual vessels. Scientists in "brain ships" decide where to fish and at what depth; production chiefs set quotas and schedules for deliveries of fish to the processing ships and refrigerator vessels. Other officials decide crew rotation. There are fleet doctors and hospital rooms. There is even a police vessel for dealing with disorder.

Philbrook's pencil fills up sheet after sheet with names and numbers of Russian ships. He adds other notes about the fishing gear, and activities aboard. The information goes to Washington to be collated with other reports from other surveillance.

He adds up the sightings after we land back at our base. "Eighty-three Soviet ships in this sector alone this day; plus other foreigners fishing."

We picked up the first big Soviet fleet about 50 miles offshore. The next fleet about 80 miles offshore; and the third fleet about 125 miles off Cape Cod.

Smallest are the purse-seiners, 125 to 145 feet long, carrying 30 to 45 crew members. Scores of these seiners work to supply big processing ships. By the smoke coming from the stacks far aft, we detect when the processing ships are cooking.

Biggest ships, in separate fleets, are the Soviet stern trawlers. They can do their own processing as well as catching. These ships are some 300 feet long. They carry up to 350 in crew. Many of the crew are women. We see the women sunbathing in bikinis as we fly over. We see helicopters on the larger vessels.

There is recreation for the crew of these big ships. We fly low over their volleyball courts, enclosed in wiremesh so the ball doesn't go out of bounds into the sea.

"The ships stay on station. The crews change," Philbrook tells me. "They take the 45 people cooped up on a 145-foot ship off after 45 days or so, and bring a new crew in. On the larger, more comfortable vessels, the crew changes every 90 days or so."

East German crews, changed every 90 days, are taken by transport vessel to Cuba, then flown home. By way of stark contrast, only a few of the 75 draggers in the Maine fleet regularly stay out fishing for more than three nights. Most dayfish only.

The Coast Guard runs other patrol missions along the coast.

The findings are distributed monthly. I quote from one typical report:

"In the Northwest Atlantic a total of 334 individual foreign fishing and support vessels were spotted this month . . . Soviet Union 204; Poland 40; East Germany 13; Bulgaria 8; Japan 13; Spain 48; Italy 7; Ireland 1 . . . The Soviets were by far the largest fleet . . . They had 156 large factory stern trawlers; 19 medium stern freezer trawlers; 10 medium side trawlers; 16 factory base ships and refrigerator fish transports, two fuel tankers and one research vessel."

This flight was made a few months before the revolutionary law was passed in Congress in 1976 which extended U.S. fisheries jurisdiction to 200 miles off our coasts. The law finally reduced the massacres of our fishing grounds by foreign fleets. The U.S. now has a measure of control over our Continental Shelf.

Why do these New England waters contain some of the richest fishing grounds in the world? Why did fish congregate here in huge quantities 500 years ago? Why are they still here today, after 500 years of constant fishing over Grand Bank and Georges Bank?

The answer lies in the nature of the ocean bottom. It is no digression to take a look here at the hidden, astonishing world of the ocean bottom; for in it lies the reason why white men first came to fish from the Maine islands.

On one wall in the office of the admiral commanding Fleet Wing Atlantic at Brunswick Naval Air Base, Maine, I saw a terrifying, three dimensional map of the bottom of the Atlantic. It hangs there because the prime mission of P-3 Orion search planes under his command in Brunswick, Jacksonville, Florida, Bermuda, Iceland, the Azores, Spain and Sicily is to maintain surveillance of Soviet submarines, loaded with nuclear missiles targeted against U.S. cities and military installations. These submarines hide deep in the strange, mountainous world beneath the surface of the Atlantic.

The Atlantic, covering 33½ million square miles, has three main parts: the Continental Shelf, the Slope and the Abyss. The Continental Shelf, which was dry land many millions of years ago, is the shallowest and smallest part, averaging only just over 400 feet deep, compared to an average of over 12,000

for the Atlantic as a whole. It occupies only about seven percent of the ocean bottom.

The Shelf deepens slowly, at the rate of about 15 feet a
mile, into the Slope. This Slope occupies only about 15 percent of the total ocean area. But in it are terrifying cliffs,
escarpments, precipitous gorges, jagged mountain peaks.

The rest of the ocean is the Abyss. Here is the pitch dark,
totally silent, unknown and alien world. Yet the Abyss parts
of all the oceans of the world are the largest part of our planet
Earth. Oceans cover 70 percent of the Earth's surface; and
the Abysses are 73 percent of the oceans.

Four and five miles down in that blackness, pressure is seven
tons per inch. Down there may be more secrets of our world
than we have found in outer space. No rage of storms on the
surface causes a ripple down there. Scientists who probe the
Abyss with seismic soundings report that much of the bottom
is covered with soft sediment, miles thick. They estimate it
takes 2,500 years for one inch of this sediment from the
Earth's surface to accumulate on the bottom of the Abyss.

That weird underwater map of the Atlantic hanging on the
wall of the submarine hunter shows that the biggest mountain
range in the world lies under the Atlantic ocean. The mountain range is 10,000 miles long and 500 miles wide, reaching
from Iceland to Antarctica. One of its biggest peaks shows to
our eyes as Mount Pico, in the Azores. From an ocean depth
of 20,000 feet, almost four miles down, the mountain races
up, breaks the ocean surface and keeps rising till it tops out as
Mount Pico, which towers 7,613 feet above the Atlantic Ocean's
surface.

Not far off the coast of Maine lies another gigantic, underwater mountain, some 13,000 feet tall, but invisible to our
eyes. It rises up out of the Atlantic Abyss into the Slope near
Newfoundland. As it rises, the water depth shallows, going
from 13,482 feet to 9,000 feet to 6,000 feet. Then the Slope
changes into the Shelf. Here the underwater mountain keeps
rising higher and higher and the ocean depth gets shallower
and shallower, until it is 400 feet, and sometimes less than 200
feet deep. This forms that huge flat underwater plateau called
the Grand Banks. Here is one of the world's richest fishing
grounds.

Shallowness is the reason fish by the billions are here over
the Grand Banks, and the other banks off the Maine coast,

such as Georges Bank, Jeffrey's Bank, Platt's Bank, the Monhegan Banks, Three Dory Ridge, Bank Comfort, the 45 Fathom Bunch and many others.

Sunlight can penetrate right to the shallow ocean bottom, and work its magic of photosynthesis through which plants can grow down there. These plants make possible the best kind of feeding ground for "bottom" fish. They are the magnets which have been attracting haddock and cod by the billions here to the Banks for centuries.

Other fish such as herring, mackerel and porgies feed closer to the surface, eating plankton and algae. The Maine waters over our Continental Shelf are rich in these fish foods too, thanks to the mingling of cold and warm currents.

Finally, these fishing Banks are very big. The Grand Bank covers over 40,000 square miles. Georges Bank, to the south, spreads across 10,000 square miles. These are the reasons why fishing fleets of many nations have been off New England shores for 500 years.

Today when fishing is good, word spreads fast due to radio telephones, spotting aircraft and even reports that fishing boats must file with government agencies.

Hundreds of years ago, news about "where the fish were at" traveled by the fishermen's grapevine.

On May 17, 1605, two years before 105 English cavaliers landed to form their "first settlement" at Jamestown, Virginia, the ship Archangel dropped anchor off Muscongus Bay, under the command of Captain George Weymouth. Aboard was a writer, James Rosier, whose job was to keep a running diary of the trip for the financial backers home in England.

Rosier wrote ecstatically about the fishing. In England, where fish was money, these words of his must have jumped off the page. Rosier wrote:

"Thomas King, boatswain, cast out his hook when we were but 30 leagues (90 miles) from land, with sails down . . . and hauled up an exceeding great and well fed cod. Then there were cast out three or four more hooks, and the fish were so plentiful and great that when our captain would have set sail, we all desired him to permit

them to fish a while longer because we were so delighted
to see them catch such large fish as soon as the hook
went down . . . One of the mates with two hooks on a
lead at five draughts together hauled up 10 fish; some
measured to be five feet long and three feet about."

In 1614 Capt. John Smith was in the anchorage at Monhegan Island, writing enthusiastically about the fishing. In
April that year, Smith reported he was drying and salting
40,000 fish and corning another 7,000 on the beach at Monhegan. He took one shipload of fish home to England, sent
another to Spain; and cleared 1,500 pounds sterling profit from
that trip alone.

The fishing harbor at Monhegan was busy. A Captain Michael Cooper was back the next year with four fishing vessels.
Then in 1616, came Richard Hawkins, son of the slave-trader
and pirate Sir John Hawkins. He sailed in with two fishing
vessels. Ten more fished close by. Sir Ferdinando Gorges had
other boats there. Capt John Smith came back, and had seven
boats built on Monhegan between 1615 and 1618. The Pilgrims
would not set foot on Plymouth Rock till 1620.

Still other evidence of the profitable fishing around Monhegan Island comes from an affadavit by Thomas Piddock. He
swore, in connection with a legal dispute, that in July 1617,
173,700 dried fish, weighing 300,000 pounds and valued at
$10,000, were shipped from Monhegan to Bordeaux, France,
aboard the vessel Jacob.

Ships' logs of the time report that during "stormes a full 30
to 40 fishing vessels may be found taking shelter in the small
harbor" at Damariscove Island, ten miles westward of Monhegan.

The entrance to that harbor, guarded by submerged ledges
well-named "The Motions" can be hazardous. To anchor 30
vessels would mean very little swinging room. Today if a
dozen boats were inside, the next arrival would seek shelter
elsewhere. If in the early 1600s 30 boats crowded in, it indicated so many fishing boats were in these waters that other
harbors were already full.

If these quotes seem suspect as exaggerations to which some
fishermen are prone, the Reverend Francis Higginson, who saw
the scene from a different angle, wrote: "The abundance of sea

fish are almost beyond believing, and sure I should scarce have believed it, except as I had seen it with mine own eyes. I saw great store of whales and grampuses and such abundance of mackerels that it would astonish one to behold . . . and an abundance of lobsters . . . For my own part, I was soon cloyed of them, they were so great and fat and luscious."

Early in the 1600s, the New England fishery was so extensive that more than 10,000 men and boys were making their living exporting fish to England and Europe. Before the 1600s ended, ten million pounds of fish were being shipped annually from here. Hundreds of fish ships were carrying big cargoes of 300,000 fish each to England, Europe and the West Indies. Their cash earnings topped $500,000 a year.

In those days, months would elapse between the time fish were caught here and the time they were eaten in England or Europe.

The way those fish were cured, or preserved, for the trip back to market may have had a lot to do with the beginnings of the first semi-permanent settlements.

English vessels did not carry nearly as much salt as Spanish, Portuguese and French vessels, because to the English salt was expensive. Salt beds were mostly around Cadiz and the Algarve in Portugal, which made salt cheap to fishermen from those regions. But the English had to import salt; had to pay more for it, and so used less. Therefore the English cured their fish differently. They used the "dry" method. The French and Spaniards used the "wet" method.

Under the wet method, fish were gutted on board as soon as caught and immediately packed layer upon layer into barrels with heavy doses of salt between layers to preserve them. No shore station was necessary.

Under the dry method, which needed far less costly salt, English vessels cured their fish on shore. Half a ship's crew worked on shore. Their first job was to cut timber and build a large wharf. The half of the crew which was fishing from the big boat and from six or seven smaller boats carried aboard, would come alongside the wharf and throw out their fish, fresh and whole. The shore party would gut and split the fish on the wharf. Then they carried the fish up the beach to the "flakes" to dry. Flakes, made from brushwood and branches, were the "drying lines." Split fish were only lightly salted, then hung on the flakes, where they were cured by the sun and dried out until they were hard, stiff and slightly cooked. To prevent them being dampened by fog or rain, the fish on the flakes were covered with brushwood or old sails. This process took several weeks. Then these fish were piled in nearby storage sheds and thousands more fish were hung to dry.

Shore duty was surely preferred by many farm boys from the West country of England: Devon, Cornwall, Somerset and Dorset. Working on shore, on a Maine island, where a fellow could stretch his legs, get a sweet smell of spruce trees, snare an animal or kill a bird for dinner, pick wild berries, was better duty than hauling up codfish all day. When night came, the shore crew preferred to bunk down in a shack on the island rather than go aboard ship to the dank, smelly fo'c's'le, crowded with men who'd been thigh-deep in fish all day.

When the time came in September or October for the fishing vessel to head home, loaded with dried cod, I suspect that there were some among the shore crew who chose to stay behind on a Maine island. A month-long crossing of the north Atlantic in October gales, in a ship loaded with 300,000 codfish, was not much to offer men who had enjoyed summer on a Maine island. Some chose to stay, until the boat came back in the spring. They might be able to make good money in the winter, too, through trapping and fur trading with the Indians. The market for beaver pelts in London was high. Thus, with no intent of founding a colony, the first, unknown semipermanent settlers began living on the Maine islands — left behind with a supply of fish, biscuit, salt pork, fish lines and a small boat. And maybe some rum.

4.

Men And Boats:
Rugged Atlantic Pioneers

On the north side of Allen Island in Muscongus Bay is a cove where I love to anchor. Most often we come to it in Steer Clear through that sweet body of water called George's Harbor. The harbor, really a narrow passage crowded with lobster traps between Allen and Benner Islands, has weather-beaten shingled cottages, barns with gaping holes and small wharves. Meadows reach down from the high ground on each island to the fish house and wharf along each shore. In summer there may be a few sheep, some laundry drying on a line, swinging in the summer breeze, signs a fishing family is on each island for the summer. There may be a skiff or two on the moorings in midstream, where the lobster boats will lay when they come back from hauling. But in winter, there is no sign of life.

The cove I like is just to the east as you come out of George's Harbor. At high water, all of it looks innocent and inviting, but when the tide drains, two sets of ledges are exposed. We discovered them the hard way one summer. We'd dropped anchor fairly far out in the cove, in the lee of the north tip of Allen, and taken the dinghy to the crescent-shaped stone beach to enjoy a swim and a walk. As we rowed back to Steer Clear, we found our boat safe but almost encircled by ledge. So we made the best of it, by rowing back to shore and exploring the island further, until the tide came in again.

We walked to the Weymouth Cross, on a hill beside George's Harbor. It is a big granite cross which commemorates the first church service held on these islands by Capt. George

Weymouth in 1607. The cross was erected over 300 years later.

The picture we envisioned of his tattered crew gathered on this empty island, 3,000 miles from their homes, on the verge of an unknown land, celebrating with a Sunday service, made us wonder what kind of men they were, where their roots lay, the kind of boat they sailed here, how they navigated, how they ate and lived and endured; and above all why they came, why they left the safety of England.

We wondered not just about the men with Weymouth, but the men who sailed here earlier with Martin Pring in 1603, who saw foxes between North Haven and Vinalhaven and first called the water separating the two islands the Fox Thorofare; the men who sailed with Humphrey Gilbert and Bartholomew Gosnold earlier; with the Frenchmen De Monts and Champlain, in 1604, and scores of others before and soon after them.

These were among the very first white men to set foot on Maine islands. It was they who built the first shacks, dried the first fish, first met the Indians, ate the first lobsters. Among them were a few who chose to stay behind when their ships sailed home. They were the lonely men who built the first winter camps, and waited for the return of their ships next fishing season. They were the men who started the early rough settlements of New England.

Who were they?

The accounts of the early voyages make almost no mention at all of the crews.

Physically, they were certainly small men by our standards today. They stood only about five feet tall, or less: for the headroom below decks was never higher than five feet. Most were fairly young; with ages running from a boy of 12 or so to "mariners" in their 20s and 30s. Almost certainly none of the crew could read or write.

It would be a mistake to think all of them were real seafarers. No more than a handful of each crew were true sailors. When Bartholomew Gosnold sailed for Maine from England in March, 1602, a contemporary wrote, "he was attended by 32 persons, only eight of whom were mariners." When Martin Pring sailed in the Speedwell in 1603, he had a crew of "30 men and boys." William Browne, sailing in Discoverer, a bark of only 26 tons, and accompanying Pring, had "13 men and a boy."

The captain was often highly educated, sometimes blue-blooded; certainly a man trusted by the financial backers in London, Plymouth or Bristol; a man who could read, write, make reports, and extract money from merchant bankers or land grants from the Court. Just below him in rank was a "pilot"; a man who had proven experience in navigation, in crossing the Atlantic on other voyages, a kind of "executive officer." Then if lucky, the crew contained a mate or two who knew the tricks of sailing and how to handle men well. On larger crews, there might be a carpenter, who could make repairs, build small boats, keep the food and wine barrels from leaking.

The rest of the crew were usually "picked up" from the waterfront wharves, taverns, jails. Often they were willing to go because the law was after them, because of shrewish wives, because creditors were about to have them thrown in jail. Some, as in every generation, sailed for the hell of it; adventure — or escape — was in their blood. Some were "pressed"; kidnapped by a "press gang" who got paid to round up men and dump them aboard.

Life aboard a fishing boat then had few good days. Most of the time, the life was hard, miserable, cold and wet. Men slept on decks or in passageways, wherever they could. They wore the same rough clothes day and night, for months on end. When they finally reached their destination at a Maine island, no city port, no tavern, no female company would be waiting to make life worth living even for a night or two. Just an island, uninhabited except possibly by Indian "savages." Once they had reached the coast of Maine, there was more work. Shore parties would tote water from cold streams, carrying heavy barrels back to the ship. Others would cut wood, for the cookstove or for repairing and building boats. The big boat would be gone, catching fish. Men with shore duty would spend the day handling the earlier catch, gutting and splitting fish, then drying the stinking mess in the sun, on rocks and drying lines.

After two or three months when the vessel was abrim with smelly fish, they'd set sail on the long trip home, perhaps another month in the stormy north Atlantic during October or November. Back in Plymouth or Bristol, the catch would be unloaded, sold; and when the money came in, deductions would be taken from their pay for the food, the fishhooks and lines they had used, and the fines they had incurred for breaking discipline. For six months' hard, dangerous, comfortless work, the pay might amount to 20 pounds.

Seamen in the Royal Navy in the 1600s were paid five shillings a month; in the merchant marine the pay was ten shillings a month. So the crew of a fishing vessel, who went "shares," apparently made twice as much money, even after deductions, provided the fishing was good, and they were still around to collect when the shares were divvied up.

However, there were compensations. First, there was likely to be plenty to drink and to eat, at least on the outbound trip. The best account of this comes from Samuel Eliot Morison's book, "The Northern Voyages." Morison quotes from the record of Frobisher's voyage to Newfoundland in 1577, and the food he put aboard.

"The ration was one pound of biscuit and one gallon of beer per man per day; one pound of salt beef or pork per man per day for flesh days; one dried cod for every four men on fast days; with oatmeal and rice if the fish supply gave out; a quarter pound of butter and half a pound of cheese per man per day; honey for sweetening; and a hogshead of 'sallet oyle' and a pipe of vinegar to last 120 men for four months."

In beer alone, that amounts to 14,400 gallons. In salt beef, it adds up to over seven tons.

But the food on long voyages went mouldy. Ferdinand Columbus says that on his father's fourth voyage: "What with the heat and the dampness, our ship biscuit had become so wormy that, so help me God, I saw many who waited for darkness to eat the porridge made of it, that they might not see the maggots; and others were so used to eating them that they didn't even trouble to pick them out because they might lose their supper had they been so nice."

The smells aboard those early fishing and exploring vessels might have been unendurable to a 20th century nose. The bilges filled with garbage, urine, vomit, defecation, food scraps. The ballast became impregnated with "pestilential funkes" and the stench was so overpowering that the ship was hauled ashore, the ballast was thrown into the tide for cleansing, and the horrible gunk on the inside of the hold was washed down with strong solutions of salt water and vinegar.

A description of "a sayler" 350 years ago is contained in Richard Braithwait's book, published in 1631 and called "Whimzies: or a New Cast of Characters."

"A Sayler," he wrote, "is an Otter or Amphibium that lives both on Land and Water . . . His familiarity with death and danger, hath armed him with a kind of dissolute security against any encounter. The sea cannot rant and roar abroad worse than hee within, fire him but with liquor . . . In a Tempest you shall heare him pray, but so amothodically, as it argues he is seldom vers'd in that practice . . . He makes small or no choice of his pallet; he can sleepe as well on a Sacke of Pumice as a pillow of doune. He was never acquainted much with civilitie; the Sea hath taught him other Rhetoric. He is most contant to his shirt and other of his seldom wash'd linen. He cannot speak low, the Sea talks so loud . . . He can spin up a rope like a Spider and down again like a lightening . . . Death hee has seen in so many shapes, as it cannot amaze him."

Aboard a 17th century boat, discipline was brutal, swift and undisputed. Captain John Smith, who sailed to Monhegan in 1614, wrote, "The Marshall (or mate) is to punish offenders and see justice is executed according to directions; as ducking at the yard arme, hauling under the keel, bound to the capsterne or main-mast with a bucke of shot around his necke, setting in the bilbowes."

It would be hard to exaggerate the hardships and perils endured by the early explorers, the early fishermen and settlers. Equally it is almost impossible to re create the ships, their daily lives aboard.

Their ships were strongly built, seaworthy; and except for the captain's quarters, totally without comfort of any kind.

In size, they ranged from about 50 to 100 feet long, sometimes 125; in tonnage from 25 to 50 or 60 tons. In those days tonnage was measured in "tuns" and usually spelled "tunnage." A tun was a double hogshead, the outsize barrel in which wine was shipped. Tunnage of a ship meant how many tuns of wine it could carry. From this developed the modern maritime ton, 40 cubic feet.

The fishing boats most often had two decks; the main inside deck laid over the holds and ballast; and the spar deck, outside, open to the weather. The seamen slept wherever they could find space to curl up on the main deck. There were no bunks and no hammocks for crew in most vessels. Only the officers had bunks. Sailors wrapped an old bit of sail or blanket over their wet clothes and made do, month after month.

At the forward end of the open deck was the galley or cook-box. Usually it was just a box with a hood to fend off the wind and sea, with a few inches of sand at the bottom of it as a base for a wood fire. One huge stew pot plus a few smaller pots and pans were all the equipment used to feed a crew of up to 50 men. In foul weather, the cook box was moved below, with a makeshift smoke pipe to carry off part of the smoke.

The ship was steered by a helmsman, out in the weather. Usually he got his steering orders from an officer who sat inside with the compass. This compass was probably a dry card type on a pivot, floating in a bowl and enclosed in a waterproof binnacle, lit by a small whale oil lamp.

The science of navigation was still new. Celestial navigation had been used for centuries, but most navigators had only the experience of sailing the western shore of Europe and the Mediterranean. Coming across the empty Atlantic however, the North Star and the sun became the best way to fix their latitude.

Even in summer, the North Atlantic can be a nightmare to sailor and navigator alike, especially in a 16th century boat. Westerly gales would batter the little bark, forcing it to drop sail and lay-by and weather out the storm for days and nights on end. Easterly gales drenched the sailors on deck with cold rain and the water seeped throughout the cold, dank ship. Northerly gales would rip sails and tear masts out of the deck. Between fronts of foul weather, fog would blot out the sun; or dead calms would put the ship in "irons," wallowing in the slow rolls of the Atlantic for day after day. Men died often. They died from storms, died from fights, died from drink, boredom and scurvy. It was not a pleasant journey to an unknown fishing ground.

Maybe this was what induced the first settlers to stay behind. Men and boys from West of England farms may have preferred to risk a winter on a secure but lonely island rather than go back aboard their fish ship for a November crossing and a winter on the docks.

Indians around a fire
Drawing by John White, 1585. White was the journalist-painter and
briefly Governor of the 1587 colony at Roanoke. His granddaughter, Virginia Dare, was born there, first English child in the New World.

Detail from an early chart

The Oseberg Ship—Norse (835 A.D.)

Norse ship, 835 A.D.
This Oseburg ship, 75 feet long, 16 feet wide, had its rudder on the right, or steer board, side. From this we get the word starboard. (Drawing by Edwin Tunis)

17th century English merchantman
Early English settlers crossed the Atlantic in ships like this. (Drawn by Edwin Tunis)

Sea monsters of North Atlantic

Woodcut in Sebastian Münster's Cosmographia, Basle, 1550. The huge monsters (top left and bottom) overturn ships. The serpents (top right), 250 feet long, climb on decks. Crabs (left center) so big, they devour a sailor.

Indians hunting deer

Drawing by Le Moyne, 1591. "The Indians put on the skins, with the heads on their heads, so they can see out . . . and thus approach the deer without frightening them."

GIOVANNI DI PIER ANDREA DI   BERNARDO DA VERRAZZANO

PATRIZIO FIOR. GRAN CAPT^{NO}.   COMANDANTE IN MARE PER

IL RÈ CRISTIANISSIMO   FRANCESCO PRIMO,

E DISCOPRITORE   DELLA NUOVA FRANCIA,

nato circa il MCDLXXV.   morto nel MDXXV.

Dedicato al merito sing: dell' Ill.^{re} e Rev.^{mo} Sig.^{re} Lodovico da Verrazano

Patrizio, e Canonico Fiorentino Agnato del Med.^o

Preso dal Quadro Originale in Tela esistente presso la sud.^a Nobil Famiglia

G. Zocchi del.   F. Allegrini inc: 1767

Giovanni da Verrazano

In 1524, Verrazano, sailing in La Dauphine, with 50 in crew, spent six months exploring North America. He came into Casco Bay, and then sailed by Monhegan, Isle au Haut, Mt. Desert. (Courtesy of the Pierpont Morgan Library, New York.)

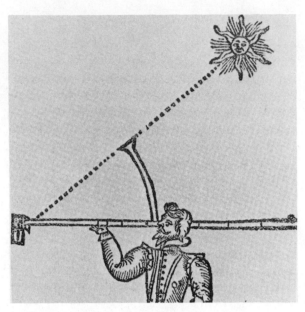

Shooting the sun
In 1595, navigators were using the Davis backstaff as a sextant.

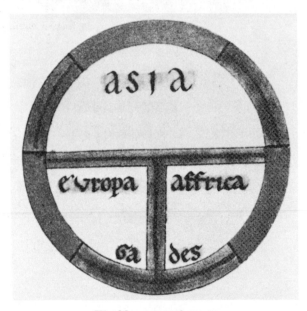

World map, 13th century
In the Middle Ages, this T-O map showed the habitable world as a circular disc floating in the ocean. Asia, Europe, Africa are divided by the Rivers Don and Nile (horizontal line) and Mediterranean Sea (vertical line).

John Cabot and three sons

Cabot, and his sons, Lewis, Sebastian and Santium, made three North American voyages before his death in 1499, sailing for King Henry VII of England. He claimed Mt. Desert for England, out of which stemmed the English claim to Maine.

5.

Sir Ferdinando Gorges:
Father Of Maine

We Americans are fascinated by the men who built our country. We're intrigued by legends of the men who plotted the Boston Tea Party; by Paul Revere and his midnight ride; by Lewis and Clark and their hard journey west; by pioneers who opened the West in their covered wagons; by the Indian fighters; by the cattle drivers, cowboys, badmen and sheriffs of the Wild West; by the aviators who first flew the mail and by ruthless money barons who built the transcontinental railroads; by the astronauts who flew to outer space and walked on the moon. We know about all of them.

Yet we draw blanks about the men who first sailed among these islands of Maine, and about their backers in England and Europe. Who financed those risky ventures? Who were the backers? Why did they risk their money to send ships to an unknown land?

Let's look at Sir Ferdinando Gorges, the man with the Spanish sounding name who, as much as any single man, was the father of Maine.

Gorges was for 40 years the one man in all England who kept faith with his dream of colonizing Maine. From the time he was 30 until he was past 70, he master-minded and financed expedition after expedition; he spent over 20,000 pounds of his own money when 1,000 pounds could outfit a transatlantic expedition; he involved his sons, nephews and other relatives in his schemes and sent many of them on voyages. He was granted king's charters, only to fight investigations before the House of Commons that would have canceled his precious land patents. Through it all, Georges clung obstinately to his dream.

A royalist to the end, Georges backed Prince Charles instead of Oliver Cromwell. Cromwell stripped him of his influence and most of his lands; he was "banished" to a small village in Somerset in his old age and he died, broke and broken-hearted.

Gorges was indeed the Father of Maine. Yet in Maine today all that bears his name is Fort Gorges in Portland Harbor, a dirty, disused, granite fort on a tiny island. He deserves better.

Ferdinando Gorges (1566-1646) was born in Somerset, in the west country of England. His Spanish-sounding name came from ancestors who'd arrived in England from Spain during the reign of Philip and Mary. Early in his 20s, Gorges received inside knowledge about the conspiracy of his friend, the Earl of Essex, discarded lover of Queen Elizabeth, to overthrow the Queen. Gorges decided to tell the Queen all he knew. Essex was disgraced and executed. As a result, Gorges became a court favorite. The Queen made him a navy commander in her last war against Spain. He fought bravely and was knighted for gallantry during the battle against the Spanish Armada. In gratitude, the Crown made him Governor of Plymouth in 1604, an important post much to the liking of the 31-year-old Gorges. For Plymouth, long a front-line defense port against the Spanish, was also becoming the jumping-off port for voyages to the New World. Gorges was already intrigued by the New World. His imagination had been fired by an Indian birch bark canoe, brought home to England by Martin Pring from his voyage to the Fox Islands (North Haven and Vinalhaven).

In 1605 Capt. George Weymouth returned to Plymouth from his voyage to Monhegan, the Georges River and the islands of Muscongus Bay. With him, Weymouth brought back five Indians, kidnapped from the New World, first ever seen in England. He presented three of them to the Governor of Plymouth, Sir Ferdinando Gorges. Gorges took the Indians into his home for three years, treated them as honored guests, learning their language so he could question them better about their country. He arranged for them to be presented to the Crown at Court and to get the red carpet treatment accorded visiting royalty. In a nation already captivated by the stories of the New World, these Maine Indians became the adulated Lindberghs of their time.

These kidnapped Indians not only excited the imaginations of Englishmen at Court and in commerce to hurry along their dreams of an English colony, but also were to have a telling influence on the good and the bad receptions by the Indians of future voyagers to Maine.

It is worth looking at the Weymouth encounters with the Indians, as told by James Rosier, the writer aboard Weymouth's ship Archangel.

In his account, Rosier says:

> "The Indians visited us on board, lying upon deck with us, and we ashore with them, changing man for man as hostages. We treated them very kindly, because we intended to inhabit their country. And they readily traded with us, the exchange of their furs for our knives, glasses, combs and toys, being of great profit to us; for instance, one gave 40 skins of beaver, otter and sable, for articles of five shillings value."

Somehow, after these first exchanges, a quarrel broke out. Rosier, perhaps trying to cover up, says little about the details. But Captain John Smith, in his "Description of New England," written a short time later, tells this story.

> "The natives came aboard Weymouth's ship and desired the captain to go and trade with their Bashaba, on the main, who was their chief lord; and he accordingly manned the yawl with 14 men for this purpose. Yet the Natives would row faster with five oars in their canoe than could our men in their boat with eight oars. At the shore was exchanged one Owen Griffin, for a young fellow of the savages. Griffin discovered their treachery, finding 283 savages, armed with bows and arrows, and without any such articles of trade as they pretended to have."

This trick "gave umbrage" to Weymouth and when natives came to his ship, he seized three of them and took two more on shore, along with two canoes, bows and arrows. Four of these unhappy natives were called Tisquantum, Manida, Skid-warres and Assecomoit, one being a Sagamore and three of the others "persons of rank." The first three were those delivered by Captain Weymouth to Sir Ferdinando Gorges, when they arrived at Plymouth.

In part as the result of new eager interest stirred by the first Indians seen in England, two corporations were formed under patent from King James I on April 10, 1606. Both had the goal of establishing colonies. One was called The London Company or the First Colony of Virginia. The other was called the Plymouth Company or "The Second Colony." The land patents for both extended from the 34th to the 45th degree of north latitude, and included all the islands within 100 miles of the coast, the whole being called under the general name of North and South Virginia.

The two corporations or colonies were carefully separated from each other, so there would be less chance of conflict between them. It was stipulated that the North Virginia Colony could colonize north of the 38th degree; and the South Virginia Colony below the 41st degree. But whoever established a colony first should have at least 100 miles breathing space; the second colony could not establish a settlement within that 100-mile limit.

Gorges, a key member of the Plymouth Company, was determined he would be the driving force to start the first colony. The patent had been granted only in April. But by August, Gorges and the Plymouth Company were ready to start. They outfitted a ship named Richard of Plymouth, put Henry Chalons in command of 31 men. Sir Ferdinando also put aboard two of his native Indians, Manida and Assecomoit, to act as guides and go-betweens with the native tribes after Chalons arrived to start his colony. The third Indian, nicknamed Squanto, went home to Maine on a later voyage. There, in the islands of Muscongus Bay, Squanto taught the English words he had learned to Samoset, the Wawenock chief. He must also have told Samoset he had been well treated by the English. For in 1621-1622, Samoset welcomed and helped the Pilgrim fathers in their struggle to survive the bad winter at Plymouth.

But Chalons and his ship never reached their destination in Maine. Chalons was blown off course on his way across the Atlantic, wound up near Puerto Rico. There his ship was captured by Spaniards and all the crew were taken prisoner.

The London Company, better financed, moved more slowly in a more ambitious way. On December 20, 1606, four months after Gorges' expedition sailed, the London Company sent out three ships and 100 would-be colonists, plus mariners, and equipped them well. In April 1607, they landed at Jamestown.

But the disaster of the Chalons voyage was not much of a deterrent to Sir Ferdinando Gorges. He just raised his sights, played for higher stakes. This time he went to his illustrious neighbor in Plymouth, Lord John Popham, Chief Justice of England, and persuaded him into active partnership. The Plymouth Company did it right this time. It outfitted three ships, gathered 120 men as colonists and equipped the expedition with a splendid array of supplies, even including cannons to fortify and defend the colony-to-be. Only two ships eventually sailed, filled with promise and hope, and backed by power and money at home. In overall command was an illustrious name — George Popham, son of the Lord Chief Justice. Second in command was Raleigh Gilbert, nephew of the famous Sir Walter Raleigh. They were determined to beat or at least equal the efforts of the London Company at Jamestown. On May 31, 1607, with bands playing, they sailed out of Plymouth harbor, made a fair crossing and by August 8, the expedition touched at Monhegan island. By the 11th, they were ashore on Stage Island, which turned out to be a poor choice. Quickly they moved to the mouth of the Kennebec River and there established Popham, also called the Sagadahoc Colony.

This, too, proved a poor choice. It was too exposed to the combined perils of the sea, the river mouth and the worst a Maine winter could throw. The sad failure of the brave Popham colony is told in the next chapter.

The failed colonists arrived back in England early the next year, with terrible tales of how no Englishman could survive winters in Maine. Their discouraging reports dampened every ardor except that of the stubborn, optimistic, determined Gorges. Although now he could raise no money from others he financed single handed another expedition in 1616. He forced 16 of his tenants and servants to sail under Richard Vines, in a small ship. It was a pitiful and meek departure from Plymouth compared to the great Popham sailing. This time Gorges at last had the good luck in men and weather that he deserved. This tiny colony succeeded at the mouth of the

Saco River. Vines sent home enthusiastic reports. But since he had been hired only as the navigator, Vines returned to England where he spread the good news in person. Enthusiasm for making a new start in the New World boomed. A bevy of new settlements began to thrive along the coast of Maine, now called New Somerset, at Kittery, Isles of Shoals, Richmond Island, Wells, York, Saco; as well as at Pemaquid, Damariscove and Monhegan Island. Gorges' fame, popularity and acclaim grew apace in England.

Outside of the book he later wrote, there is little first-hand information about Gorges. I like to imagine Sir Ferdinando at home and at business. He was 50 years old when Vines settled the colony at Saco. Because he was Governor of Plymouth, his working days must have been spent close to the harbor, concerned with maritime business. He'd surely oversee all military and naval defense aspects of the busy port. This would keep him in contact not only with local commanders, but with Admiralty officials in London. As men o' war, merchant ships, exploring ships or even fishing vessels, freebooters and raiders sailed home into Plymouth, their captains would pay their first calls on Gorges, as Governor. They'd talk the day and half the night through, with Gorges firing questions about where they had been, what ships, what people, what weather, what strange shores they had encountered. Together, he and the skippers would pour over charts. Voyaging was his business and his avocation.

Yet Gorges was probably regarded as a bit of a crackpot; at best an eccentric. For this man had a fixation about the New World 3,000 miles away. In his home, probably one of the grandest in Plymouth, Gorges surely had a workroom, crowded with all the information he could get about the New World, particularly Maine and New England. He brought returning captains into that room and pumped them for all they knew; showed them reports from other captains, and the courses they had sailed, the charts they had drawn, and asked for comments and comparisons.

In London business circles and at the Court, first of Queen Elizabeth, then of King James I, then of Charles I, Gorges must have had a mixed reputation. He was a good-looking ladies' man. He'd been knighted for gallantry in battle. He'd been wounded and briefly captured at Lille. He'd been a navy officer. Yet at the same time, Gorges was a west countryman;

his job was far off in the provinces, as Governor of Plymouth.
Above all, he was, to the courtiers and financiers, a man with
a dream, a fixation on colonizing almost unknown places across
the Atlantic. Given a chance, he'd bend anyone's ear for hours,
trying to persuade them to invest in yet another expedition.
He had persuaded such big names as Sir Humphrey Gilbert,
Lord Chief Justice Popham and the Earl of Southampton to
put up money. Gorges, and they, had once had clout at the
Court, too. They had quickly obtained royal charters and
patents from the King for their risky ventures. And Gorges
knew how to promote his wild schemes; the way he had pa-
raded those wild Indians about London, even had them wined
and dined at the Palace, was an example of what his enthusiasm and persistence could accomplish.

But . . . what did he have to show for it? Not money, certainly. No gold, no silver mines, no rich cargoes of spices and
jewels as had come from Cathay, the Levant, Mexico and Peru.
Just a few boatloads of fish and some furs. He'd lost his own
shirt, along with the shirts of others, in backing that disas-
trous attempt to colonize at Popham. His people had hugely
suffered there in the first winter. They had come home with
stories of terrible cold in a cruel land. Yet the obstinate man
wouldn't learn; he had gone ahead again, alone, because he
couldn't any longer obtain partners. The dreamer had mortgaged his property and gone into debt to send still another
expedition out. A tiny affair of one small boat with 16 of his
own tenants as colonists, this time their reports trumpeting
their success under an unknown leader called Vines. Vines
was, in fact, a tenant farmer of Gorges'.

Gorges, too, must have had moments when he felt like giving up his dream. He had sunk money into expeditions, waved
goodbye to his ships; and then waited; waited, impatiently and
anxiously for some word back. At best the wait lasted three
or four months. Then when the news finally came, it often had
been dismally bad.

But this time, the news from Vines was good. What would
it lead to? Weymouth, back in 1606, had brought home glowing reports from Muscongus. Those had persuaded Gorges to
form the Plymouth Company, which had hit disaster at Popham and gone broke. Then Gorges had backed three expeditions by Capt. John Smith, best of all the captains. All three
had failed. The first failed almost before it began, with Smith's

ship wrecked off Land's End, just down the English Channel from Plymouth. A second hit the skids when ship and crew were captured by French pirates. The third, a sizeable venture with three ships financed, was locked into port so long by bad weather that the other investors gave up and canceled the effort. The list was depressingly long; the Nicholas Hobson expedition had been driven off by attacks from Indians; mutiny aboard ship had ruined the effort by Capt. Edward Rocrafot; plague had decimated yet another try.

But now, with Vines, there was good news at last. Small as the colony was, it was enough to keep alive Gorges' dream, to fan the flame of hope and adventure in others. There followed a minor boomlet during the 1620s, with scores of ships coming to Maine to fish, to trade trinkets for furs, to establish small settlements. But, as is often the case, when public interest peaks, the politicians get involved. By this time, Gorges was the target of political infighting, some of it from the financiers, some in the House of Commons.

The problem was that as settlements in Maine grew, so did bickering among them. New authority had to be established for the orderly conduct of business between the settlements and England. The revived Plymouth Council sent over a new team of "managers." Robert Gorges, son of Sir Ferdinando, went to New England as Governor-in-Chief. Under him was Christopher Levett, as governor of the New Plymouth area; and Francis West was made Admiral of New England, with orders to make even small fishing vessels pay $100 for licenses to fish. (He was never able to enforce payment from the independent fishing boat captains.) And to make a neat package of politics, commerce and church, the Plymouth Council sent an Episcopalian minister to supervise all the churches. The local churches in the settlement were even more obstinate against supervision than were the local fishermen. The minister met no welcome and returned home in disgust.

Complaints from the growing settlements poured into Parliament. As head of the Plymouth Council and the long-time expert, Sir Ferdinando was hauled to the bar of the House of Commons. The charge against him was that he and the Plymouth Council were running the New World for their "own private gain"; were usurping the powers that properly belonged to the government. He was told to surrender forthwith the patent, or charter, of the Plymouth Council.

Gorges did a commendable job, according to contemporary accounts, of defending himself and the Council. But the political heat was on. Within a year his son, Robert Gorges, was recalled from his position as Governor-General of New England. The effort at establishing an overall government, controlled from London, collapsed. (Not until March 4, 1628, was a Royal Charter issued by which a full-fledged colony was established under the name of The Massachusetts Bay Colony, and civil government truly established.) Maine, though it had no such name then, and was part of The Massachusetts Bay Colony, was in the news. Money was being made there. The fish and the fur and the timber business were all showing a profit. The number of boats, of settlers, of settlements along the coast and among the islands were increasing every year.

Sir Ferdinando, now 60, had a tiger by the tail. But the administration of it was chaotic.

The House of Commons hauled Gorges before the bar again in 1634. Like Congress today, the English politicians of 1634 reacted to public complaints and accusations by staging an investigation. They ordered Gorges to appear as a major witness. Furthermore, the House of Commons was jealous. Altogether too many Englishmen were leaving for the New World. So many were emigrating that in 1633 the government acted to stop the exodus. Several ships, loaded with passengers and cargoes and ready to sail, were held in the Thames. Members of Parliament were personally jealous, too, of the vast tracts of land held by Gorges and other Plymouth Council members under grants from the king. In small England, the size of those land grants — some as big as England itself — were grounds for jealousy. According to parliamentary records of the time, the investigation of the Plymouth Council by the Commons must have been similar to some present-day congressional antitrust hearings. Their goal was to break up the holdings and the monopolies of the Plymouth Council.

Gorges, in his testimony before them, must have sounded much like today's conglomerate executive defending himself and his corporation against accusations of making too much money. Gorges reminded the Commons of his long, untiring, often unrewarding efforts against odds to advance England's interest in America.

"I have spent well in excess of 20,000 pounds of my own estate and 30 years, the whole flower of my life, in promoting new discoveries and new settlements upon a remote continent, in the enlargement of my country's commerce and domains; in the carrying of civilization and Christianity into regions of savages," he said.

Gorges emphatically denied that he and his associates had run a monopoly or grown rich doing it. "Disbursements have far exceeded receipts," he cried. He said that his colonists had too often proved "indolent and wasteful," and as for mismanagement, he claimed "no superintendent could control their erratic dispositions, or prevent their changes of abode from place to place." He sought sympathy from the investigating politicians by recounting how the French and the Indians were "creating mischief" and "encroaching upon our rights."

But the Commons was determined to dissolve the Plymouth Council, and did. In an antitrust measure, it divided the council's huge original holdings into 12 Royal Provinces. On February 3, 1635, Gorges and others who earlier had been granted enormous lands would have to give them up and draw lots for smaller holdings in the presence of the king — something akin to the way the United States today auctions off rights to oil exploration in the offshore banks area. In each Province, each previous owner was to be entitled to only 5,000 acres in lieu of his previous far greater holdings; and in each Province, 4,000 acres were to be set aside for a capital city for the new governor and government of that Province. Each landowner would send over 10 men at his expense to help build the city, and in each Province, 10,000 acres were to be set aside for the foundation of churches and the maintenance of clergymen.

On April 25, 1635, with Gorges and 15 other members present, the Plymouth Council held its last meeting.

"We have been bereaved of friends, oppressed with losses, expenses and troubles; assailed before the Privy Council and the House of Commons again and again, with groundless charges; weakened by the French and other forces without and within; and what remains is only a breathless carcass. We therefore now resign this Patent."

Sir Ferdinando, though head of the Council and a prime target, was above all a survivor. He stayed close in his loyalty to King James, while fighting the Commons. He remained, to his later peril, a staunch royalist. And in return, the King now appointed Gorges his Governor General over all New England.

For the aging Gorges, this was the highest honor. At last he would sail to the New World, as the ruler. Exulting, he made all preparations to depart. He would sail in splendor, too, with the King's blessing and aboard a new man o' war.

At its launching, his new ship met disaster. She flipped on her side and was crushed.

Gorges, who had devoted a full 40 years to his dreams of colonizing this coast, was destined never to set foot on Maine shores. He died in 1646, at age 70.

Gorges' first book, "Discovery and Plantation of New England," published in 1622, read like a sales prospectus.

"The place," he wrote, "is not only seated in the temperate zone but, as it were, in the middle part thereof, standing 20 degrees from the fiery tropics and as much from the freezing Arctic Circle, yet under the same course of the sun as Constantinople and Rome . . . The maritime parts thereof are somewhat colder . . . for the beams of the sun are weakened partly by . . . being laden with the moisture it exhales out of the vast ocean.

"Indeed the hot countries yield sharper wits but weaker bodies and fewer children. . . . But this country is so temperate that it seemeth to hold the golden mean. . . . The people there are tractable, if they be not abused, to commerce and trade with all. . . . The seas are stored with all kinds of excellent fish. The country aboundeth with a diversity of wildfowl, such as turkeys, partridges, swans, cranes, wild geese of two kinds, wild ducks of three sorts, many doves, especially when strawberries are ripe.

"There is also a certain beast that natives call a moose. He is big-bodied as an ox, headed like a fallow deer, with broad antlers, which he sheds every year. . . . He hath a great bunch of hair hanging down under his throat; his skin maketh very good leather and his flesh is excellent good food. . . . There is hope that this beast may be made serviceable for ordinary labor with art and industry. . . . We have succeeded in bringing ourselves into familiarity with the natives, which are in no great numbers along the coast for 200 leagues (600 miles) ; and we have now dispatched some of our people of purpose to dive into the bowels of the continent, there to search and find out what port or place is most convenient to settle our main plantation in. . . ."

The salesman's optimism is gone from his later book, written in his old age, and published 10 years after his death. Here his writing is tinged with the melancholy of a man who dreamed so persistently, worked so hard, but never saw the land he'd helped to father 3,000 miles across the Atlantic.

"We have," he wrote, "been endeavoring to found plantations in a wilderness region, where men could hardly be hired to stay, or induced to become residents. . . . We have made the discoveries and opened the fields for others to harvest. Trade, fishery, lumber, these have been the phantoms of pursuit."

Provence of Mayne

This beautifully illustrated color map and chart is from among those collected by the father of Gov. Percival Baxter of Maine and is now in the Maine State Archives. Date is probably late 16th century.

Mariner's compass
From the Rittal collection in Bath Marine Museum, Maine. Francis
Rittal of Dresden, Maine, a shipmaster, decorated his navigation book with
watercolors. These and other treasures from his attic were given by his
descendants, Carrie R. Groves and Gladys R. Castner.

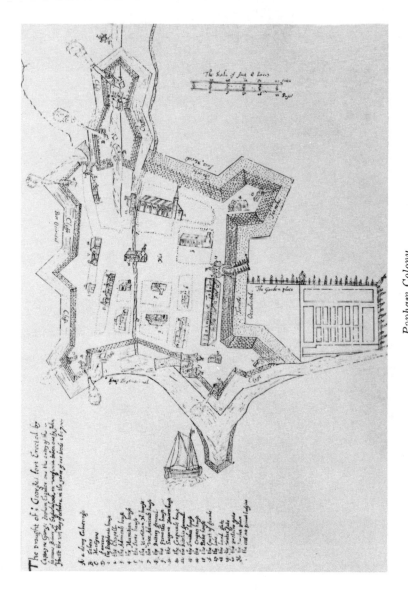

Popham Colony

Drawing of St. George's Fort, Popham (Sagadahoc) colony, 1607, from the Archivo General de Simancas. The map shows 20 buildings and installations. Map was discovered by J. L. M. Curry, U. S. Minister to Spain.

Sailors' punishments
One sailor's hand is impaled to mainmast; one is being keel-hauled under
the boat, third, at stern, is being dunked till almost drowned. (From
Historia de Gentibus Septentrionalibus, 1555.)

Signatures of Maine founders
John Popham, Christopher Levett, Ferdinando Gorges, George Weymouth.

Cod fishing in early times
The process is to offload fish from small boats to cutters on wharf; then to the salting box; on to the splitters; finally to the drying flakes. (Moll's map, 1700.)

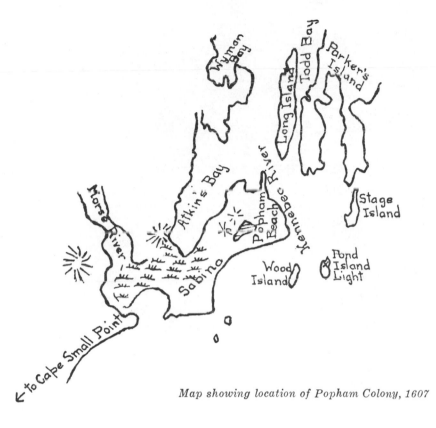

Map showing location of Popham Colony, 1607

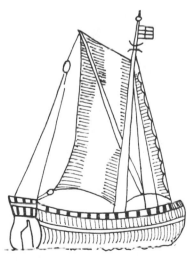

Sketch of vessel at St. George's Harbor, 1607

The pinnace Virginia, built 1607
The Virginia was the first ship built by the English in North America,
at Popham, 1607. This photo, courtesy of the Bath Marine Museum, is of
a model at the Bath Iron Works, Maine.

6.

Popham, 1607:
Why The First Colony Failed

Popham. The name is unknown in most classrooms and history books of America. But the Popham colony in Maine was the first effort at establishing a permanent English colony in this nation after the Lost Colony of 1585.

Before colonists went ashore at Jamestown, and almost 14 years before the Pilgrim Fathers set foot at Plymouth, the first American colony was begun on the banks of the Kennebec River, near the little town now called Phippsburg.

The Popham colony was a full-fledged, well financed, well planned undertaking, involving some 124 people, two ships, and some of the foremost names in England.

The Maine colony began well enough in August, 1607. A fort, defended with cannon, was quickly built; homes, meeting houses, warehouses were built within its walls. Friendly contacts were made with nearby Indians. During its early months, the Popham colony was off to a good start, better probably than the start of the later colonies at Jamestown and at Plymouth.

But thirteen months later, the Popham colony was abandoned. Had this brave first effort succeeded, American history might be different. Popham, instead of Jamestown and Plymouth, would be featured in every history book. Throngs of Americans would be visiting this remote peninsula in Maine to see where their nation began. Instead they make their pilgrimages by the millions to Plymouth Rock and Jamestown, and Popham is known only to a few; and then largely for the magnificent white sand beach and state park which bears its name.

What went wrong? Why did the Popham colony fail?

The strange fact is that all the first European colonies were pitched on some of the worst possible sites: Douchet Island on the St. Croix River, Roanoke Island, Plymouth, and Popham. Hindsight soon told all the early colonists they had chosen badly. But as they approached little known land after hard voyages, their sites looked as good as any other bit of unknown territory.

Certainly the site of the Popham colony was not the best choice. A few miles upriver from the mouth of the Kennebec, the site was on an open bluff which may have looked splendid in August and September when they landed, but during winter it was exposed to bitter weather and biting winds. This caused suffering, and the colonists later complained that winter was their downfall. Indeed, that winter of 1607 was a severe one, even in England. But if the weather had been terribly bad, the colony could have moved further up the Kennebec, which they explored as far as Augusta or to the sheltered islands in Muscongus Bay, which Weymouth had suggested. The site near the mouth of the Kennebec, however, offered a good location for trading with the Indians and good fishing grounds.

The prime reason for failure lay not with weather or sickness or site, but with the character of the colonists and their leaders. They were not of the right stuff. They failed to form themselves into an effective, pioneering community.

George Popham, the leader, was described by Sir Ferdinando Gorges as "an honest man, but old and of an unwieldy body, and timorously fearful to offend or contest with others that do oppose him." Popham was to die of ill health before the winter was out. No one else died from illness.

His second in command, Raleigh Gilbert, then took the leadership. Gorges described him as "desirous of supremacy and rule, a loose life, prompt to sensuality, little zeal in religion, headstrong and of small judgment and experience, but in other ways valiant enough."

Whatever his qualities, Gilbert too left the colony a year later to return to England because of his brother's death there.

As to the 120 "landsmen and sailors," they were a mixed bunch: Some good men, some adventurers, some men who headed out to a new world because they were in trouble in the old world. Bickering broke out early, aboard ship on the voyage. After they went ashore, according to Gorges, discordant elements caused trouble "by the want of understanding of some to perform what they were directed . . . from whence did proceed confusion and faction." Captain John Smith in his book "General History of New England," wrote that the colonists "were glad to send all but forty-five of their company back to England" before they'd been at Popham even four months. According to writers of the time, "the company was comprised of the vagrant and the dissolute."

If you sail by that Popham colony shore today, or walk the ground near Phippsburg where the first fort stood, there is little to mark the first American colony. In a nation which adulates success, we bury failures. The Popham colony is buried in most history books. Yet it should not be forgotten.

Preparations for the Popham expedition began in 1605, in a wave of enthusiasm and optimism. Entrepreneurs in the west of England had read the glowing account of Weymouth's voyage the year before, as told in Rosier's "True Relation," and they were eager to finance a major effort to start the first colony. They formed the New Plymouth Company. In the forefront was Sir Ferdinando Gorges and his powerful neighbors in Plymouth, the Popham family: Sir John Popham, Lord Chief Justice of England, and his seafaring relative, Captain George Popham, and Raleigh Gilbert. The Popham influence cut through royal red tape at the court of King James. Within eight months after Weymouth returned from his voyage, King James had granted a new charter to New Plymouth Company. This document, dated April 10, 1606, was the king's permission to establish a northern colony in Maine. Six months after the king had signed it, a ship was on its way on a scouting mission, to reconnoiter the best site. This ship was under the command of Thomas Hanham, son-in-law to Sir John Popham, and aboard as pilot was the experienced Martin Pring, who had sailed the Maine coast three years earlier. By the time Hanham and Pring were back, Gorges and the Pophams were far along with the organization of 120 men willing to blaze a new colony and with equipping the three ships that would carry them to the Maine site recommended by Hanham and Pring. The spot they urged was on the banks of a broad, navigable, pleasant river called the Sagadahoc or Kennebec.

The New Plymouth Company, with Gorges and the Pophams at the helm, spared no expense in preparations for the first colony. They obtained three ships — Gift of God, Mary and John, and a third unnamed pinnace. The leader, Captain George Popham, kin of the Chief Justice, picked his second-in-command, none other than Raleigh Gilbert, an experienced sailor and nephew of the famous Sir Walter Raleigh. Together they recruited their key subordinates. Edward Harlow was chosen as master of ordnance, in charge of 12 cannons and other firearms; Robert Davis was sergeant major and in command of the militia, which would protect the colony; Ellis Best was marshal. John Scammon was the scribe and lawyer, secretary of the colony; James Davis was named to command the fort; Gome Carew was "chief searcher," in charge of exploration and mapmaking; and John Digby was master carpenter and shipbuilder.

The ships were well provisioned and carefully stocked with guns, cannon, utensils of all kinds, and knives, beads, mirrors for trading with the Indians. Everything money and planning could do to establish the first permanent colony was done.

On May 31, 1607, the Gift of God and the Mary and John, with more than a hundred sailors and settlers, sailed from Sutton's Pool in Plymouth, the very place from which the Mayflower with her company of 102 Pilgrims was to sail 13 years later.

The Atlantic crossing went well. The ships reached the Azores in 24 days, and the crews landed to stock up on fresh water and more firewood. Soon thereafter the two ships got separated. Popham in the Gift of God sailed to Matinicus. Gilbert in Mary and John made Nova Scotia at the end of July, and went ashore to again replenish fresh water and firewood. Then Gilbert coasted through the Maine islands and on August 5 the two ships rejoined near Allen Island, as advised by Captain Weymouth who recommended George's Harbor there. (Frequently it has been reported the ships anchored off Monhegan, some four miles further out to sea. But the discovery in 1875 at Lambeth Palace, London, of a ship's journal kept on the trip by James Davis, indicates the true anchorage was in George's Harbor, the rendezvous recommended by Weymouth, who had held his first church service there.)

This was home territory to Skidwarres, an Indian aboard Gilbert's Mary and John. Skidwarres was one of the five Indians who had been captured by Weymouth. He'd been taken to England and given to Gorges, who was now returning him to Maine with the expedition.

Skidwarres immediately wanted to make contact with his tribe. Anxious to please him and to get off to a good start with the native Indians, Gilbert lowered one of the ship's small boats, even though it was already after midnight. A few sailors rowed Gilbert and Skidwarres to wherever the Indian would guide them.

An account written at the time says they rowed "past many gallant islands" that August night and finally landed at the spot where New Harbor stands now. Skidwarres led the party across the peninsula "for near three miles" to the Indian encampment at Pemaquid.

Now the story becomes almost too good to be true. The chief of the Indians at Pemaquid was none other than Nahanta, another of Weymouth's captives, who had been returned home the year before by Hanham and Pring on their voyage. The reunion of Skidwarres and Nahanda around dawn that August morning must have amazed Gilbert.

With Skidwarres as interpreter, Gilbert met for two hours with Nahanta. Then Skidwarres led them back to the boat at New Harbor and they rowed the long eight miles back to Georges Harbor at Allen Island bursting with the news of the encounter with Indians.

Next day, being Sunday, August 9, the crews went ashore to hold a thanksgiving service for a safe crossing. For most men, it was the first time on dry land in over two months.

On Monday, Popham and Gilbert left in a shallop, with 30 men to pay a joint official call on Nahanta and the Indians at Pemaquid. But the meeting was not cordial. The Indians, remembering well that white men had captured Nahanta, Skidwarres and three other Indians, gave Popham a chilly welcome. The whites spent the night well removed from the Indians on the Pemaquid shore and rowed back to the ships next day.

The men aboard had rested from the Atlantic voyage. Summer was nearing its end. So on Wednesday, the two vessels upped anchor and headed closer to their desination, Sagadahoc, an older name for the Kennebec River.

That night, they were hit by a bad storm off Seguin — a nasty piece of water even to those who know it well. The next days were filled with local reconnaissance in various directions by Popham and Gilbert and crews in small boats. They made their first camp on Stage Island, found its six acres too small and the supply of fresh water unreliable. Finally, a location on the west side near the mouth of the river was chosen for their new home.

On August 19, the entire company assembled on shore. The preacher held a religious service, asking blessings on this first colony. Then the formal articles of government, as issued by the King and by the Plymouth Company, were read. They are long and were undoubtedly boring for the colonists to hear; but they symbolized the formal beginnings of the first colony.

Immediately work was begun on building a fort. Other work crews began unloading the ships. A flag was raised. A plan for location of cannons, storehouses, and dwelling houses was marked on the ground.

By now it was September. In those early days of autumn, 1607, supplies were toted ashore. Men hauled cannons off the ships, rafted them ashore, and wrestled them into position on the new fort. Others in small boats scouted the nearby islands and up river, making contact with Indians through their own Indian interpreters. Within a few weeks, the fort was roughly in place, a central meeting house, a warehouse plus numerous outbuildings and barracks were completed. Ship's carpenter Digby and a crew set to work building the first vessel made by white settlers in North America, a 30-ton pinnace, which they christened Virginia. They built her well, for she sailed back and forth across the Atlantic for 20 years, often hauling supplies to colonists in Jamestown, Virginia.

By early December, the colony was in business, with a fort, a big new boat, numerous small boats, storehouses, dwelling houses, and water wells. The firewood was stacked and the cannons were in place. The mother ships had been fully unloaded.

On October 8, the Mary and John, one of the ships which had brought them, sailed home to England. She arrived back in Plymouth December 1, with news and a daily diary of the colony's doings, kept for Sir Ferdinando Gorges.

Before the second ship left on December 13 to return home to Plymouth, the colony's leader, George Popham, wrote a letter to King James, to be hand carried to Court by the ship captain. That letter and the writing of it is worth recalling. Popham's letter was the first state document written from an American settlement to the King of England. Popham made the most of the occasion; he wrote the letter in Latin. But he filled it with white lies, and embroidered it with outrageous compliments to His Majesty: all, perhaps, in the cause of getting continued support from the Crown.

It is a curious picture . . . Popham in a crude hut on the Maine coast in cold December, penning his letter in Latin to the King of England.

"I have thought it should be made known to your Majesty that here among the Indians, that there is none on the world more admired than King James . . . My well-considered opinion is that . . . the empire of your Majesty may easily be enlarged and the welfare of Great Britain speedily augmented in these parts. So far as relates to commerce, there are in these parts shagbarks, nutmegs and cinnamon, besides pinewood and Brazilian cochineal and ambergris and many other products of great value, and these in the greatest abundance.

"Besides, they positively assure me that there is a great sea, large, wide and deep only seven days journey from our fort. This cannot be other than the Southern Ocean, reaching to the regions of China, which unquestionably cannot be far from these regions."

George Popham filled his Latin phrases with more flattery than truth and dispatched them with Captain Robert Davis, who was returning to England with the second ship that had brought the colonists here. That ship, Gift of God, also carried home fifty or more discontents or troublemakers from the embryo colony.

Then came winter. That winter of 1607/8 was one of the meanest and coldest. The houses built by the novice colonists were ill-equipped to withstand the ice, snow, sleet and raging winds and storms from the ocean. The shivering colonists found how big a mistake they had made by choosing to settle on one of the most exposed spots along the coast, rather than a snug cove further up the Kennebec or in Muscongus Bay, as Weymouth had advised. Food became short. The ill-dressed, hungry, cold settlers began to get scurvy, which further weakened them.

According to some contemporary accounts, perhaps only 45 men were left at Popham by Christmas 1607, out of the 100 and more who had sailed. The others had gone home on the Gift of God, when she left on December 13.

It was quickly apparent to Gorges, when he read the daily diaries brought home on the first returning ship, that all was not well with the colonists. The news brought back by the second ship and the discontented returning colonists in February was worse. As for "return on investment," there was nothing in the cargoes beyond some furs, some fish, and some sassafras to kindle hope of wealth.

Clearly, there had been trouble between the colonists and the Indians, though accounts differ in detail. In a winter of bad weather (it was a freezing cold winter in England, too), this meant that Indians would not be a source of food supplies needed by the colonists.

Purchas, in his book "Pilgrimmes," published in 1614, reports "a quarrel fell out between the colonists and the Indians" wherein one colonist was killed and others driven from the fort. The Indians took over the fort briefly. They broke into barrels of provisions and supplies. One barrel contained gunpowder, which caught fire, blew the fort to pieces, killing several Indians. Clearly such a fearsome accident would have created mistrust and suspicion on both sides.

Another incident, reported in the book "King Philips' War," caused more Indian death and injury. A number of Indians came to the fort to trade. The colonists asked them to help drag a cannon up an incline. They agreed. As they were doing this, the cannon fired by accident, killing one Indian and wounding others.

It does seem certain that from whatever cause, the Indians turned hostile, fire destroyed the main building, and the colonists lost a great part of their supplies in midwinter.

But despite bad news, despite the return of discontents aboard the Gift of God in February, Gorges and Popham planned to send out fresh supplies promptly to the Popham colonists. They laid plans for more men, ships and provisions.

Then misfortune hit in a series of deaths. First the leader of the colony, George Popham, died. He was an elderly man, with a physique unsuited, at best, to a cold first winter in a new, rough fort on the Maine coast.

In England, Sir John Popham, Chief Justice of England, and a major backer in the Plymouth Company, died too.

Then Sir John Gilbert died in England. He was the brother of Raleigh Gilbert, who had succeeded George Popham as leader of the Popham Colony. When this news reached Gilbert in the summer, he felt he had to hurry home to England to take care of his brother's estates, to which he was heir.

This was the final blow to the Popham Colony. They'd had a tough winter; they'd had skirmishes with Indians; their first leader had died; their next leader was leaving. They could see no future but more trouble and more hardship in their outpost. One year and one month after they had landed, the Popham contingent left. The first colony in America had failed.

7.

Isles Of Shoals:
A Stern
And Lovely Scene

The islands of Maine begin and end with names of sea magic. Cross the water boundary from New Hampshire and the Maine islands start immediately with Appledore, Duck, Cedar and Smuttynose, in the Isles of Shoals. Cruise east among a thousand islands, in and out of coves and inlets of Maine's rugged coast for almost 3,000 miles and you end up at Campobello, just across the water boundary with Canada. From the Isles of Shoals to Campobello — could there be more beautifully named beginnings and endings?

The Isles of Shoals is the magical, mysterious name for those nine small islands, nine miles to sea from Kittery, which rise weirdly, wonderfully white from the ocean. They came close to being stuck with the name "Smith Islands." Captain John Smith, that insatiable seafarer who'd helped settle Jamestown in 1607 when he was 26 years old, spent years voyaging the Maine coast, exploring and charting its islands. He never involved his own name in any of his charts until he sailed to these bare little islands. Their strange and wild white-rock beauty won his heart and stirred his ego; and he named them Smith's Islands. The name didn't last.

Early fishermen changed the name to Isles of Shoals, not because of its pretty sound but because the ocean becomes suddenly shallow, or shoals, here. Nine treacherous ledges surround the nine islands. The only harbor is Gosport Harbor, bordered and protected by Star, Cedar, Smuttynose, and Malaga islands. The boundary line between Maine and New Hampshire runs through Gosport Harbor, giving the five northern islands to Maine — Appledore, Duck, Cedar, Malaga and Smuttynose; and the four southern islands to New Hampshire — Star, Lunging, Seavey's and White.

God must have loved these strange, stark islands, for He made them from a white shining, banded, metamorphic rock, in startling contrast to the dark granite of most Maine islands. Birds love them, for over 140 species have been sighted here. So do plants and flowers, with over 250 varieties finding places to bloom here, even though the islands are bare, rocky, almost barren of trees, but thickly covered in places with low bushes. Herring gulls and great black-backed gulls by the thousands, six kinds of herons, guillemots, snowy egrets, eider ducks, song sparrows, yellowthroats, red-wing blackbirds, cormorants and spindly legged sandpipers abound. Because there are so few trees, the islands seem barren at first; but the meadows of Appledore sprout clover, stitchwort and ox-eye daisies. Iris bloom among the duckweed, loosestrife and arrow-grass in the swampy areas. In summer wild roses, wild strawberries, bachelor buttons, buttercups, lilies of the valley, morning glories and tiny scarlet pimpernels flourish on these rocky, inscrutable islands.

Early in the 1600s, fishermen from England began using the Isles of Shoals regularly. In 1623, Christopher Levett, commissioned by Sir Ferdinando Gorges to start a settlement and a church in the Province of Maine, wrote of the Shoals: "The place is found to be a good fishing place for six shippes, but more cannot well be there; for want of a good stage-roome, as this yeares experience hath proved. The Harbor is but indifferent good. Upon these Ilands are no Savages at all."

By 1628, so many fishing crews were using the Shoals, they were able to support two tavern keepers. The needs of the spirit as well as the flesh were catered to. The Reverend Jedediah Morse wrote that a meetinghouse was built before 1640, with the Reverend Joseph Hull as its minister. The good minister was sued by Gorges in 1646 for possession of a 20 acre marsh. Three Kelly brothers, the Oliver brothers and the Seeleys, and the three Cutt brothers from Wales, were all established fishermen who were playing active roles in life on the Shoals during the 1640s.

Men have always loved the Isles of Shoals. But women have not. The early settlers, all male, banned women from setting foot in their Eden. A strange court record of 1647 contains a lawful complaint from Richard Cutts and John Cutting, settlers on Hog Island (now prettily changed to Appledore), against their neighbor, John Reynolds.

"Contrary to an act of court, which says that no woman shall live on the Isles of Shoals, John Reynolds has brought his wife hither with the intention that she live and abide here . . . He has also brought upon Hog Island a great stock of goats and swine, which by destroying much fish, do great damage . . . and spoil the spring water . . . Your petitioners therefore pray that the Act of Court be put in execution for the removal of women from inhabitating here; and that said Reynolds also be ordered to remove his goats and swine from the island without delay."

The court ordered Reynolds to get rid of his goats and swine within 20 days, "but as to the removal of his wife, she may remain and enjoy the company of her husband, if no further complaint be brought against her."

That was the end of the ban against women. They came. Soon they had the upper hand on the Isles and in Court. Later court records show many men from the Isles were being sentenced to the lash for abusing their wives. Further, the Isles of Shoals women forced their men to ignore a court order which required them to build a "ducking stool for scolds and brawling women."

One of the first big fortunes made in Maine began in the Isles of Shoals. A young immigrant from Cornwall, England, named William Pepperrell settled on Appledore in 1676 and began curing and dunning fish on its sweeping rock ledges. His specialty was to cure them the Appledore way — light on the salt and heavy on the sun; then bury them in salt hay until the flesh turned the color of brown sherry wine.

This trick — called dunning — tickled the palates of the wealthy in Europe and Pepperrell's dried fish fetched premium prices in Spain.

His son, another William, was born at Kittery Point in 1696 and grew up to lead three thousand Maine men in battle, to storm and capture the French fortress of Louisburg, on Cape Breton, in March 1745. He became a hero and was invited to sail to England for a hero's welcome, where he was the first American to be created a baronet by the King of England. The boy from the Isles of Shoals was made Sir William Pepperrell by King George II. For a hundred years, the Pepperrells prospered in Kittery, amassing a great fortune. Col. William Pepperrell built the Pepperrell mansion in 1682. Lady Pepperrell built her house in 1760.

In the American Revolution the Pepperrells lost their wealth, estates and deer parks in America, because they picked the wrong side and stayed loyal to King George III of England, largely because the king's father had made their grandfather the first baronet in the New World.

There is an interesting conflict in the contemporary records about how poor or how prosperous the Shoals were during the early 1700s. A French vessel which visited the Shoals in 1702 reported prosperity: "There are at these islands about sixty fishing shallops, each manned by four men. Besides these, are the masters of the fishing stages, and as they are assisted by the women in taking care of the fish, there may be in all about 280 men." The Rev. Jedediah Morse reported the Shoals were curing up to four thousand quintals of fish (about 448,000 pounds) in the 1730s and were selling many big boatloads of their famous dunfish to Spain and cod to the West Indies market.

The islanders however told a different story. They cried poor, especially when threatened by a new tax. In a petition of April 22, 1721, the inhabitants of Gosport protested: "The people here are very few in number and most of them are men of no Substance, live only by their daily fishing; and near one third of them are single men who threaten to leave if taxed, which will prove our utter ruin. . . . They live on a Rock in the Sea and have not any privilege of right in common lands, as other Inhabitants in the respective Towns have . . ."

In 1761, it was Kittery's turn to cry poor, to plead for a reduction of taxes, saying of the Isles of Shoals: "There was seldom more than ten or fifteen persons ratable there, and they were all poor, had about three or four boats for fishing, and they never paid half the rates and taxes that was added to the Town . . ."

The Reverend John Tucke, a Harvard graduate, became minister on the Shoals in 1732 and he introduced a new orderliness of life. Tucke was the first to record marriages, births, baptisms and deaths among the islanders; and he began the first town meetings. Under him a new ordinance was passed which made liable to fines any fisherman "who spelt any fish above hie warter marck and Leave their heads and bonese. . . ." Tucke ministered to the Shoals for forty years, until his death there in 1773. An indication of how much the islanders liked and respected him is the fact that they paid him his salary in quintals of the prized dunfish.

The death of the Rev. Tucke marked the end of an era for the Isles of Shoals. Within two years, the American Revolution began, and its repercussions hit the Shoals hard. Almost everyone living on the islands was evacuated during the Revolution. A government order said "the islands afforded sustenance and recruitment to the enemy"; and commanded all islanders to quit their homes and move to the mainland. Some floated their homes by raft to Kittery and Portsmouth.

This was no minor evacuation. About 600 families were crowded on these small, lovely islands before the Revolution. Today there are no year-round inhabitants.

The Shoals enjoyed more than a hundred years of growth from the early 1600s as one of the nation's early island settlements. But at the time of the Revolution, the islands hit the skids. With the hundreds of Shoalers now scattered to new homes and with new ties along the coast, few returned after the Revolution. The islands became a rough hangout of bad repute. The rag-tail population which drifted back was considered depraved, drunken. The men were suspected of setting out false lights to entice stormdriven ships onto the rocks, and then looting them.

By 1820 however, a big effort was made to bring Appledore back. The burned-out church was rebuilt; town meetings were begun and improvements in living, fishing and schooling were started. New settlers came.

The big change took shape in 1839 when Thomas Laighton, a New Hampshire politician, obtained appointment as lighthouse keeper on White Island. Laighton, who had a good nose for real estate, bought half of Appledore, and three other islands on the Maine side of the state line, Smuttynose, Malaga and Cedar. Laighton took his wife, Eliza, their 4-year-old daughter, Celia, and infant son, Oscar, with him and moved to his job as keeper of the White Island Light.

Laighton was a hustler. Keeping the light was not work enough to occupy him full time. He was elected to the New Hampshire legislature in 1841 and to the Portsmouth Board of Selectmen. He worked to revive the fishing business. Then he took the wild, bold step of building a small hotel on Appledore in the 1840s. Summer people filled it. By 1848, Laighton built Maine's first island resort hotel, called The Appledore House, which in time became a famous trend-setter, a magnet for artists, authors and the whole "culture crowd" of 19th-century New England. This transformation of the Shoals was due in great part to his daughter, Celia Thaxter.

Young Celia, who came as a baby to White Island Light, moved with the family from White to Appledore and the little Mid Ocean Hotel when she was 12. After the bigger, grander Appledore was opened, she became the hostess. An attractive girl as hostess in a Maine island hotel made news. She began writing poetry about the life, the plants, the birds on the Isles of Shoals. Her poems were published and well received in the Atlantic Monthly. Celia, who at 16 had married Levi Thaxter, attracted the lions of the literary and art worlds, the movie stars of their day, to stay at the Appledore. Soon the hotel register was signed by Nathaniel Hawthorne, James Russell Lowell, Richard Henry Dana, Harriet Beecher Stowe, Franklin Pierce, Samuel Longfellow, William Dean Howells, Sarah Orne Jewett and Frances Burnett (of Little Lord Fauntleroy fame). Artists such as Childe Hassam, A. T. Bircher, Olaf Brauner and William Morris Hunt came to paint.

The Appledore House was constantly enlarged, with two wings, a dance hall, billiard room, a huge verandah and heating and lighting system. The Reverend A. M. Coulton in a letter dated July 23, 1873, described it:

> "Appledore House is a finer hotel than can be found else-where on or near these eastern shores. . . . It is a first class house, and will compare favorably with the United States and the Grand Union in Saratoga . . . abundance of sofas . . . bible in every bedroom . . . billiard-saloon,

bowling alley, ball-room, a band of music and bar . . .
this last in the rear basement. . . . Our company at this
hotel now number three hundred — from St. Louis, Chicago, Philadelphia, New York. They are the choicest
. . . representing millions in wealth."

The Shoals, once a rough fishing settlement, was now promi-
nent on the social map. Boston promoters even staged illegal
prizefights on Smuttynose, with steamers bringing the bloods
of the sporting world up from Boston and New York, much to
the fury of Cedric Laighton, the great hotel keeper at Appledore House.

Competitors built new resort hotels, the big Atlantic House
and the Oceanic, nearby on Star Island. By 1875, Celia's
brothers, Cedric and Oscar, bought them out. The Laightons
ran the Star Island hotels until 1916, when for $16,000 they
sold Star Island and the hotels and cottages to a religious
group. The Unitarian-Congregational Star Island Corporation
soon transformed the Isles again — this time into a kind of
religious retreat.

Then this era on the Shoals abruptly came to its end. The
Appledore burned to the ground in 1914. Cars, rather than
trains and boats, became the summer transportation for vacationing families. Bigger, newer resort hotels lured away the
summer trade from the islands to the mainland. The Laightons died. Father, mother, Celia, and her brothers (Oscar lived
almost to his 100th birthday) are all buried in the Laighton
family cemetery on Appledore. A museum in Celia's memory
was built on the ruins of the famous Appledore hotel. The
garden in front of her cottage, made famous with her book in
1893 called "An Island Garden," has been recreated, with
plantings based on her text and the Childe Hassam illustrations in her book.

Cottages from the days of the hotel have been restored, af-
ter years of vandalism. They are used by the Shoals Marine
Laboratory, established in 1973 by the University of New
Hampshire and Cornell University.

Part of Appledore Island is now a heron rookery and the
great nests of helter-skelter twigs mark where generations of
long-stemmed herons hatch.

Smuttynose

Across a narrow channel lies Smuttynose Island, smaller than Appledore, and named for the black ledge which sticks like a landmark into the sea. Seamen gave it this apt descriptive nickname when they first came to the Isles of Shoals some 370 years ago. Official records from 1684 show the Court of the Western Islands sat at Smuttynose and tried cases here.

Pirates supposedly buried treasure on Smuttynose. That killer-pirate Edward Lowe, so brutal and bestial that his men mutinied and set the rascal adrift in a small boat, committed murder at Smuttynose in 1722. The beautiful fair-haired girl whom he murdered is said to haunt the island, guarding the hidden treasure of Blackbeard. Many have searched but none have found much treasure. However, Captain Samuel Haley, who lived on Smuttynose early in the 1800s, did find four bars of silver buried beneath a rock. The captain used the money to build an expensive breakwater to provide shelter for the fishermen on his island and nearby Star Island. Today, you can safely anchor there at Gosport Harbor and see to the bottom, 20 feet below. Elsewhere, the bottom is solid rock, sometimes deceivingly covered with kelp, neither of which will hold an anchor.

Horror struck in the upright life of Captain Haley on a winter's night early in 1813. The Spanish ship Sagunto headed for a light, which they thought was a beacon, burning in a window above Captain Haley's mill, and hit hard on rocks and ledges on the eastern shore of Smuttynose. The shipwrecked sailors, freezing in the winter gale, struggled ashore and tried to crawl through deep snow to the light in Haley's mill. But they collapsed and froze to death, while Captain Haley slept nearby, unaware. In the morning, Haley found the bodies of the fifteen Spanish sailors. He gave them all he could give them — a decent burial on Smuttynose. Their graves can be seen today, marked by one of Haley's mill stones. Walk by the graves and down to the shore on a winter's night, and you may see the ghosts of the Spanish sailors, hailing passing ships, seeking one that will carry them home to Spain.

Murder of the foulest kind was committed on Smuttynose on the night of March 5, 1873. A man named Louis Wagner knew the island men were away fishing and Smuttynose was deserted except for two women, Karen Christensen and her sister-in-law, Anetha Christensen. Wagner had heard the women had a strong box filled with money. He stole a dinghy from the waterfront at Portsmouth and rowed the nine miles out to Smuttynose. He murdered the two women with an axe. But a third girl, Maren, and her dog escaped through the snow and hid in rock crevices by the shore. Wagner, his foul murders done, rowed the nine miles back to Portsmouth in the nighttime. At daybreak, Maren and her dog climbed out from the hiding place and she screamed and waved to attract fishermen coming down to the shore on Appledore, across the channel. They rowed across; she led them to the bloodstained house; they saw and never forgot the sight of the bodies of the two dead women, hacked by Wagner's axe.

Wagner was caught, tried and sentenced to death, the last man hanged in Maine. His story is an interesting episode in Maine history.

Wagner's trial took nine days. But the jury took only 55 minutes to bring in a verdict of "guilty of murder." Yet many in Maine contended Wagner could not have committed the murders. They thought no man could row nine miles out to Smuttynose, commit two murders and then row nine miles back to Portsmouth in the time for which Wagner had no alibi.

The law of Maine on the statute books then was clear and curt: Anyone found guilty of murder should hang by the neck till dead. But, to minimize chances of hanging the wrong man, the law also required that the hanging should not be carried out for at least one year. Wagner's lawyer appealed the sentence, asking for life imprisonment instead of death. Opponents of the death penalty added their pleas. A two-year delay followed. Wagner waited in his jail cell in the Maine prison at Thomaston.

Another prisoner in Thomaston, named Gordon, awaited execution along with Wagner. Both men were in their 30s. Finally Governor Dingle signed both death warrants. Gordon tried to commit suicide, by stabbing himself on the day of the hanging. But he was carried to the gallows, bleeding and unconscious, side by side with his fellow prisoner, Louis Wagner. The hangings were carried out under supervision by the sheriff, his deputies, and twelve witnesses, the prison doctor and other state officials who by law had to witness the execution. The bodies, with no relatives to claim them, were sent to the Maine Medical Society for dissection. In 1887, Maine outlawed the death penalty, in part because of the outcry against the hangings of Gordon and Wagner. The Smutty-nose murderer was the last man legally executed in Maine.

No one lives in winter on the Isles of Shoals today, except the Coast Guardsmen manning the White Island Light and Dave and Edith Pearson, caretakers on Star Island. Today the little islands are only a summer paradise. But for over 370 years, families lived through terrible winter storms which bombarded the Shoals. The storms, as much as the summer flowers, are part of the Isles of Shoals.

Celia Thaxter, who went to the Shoals with her father as a 4-year-old in 1840 and died on Appledore in 1894, describes a Shoals storm in a letter to a woman friend.

"I know you thought of us in the terrific storm yesterday . . . Had it continued another 24 hours, it would not have left a stick or stone on the Shoals. It is utterly indescribable. All of the islands were lost in clouds of flying foam. Our yacht, the Lone Star, sank at her moorings and is lost. The wind and water were blown through the house . . . You remember Londoners' Island (Lunging Island), where you and I went for morning glories? . . . A brig lies there smashed to atoms, eight men drowned, but one alive to tell the tale. She struck at 8 a.m. in broad daylight, but thick fog, on the outlying rocks of White Island; a breaker carried off part of her stern and drowned five men. Then she rolled and wallowed to Londoners' and went ashore there . . . There the brig was smased in two . . . three more men were drowned. I have been over to see the wreck . . . the huge vessel lay not far from our morning glory garden. Crushed like an eggshell . . . her huge beams snapped like sticks of macaroni; such a total and gigantic destruction is not to be described . . . Her sails strewed the whole beach, she was one heap of splintered fragments. Eight men dead, lying about the ledges; everywhere I feared to see a ghastly face, a hand, a foot. One thick grey vest lay in a pool and stared up at me with ghastly white horn buttons. Iron bolts four feet long were twisted like hairpins. The brig was 40 days out of Liverpool to Boston, loaded with salt.

"It has stormed five days, wearily, wearily. The face of the gale was awful to behold — the sea black, swollen, angry, streaming with hoary vapor from the cold, and flinging broadsides of freezing spray all over the island; snow falling, hissing, whispering, lashing the windowpanes; the noise of the breakers booming and thundering; and the voice of the wind wailing, howling, expostulating, shrieking.

"Tonight the world is calm in comparison. Just before sunset, I ventured out. Solid ice about the island shore; wharf and crane a mountain of solid saltwater ice; snow everywhere; the sea dull olive green and black; a rift of stormy grey in the sky. A huge black shag rose from the rock opposite me and flew ponderously away. The gulls soared and shrieked. I ran back and crept to the fireside."

At times close to a thousand people lived happily on these Isles of Shoals. During 370 years scores of ships have been wrecked here. Today old headstones in the island cemetery tell the story; the graves of sailors shipwrecked and drowned here; and the tiny headstones of infant children who perished from some forgotten plague. Yet poets and artists have written and painted paeans of praise to the strange, hypnotic beauty of these remote Isles of Shoals. Robert Low described them:

"A heap of bare and splintery crags
  Tumbled about by lightning and frost,
  With rifts and chasms and storm-bleached jags
  That wait and growl for ships to be lost."

Legends and ghosts abound on the Isles of Shoals. Where the sea pours onto Appledore is a ghostly spot named Betty Moody's Hole. The legend is that Betty Moody fled here with her little children during an Indian attack on the Shoals. They hid in this cleft in the rocks. Through the long night, Betty Moody heard the Indians on the rampage. Her children, cold and frightened, would break out crying. When a band of scalp-hunting Indians came searching for survivors among the chasms on the shore, one child cried out; and kept crying despite Betty Moody's efforts to stifle the cries which would guide the Indians to her children. In a desperate move to preserve the safety of their hiding spot, Betty Moody is said to have slit the throat of her wailing baby. That wail can be heard some nights now, if you walk the shore.

The pale ghost of Constable Babb also walks the moon-lighted shore of Appledore. Babb, island constable when the Court of the Western Isles convened here in the 1680s, had witnessed such fearful crimes that now, 300 years later, wearing a bloody butcher's smock and wielding a long knife, he walks the Isles of Shoals in an eternal round of vigilance against more crimes.

The U.S. Navy began close to the Isles of Shoals. In 1776, the Continental Congress ordered the new nation's first frigate Raleigh, 32 guns, to be built in frantic haste at Badger's Island, nine miles from the Isles of Shoals. Within 60 days, she was launched. No sooner was she off to war than the famous sloop of war Ranger was laid down on her blocks at Kittery. Ranger was launched in May, 1777, with Captain John Paul Jones in command. Ranger was followed by Congress, 74 guns; then America, also commanded by John Paul Jones. Then, in 1798, Crescent, 32 guns, and Portsmouth, 24 guns, were launched here.

In 1800, the government bought Dennett's Island for $5,000. Ever since then, the Kittery Yard has been prominent in American naval history. The keel of the first steam side-wheeler the USS Saranac was laid here in May, 1847. Old Ironsides, officially the USS Constitution, was rebuilt at Kittery. She is now anchored at Boston, the oldest ship in the Navy.

In the Civil War, more than 2,000 men worked at the Kittery Yard; in World War II, over 25,000. Kittery built the first submarine, the L-8, launched in April, 1917. Before 1941, Kittery had built 33 submarines. During World War II, the Kittery Yard built 75 submarines, cutting construction time from 469 days down to 173 days. Kittery built the early nuclear-powered submarine Swordfish, launched here in 1958. Today, 6,000 work there on the newest of guided missile submarines.

Coming in from the Isles of Shoals on my boat, I sometimes stop at the town wharf at Frisbee's store for supplies. This fine old store in a seafaring town still serves customers from the wharf as well as from the road on Kittery Point.

This is the oldest family grocery store in the United States. I spent two hours talking with Frank Frisbee and his brother, David, and their children, who operate the store today — fifth generation of Frisbees working here in 150 years.

Frisbee's was first opened by Daniel Frisbee in 1828, when John Quincy Adams was President and Maine was just eight years old as a state. The family store is now run by the fourth successive generation, Frank and David Frisbee, helped by their children, the fifth generation.

Frank Frisbee, boss of today's store, keeps a library of Frisbee memorabilia.

"The stock in trade of the store in 1828 included skunk oil, gunpowder, flints, ox yokes, bear grease and lots of rum . . . Great schooners, home from voyages across the world, unloaded their cargoes at this wharf. We had barrels of molasses, rum, spices, and all kinds of drygoods and dress materials to sell, straight from the ships.

"Frisbee's was a ship chandlery then as well as a grocery and drygoods store. Our great-grandfather did a handsome business in stocking out-going vessels."

Today a corner of the grocery is filled still with ships' supplies — marine paints, caulking compound, nails and rope. Frisbee's still has one foot in the sea, supplying food, drygoods, wine, beer and fuel to the boats which come to their float.

"When we were putting in new foundations in 1954, on the site of the very first Frisbee store, we found six bottles of rum, carefully and safely hidden. We sniffed the rich old rum but didn't have the courage to drink it," says Frank Frisbee. Nearby is the Frisbee School, named for their great-grandfather, Frank Frisbee.

From the wharf, back of Frisbee's, you can look out to the Isles of Shoals. Stand quietly and in your mind's eye you may see the old sailing vessels of the first settlers in the early 1600s. Now there are moorings out here for over 211 boats — sailing craft, pleasure cruisers and lobster boats.

"Each morning up until World War II, the store sent a man with a horse and wagon to knock on customers' doors. He'd take their orders and deliver the goods later in the day," says Frank. "I helped make the deliveries as a boy."

The old ways have, of course, changed. But despite changes, Frisbee's still has a very special atmosphere that rightfully clings to the oldest family grocery store in the United States. Frank and David wear neat short-sleeved shirts, always wear ties. They wear the long white aprons that have been the traditional hallmark of grocers.

"We still make the Frisbee corned beef for which customers drive hundreds of miles," says David. He explains how Frisbee's have been making it for one and a half centuries.

"We start with cold fresh clear water. Add salt and keep adding until it is salty enough to float a potato. Sometimes we use an egg instead of a potato. Then we put in first-quality beef, about four pieces weighing 10 pounds each. We put the beef into the brine on Monday and by Thursday it is ready — Frisbee's famous corned beef."

The famous and wealthy who used to summer in vast rambling summer cottages were customers at Frisbee's. Old account books tell the story of enormous orders from the estates of John M. Howells, designer of New York skyscrapers and son of William Deal Howells, the 19th-century writer; and from the homes of Mrs. Decatur Wright, Mrs. Anna Payson, Ambassador Edward Crocker and dozens more. Theodore Roosevelt and Margaret Truman and Mark Twain and the great eagle carver John Bellamy have all been customers of Frisbee's.

Across the road from the store is a headstone, in memory of Sir William Pepperrell, 1696-1759, a leading figure in the colonial days of Kittery Point. His birthplace, his mansion and his tomb all are close to Frisbee's store — a store built on land confiscated from the Pepperrell family at the time of the American Revolution.

"We take care of his marker and his tombstone now," says Frank Frisbee.

Here on the southernmost tip of Maine, is a comforting sign of continuity in a rather rootless world.

Before I went to Frisbee's store, I'd seen a small lobster boat hauling traps off Appledore, and had done a double-take. Clearly a woman was running the boat and doing the hauling, single-handed. I made it my business to talk with her.

Yvonne Sullivan was a brown-eyed blonde.

"Lobstering is a great job for a girl," she told me. "I paid for my new 22-foot boat in two years, thanks to my lobstering. I wish I had started fishing a long while ago. I've been married to Rodney Sullivan 15 years and helped him lobster often. But I didn't start going on my own till 12 years later. I began small, in a skiff with just a few traps and gradually added more. Then I got my own 22-foot fiberglass boat and I'm setting out 250 traps. Hauling 100 traps a day."

Dozens of women go lobstering along the Maine coast. Most go with their husbands, as helpers on fine days. Others have a skiff and an outboard, and fish a few traps close to shore. Very few have their own lobster boat, their own traps and go single-handed several miles off the mainland as Yvonne Sullivan does.

"She is a darn good, serious lobsterman," I was told by her neighbor, J. Russell Smith, who retired after 36 years building submarines in the Kittery Navy Yard. "There are not many as good as her."

Yvonne talked about lobstering from the Sullivan cottage out on Appledore Island in the Isles of Shoals.

When it comes to lobstering, the Isles of Shoals are a bit like Monhegan farther down the coast. By tradition the Shoals are sovereign territory. "You don't set traps close in to the Shoals unless your family comes from one of these islands."

The Sullivan family does indeed belong on Appledore Island.

"Rodney's father fished from there. And his father before him. On back through generations, Sullivans have fished from Appledore. Now Rodney and I live on Appledore and lobster out of here from May till November," said Yvonne Sullivan.

Rodney goes in a bigger 37-foot boat, fishes more traps farther out.

"I only lobster in summer, from Appledore, and my traps are within two miles of the island. I make all my own traps. Built 50 new ones this winter. Rodney hires men to build his for him. But I have to buy the heads. I plain can't knit the heads."

There are only three cottages and a Cornell University marine research station on Appledore now. On nearby Smuttynose, the Foys are the only family there. Again it is their fishing territory, because generations of Foys have lobstered from Smuttynose.

One man had bad luck fishing in the waters around the Isles of Shoals. In President George Washington's diary for November 2, 1789, he wrote: "On my way to the mouth of the harbor, I stopped at a place called Kittery, in the Province of Maine . . . Having lines aboard, we proceeded to the Fishing Banks a little without the Harbor and fished for cod; but it not being a proper time for tide we caught only two."

Scientists share Appledore with fishermen today. Cornell and the University of New Hampshire have been operating research laboratories on the Shoals in summer. From time to time, the Shoals Marine Laboratory publishes its technical research into marine organisms, plant and bird life. The northern end of Appledore has been declared a Critical Natural Area by the state of Maine to protect the natural heron rookery there. Botantists have reconstructed the 1890s garden with the same types of plants and flowers and shrubs which Celia Thaxter tended with so much care and so much success.

Star Island has for over 80 years been a center for summer meetings of religious groups. The tradition started in 1896, when Thomas H. Elliott, of Lowell, Massachusetts, proposed bringing a large group of Unitarians to the Shoals. Oscar Laighton was cautious. "What's a Unitarian?" he asked.

"Are they good people? It won't do to introduce any rough element."

The coming of the Unitarians to Star Island, and their subsequent purchase of the hotel properties there, has added an entirely new dimension to the Shoals, turning Star Island into an island almost totally devoted to religious teaching. Over 300 people, engaged in various religious conferences and retreats, are on Star Island every summer month.

Worst shiver and shock to hit the Shoals came in the winter of 1973. It was not a storm of nature, but a scheme by oil men which shook the Shoals. Olympic Refineries, then controlled by Aristotle Onassis, proposed bringing supertankers to a docking station they would erect near the Shoals; then unloading crude from them by underwater pipeline to a 400,000 barrel-a-day refinery, to be built on the mainland at Durham, N. H. Each supertanker would have been as big as two or three of the islands. The supertankers plus their support vessels and equipment would have occupied much of the ocean near the Shoals. For 90 days a battle was waged between those who wanted the jobs and money promised by the refinery and those who feared the possible consequences of supertankers and oil refineries. When the critical vote was taken at the Durham town meeting, the town refused to grant the required rezoning permit by a vote of 1,254 to 144. The oil project was dead.

The Isles of Shoals, which can be easily reached by sightseeing boats from Portsmouth, are now on the National Register of Historic Places. In rather dry and musty words, the Historic Register states: "The Isles of Shoals, though small in area, barren in appearance, and possessed of an inhospitable winter climate, have exerted an historic and cultural influence that is disproportionate with their modest area and resources."

Indeed they have.

Isles of Shoals Light

The heyday of the Isles of Shoals as an early resort with great hotels began here. Soon after Thomas Laighton became keeper of the White Island Light in 1839 he started the first of the great resort hotels of Maine.

Fort Gorges, Casco Bay

This vast granite fort, long abandoned, is the only major landmark in Maine named for Sir Ferdinando Gorges, the father of Maine.

Portland Head Light

The oldest lighthouse in Maine, this was finished by order of George Washington and first lighted Jan. 10, 1791. (Gannett file photo)

Departing Portland

Portland Harbor has been among the busiest commercial and naval ports in the United States. Cargo ships once carried millions of tons of wheat and lumber from here; Atlantic convoys in World War II shaped up here; in the 1970s, 500 tankers a year unloaded oil here. *(Gannett file photo)*

Peaks Island House and Annexes
Copyrighted by W. D. Hanson, 1906

Peaks Island as a summer resort
Old postcards from the Maine Historical Society show some of the resort hotels and the famous Gem Theater which attracted thousands of people daily to the islands of Casco Bay.

Boat Landing, Peaks Island, Me.

Leading Hotels and Boarding Houses

ALONG THE ROUTE OF
CASCO BAY STEAMBOAT COMPANY

CUSHING'S ISLAND

Ottawa House, Chas. E. Davidson; accommodation, 250; $3.00 to $4.00 per day; $15.00 to $30.00 per week, single; $25.00 to $40.00 per week for two persons; special rates for season patrons.

PEAK'S ISLAND. Forest City Landing

Peak's Island House, ⎰ R. E. Rowe; accommodation, 600; $2.00
Coronado-Union House, ⎱ to $3.00 per day; $12.00 to $17.00 per week, single; $22.00 to $30.00 for two persons.

Inness House, Mrs. Sarah Inness; accommodation, 50; $2.00 per day; $8.00 to $10.00 per week.

Avenue House, M. C. Sterling; accommodation, 60; $2.00 per day; $8.00 to $10.00 per week.

Harbor View House, Fred E. Milliken; accommodation, 40; $2.00 per day; $9.00 to $12.00 per week.

Bay View House, W. S. Dyer; rooms only; accommodation, 60; $3.00 to $4.50 per week.

Brackett House, J. F. Brackett, rooms only; accommodation, 20; $2.00 to $3.50 per week.

Speed House, Mrs. George Speed; rooms only; accommodation, 20; $2.00 to $4.00 per week.

Cliff Cottage, Robinson Sterling; rooms only; accommodation, 20; $2.00 to $4.00 per week.

Hillside Cottage, William J. Gardiner; accommodation, 16; $1.25 per day; $8.00 per week.

Central Cottage, N. C. Skillings; rooms only; accommodation, 20; $3.00 to $4.00 per week.

Summer Retreat, Mrs. Fisher; rooms only; accommodation, 15; $2.00 to $4.00 per week.

Toronto Cottage, A. V. Ackley; rooms only; accommodation, 12; $2.00 to $3.00 per week.

Willow Cottage, Josiah Sterling; rooms only; accommodation, 12; $3.00 to $4.00 per week.

Mineral Spring House, A. T. Sterling; accommodation, 25; $1.00 per day; $7.00 per week.

TREFETHEN'S LANDING

Oceanic House, Mrs. R. T. Sterling; accommodation, 50; $2.50 per day; $12.00 per week.

Valley View House, Mrs. M. E. Brimmer; accommodation, 50; $2.00 per day; $10.00 to $14.00 per week.

Oak Cottage, Mrs. H. T. Blake; accommodation, 20; $2.00 per day; $10.00 to $14.00 per week.

Hillside House, John Peterson; rooms only; accommodation, 12; $3.00 to $5.00 per week.

Colonial House, Mrs. W. H. Trefethen; accommodation, 20; $8.00 week.

EVERGREEN LANDING

Knickerbocker Hotel, Mrs. J. H. Anderson; accommodation, 75; $2.00 to $3.00 per day; $10.00 to $15.00 per week, single; $20.00 to $30.00 for two persons.

LONG ISLAND. Ponce's Landing

Granite Spring Hotel, E. Ponce; accommodation, 150; $1.00 to $3.00 per day; $7.00 to $18.00 per week.

Dirigo House, Mrs. Joseph Perry; accommodation, 100; $9.00 to $12.00 per week, single; $17.00 to $20.00 for two persons.

Casco Bay House, Charles E. Cushing; accommodation, 60; $1.50 to $2.00 per day; $9.00 to $12.00 per week, single; $16.00 to $20.00 for two persons.

For further information, address

C. W. T. GODING, Gen. Mgr.

CASCO BAY STEAMBOAT COMPANY,
PORTLAND, ME.

Room and Board $4
More than 20 resort hotels and boarding houses on Casco Bay islands catered to summer vacationers. Some had hundreds of rooms and prices ranged from $2 to $4 a day, as listed on this old ferry timetable.

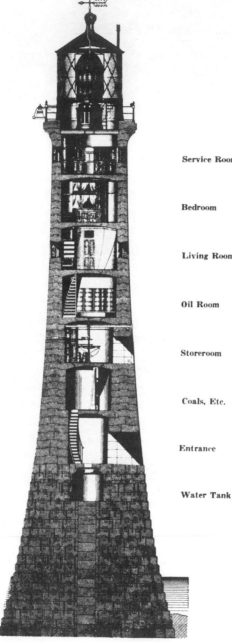

**INTERIOR
OF A STAG LIGHT**

Service Room

Bedroom

Living Room

Oil Room

Storeroom

Coals, Etc.

Entrance

Water Tank

Interior of a stag light
This schematic drawing shows the amount of stair climbing a keeper
faced each day. (From Robert T. Sterling's "Lighthouses of Maine")

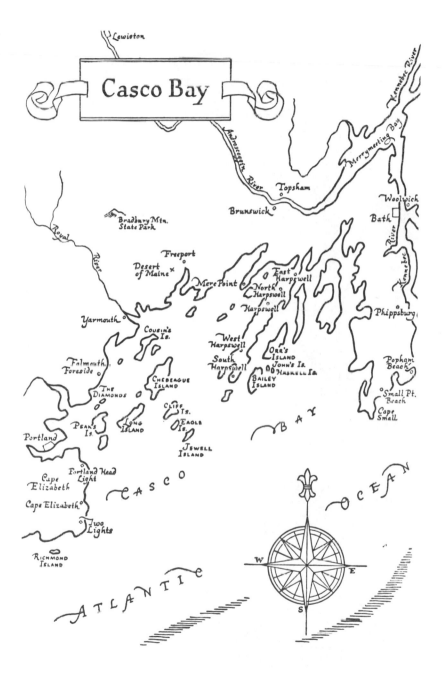

Casco Bay islands
This shows locations of islands featured in Chapters 8 and 9.

Chebeague Island ferry dock

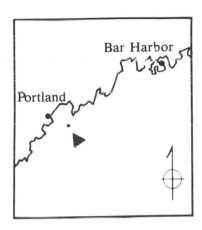

8.

Casco Bay Islands:
Cinderella Of Maine

Certain tribes of American Indians can be very discriminating in island real estate. One tribe sold Manhattan Island cheap, but another fought hard to hold onto the islands of Casco Bay. The Indians who loved Casco Bay islands christened this glorious huge bay "Ancocisco," which means "Place of the Herons." White men, unable to twist their tongues around that word, corrupted and shortened it to "Casco."

Like many places with name origins obscured by history's mists, Casco Bay has proponents for another name source. They say Spanish explorer Estaban Gomez named it "Bahia de Casco" because of its shape resembling a helmet. Take your choice.

Indian Chief Madockowando was top man on Chebeague Island when the first white settlers came in the 1600s. Each June in those days, Madockowando led his people from the inland forests to the bay. In a long line of birch bark canoes the Indians would paddle down river and cross the open water to Great Chebeague to make their summer headquarters on its shores. All summer the men caught fish from Casco Bay in tremendous quantities, while their squaws on shore dried much of the catch for eating during the inland winters; the men hunted porpoises, and turned their hides into a winter necessity, snowshoes; they killed seals and a whale or two, extracting oil for their cooking and to use as medicine. Like Chebeague islanders today, the Indians enjoyed summer in the islands, lying in the sun and swimming from the beaches.

On feast days Indians from other islands gathered on Chebeague over 400 years ago for days and nights of games, visiting, and partying. Dig in the island soil today, and you may still spade up tools and cooking utensils those Indians used here.

Indians sold Manhattan Island in 1624 to Peter Minuit for $24. But as late as 1870, a small group of the Maine tribes still summered on Great Chebeague.

Today no Indians come to Chebeague. But 2,000 whites summer here; and 400 live here year round. If you go down to the island wharf and wait there for the ferry to bring its load of supplies and passengers out from Portland, you'll probably meet Doughtys or Rosses, Seaburys or Rickers, Bennetts or Webbers and a Johnson or two. These families have been on Chebeague and other islands of Casco Bay for hundreds of years. Their names are synonymous with good pilots, and good fishermen. Their roots go deep into Chebeague's past. That is a long way back.

Great Chebeague, the biggest of some 180 islands in Casco Bay, is four and a half miles long, a mile wide, with a land area of 2,800 acres. The recorded history of the island dates back to before the Pilgrims landed at Plymouth Rock. Then Chebeague was listed as a "colony of the Royal Crown of England" and its first white proprietor was the father of Maine, Sir Ferdinando Gorges. But not for long. In 1650, he sold out to a Boston merchant named Merry, thereby starting a trend of island selling. Merry never set foot on the island, but he boosted his ego by changing its name from Chebeague (Indian word for cold spring water) to Merry Island. However, money spoke louder than vanity to Merry. He sold the island at a profit for $500 to another Boston businessman named John King. Then King sold at a profit to Walter Gendall of Yarmouth. He held it despite the inconvenience that he was charged with treason at the time by a Massachusetts court, and had to pay over 20 pounds to buy his pardon. But the Indians didn't pardon Gendall; they killed him. And soon Chebeague's name changed again, strangely this time. The island was given to two deacons of the First Church of Boston as "recompense for their goodly deeds," and was renamed "Recompense Island."

But only briefly. On shore, where Stroudwater stands now, between downtown Portland and the jetport, big money was being made in cutting and shipping tall pines for the masts of the English navy. Since 1691, all white pines with a diameter of 24 inches at one foot above the ground, were reserved for the English Crown and marked with the King's Broad Arrow. Colonel Thomas Westbrook was one of the men making small fortunes from shipping out the tall white pines. A mast tree 120 feet tall was worth $500. A 75-foot tree for a bowsprit fetched $200, and a spar fetched up to $100. In 1772 Maine shipped 382 masts, 69 bowsprits and 451 spars to England and earned over $200,000, a very big sum in those days. With some of those profits, Col. Westbrook bought Great Chebeague. But business on the mainland was too hectic for him to settle out on an island. None of the early owners had the good sense of the Indians to really enjoy this lovely island. That had to wait until Scotsman Ambrose Hamilton arrived.

Hamilton built a log house on the north end, fathered 12 children and became grandfather to 71. Hamiltons built and made famous the Chebeague stone fleet. By the 1850s, over thirty Hamilton stone sloops, the Mack truck of their time, were hauling heavy loads of granite from Maine quarries to be made into some of the greatest buildings of their time. One Chebeague stone sloop, the Addie Snow, is believed to have sent the 291-foot passenger ship Portland to the bottom in the great storm of 1898, one of the worst tragedies at sea. The theory is that the Portland, in zero visibility, heavy seas and a howling gale, collided with the granite-laden Addie Snow, caved in from the impact, and sank with the loss of 175 lives.

Exactly how or where the Portland was lost had been a mystery for half a century. Then in November 1944, a scalloper out of Rockland was dragging off Cape Cod and brought up the Portland's bell in her net. With the ship's bell as evidence of exactly where the Portland sank, Edward Rowe Snow, who has written fine books on New England's coast, sent down divers to find out if any more of the Portland lay on the bottom. The divers found the bow of the Addie Snow embedded in the side of the Portland, indicating a terrible collision and immediate sinking. All lives on both ships were lost. In another tragedy in a winter sea, ocean spray froze on the masts and decks of a Chebeague stone sloop outside of Boston Harbor. Tons of ice weighed her down till she became helpless in the breaking, freezing seas. Capt. John Ross and his two sons, John and Walter were found aboard, frozen to death, encased in ice on the rigging.

A gentler side of Chebeague, the summer cottage colony, began a hundred years ago. Hotels, a golf course, swimming beaches, boat slips and yacht moorings in Chandler's Cove multiplied as the summer folk moved in. One of the earliest was Dr. L. L. Hale, who came to the island to practice medicine in 1884, and doctored island families for 31 years. Early in the 1900s Ellis Ames Ballard, a wealthy Philadelphian, built a splendid summer house on Indian Point, spent some $40,000 (a big sum 80 years ago) on it and called it "Khatmandu."

Ballard lavished special care on a great oak tree which stood alone on Indian Point, a seamark for generations of fishermen in the Bay, The story goes that in 1791, when Wentworth Ricker came to settle on Chebeague, he found a tiny oak growing in his garden plot on Indian Point and nursed it along with loving care. When Ballard bought the land, over 100 years later, the tiny tree had grown into a massive oak. A survivor of a century of hard weather, age was taking its sad toll of the great tree. Ballard brought tree experts to the island to doctor the massive lone oak. It recovered and lived to survive hurricanes which since then have demolished younger trees in more sheltered spots.

Great Chebeague is only a few miles away from the heart of Portland, yet it has managed to retain qualities of a remote island of special beauty. But that was threatened in the 1950s, when some Chebeague islanders started a campaign for a bridge to link the island closer to the prosperity and business of downtown Portland. Howard Beehler and F. E. Repetto, strong advocates for a bridge, argued that there were too few ways for young people to make a living on Chebeague except as caretakers for summer folk. They pointed out that a bridge already linked nearby Cousins Island to Littlejohn Island and thence to the mainland. They argued that since only a sandbar separates Littlejohn from Chebeague, a causeway with only a couple of spans could link Chebeague to Littlejohn and thence to the mainland. With a bridge like

that, they said, Chebeauge could grow from a year-round population of 400 to one of 4,000. The Chebeague bridge lobby
succeeded in persuading one state legislature to authorize such
a bridge, only to have the proposal defeated in a statewide
referendum. Today it is still a ferry which links the island to
the mainland. You cannot drive your car to Chebeague yet.

The island the Indians loved so well for so long is still a
true island. But the pressure for a bridge is likely to be revived. As Portland more and more becomes a favorite, ex-
panding city, the urge to live on a nearby island, yet drive to
work, will become more powerful. The pressure for such a
bridge may come not only from people on Chebeague. Just
across the channel from Great Chebeague lies Long Island,
the 650-acre 'oil' island, a part of the City of Portland. Already
there are 300 houses and buildings on it, with an assessed
valuation topping $4 million.

At low tide, a sandspit connects Great Chebeague to Little
Chebeague. One summer night we anchored off the magnificent beach at Little Chebeague and spent the night aboard
Steer Clear. Almost half a mile long, shaped like a shallow
crescent, the beach uncovers as the tide drops until it is 200
feet wide from dunes to low water mark. I've gone back in
the log of Steer Clear to refresh memories of that day and
night.

"Anchor down by 3 p.m. Elmore Wallace, who is
cruising with us for the week as the expert with local
knowledge, says when he was a boy 50 years ago, he
used to row over here from his home on Long Island
and get milk from the cows the farmer kept in the
meadows on Little Chebeague. It was a big farm then.

"We rowed ashore in the dinghy and wandered those
meadows. The grass is shoulder high now. Small mice
scuttle in it. Young birds who can't yet fly seek shelter
in it, after crashing from wobbly takeoffs. The warm
smell of hot summer lies fragrant on the meadow this
afternoon. Ancient shutters creak on broken hinges in
a vandalized house, as the breeze from the sea stirs

up a moaning through the gaping walls. But it is not eerie or ghostly in these abandoned meadows, and there is no meanness in the tumbled down porches; just a whisper of sorrow that the joy and happiness which once filled these houses and the young people who once lived in them are gone.

"Two kids have been laughing and playing on the beach all this afternoon. Now their father rows in from his sailboat and fetches them. They up anchor and depart. Little Chebeague is ours. We sit in the cockpit and watch the sun sink; then the moon rise; and feel the summer air cool, and hear the bell buoys clank. The night is so quiet and still that we can hear voices of youngsters on Long Island, across the water, calling goodnights to each other."

Below this entry in the log, a sheet of paper has been pasted in. On it are notes made after I'd gone to City Hall to find out more about Little Chebeague.

"The island, empty and vandalized in the summer of 1970, was loved and cared for in 1890. Over a dozen fine homes stood here; today we see only their sad skeletons or their foundations and remnants of once lovely gardens of roses, lilacs, and day lilies. For a while after World War II, the island was used as a training camp for prizefighters. Before that, the navy, which had installations and men on nearby islands, used Little Chebeague for rest and recreation. The navy set up a firefighting school for training sailors to become firefighters on aircraft carriers. The strange steel hulk on the beach was where fires were set, only to be put out in practice training.

"City Hall Records show that anyone could have bought this gem of an island for a song in the 1950s. The federal government offered it for a dollar to the State of Maine, then to the City of Portland. Neither would take it. So it went on the auction block. Mainers didn't think enough of it then to buy it. So this 200-

acre island beauty was sold in 1951 for $6,250 to John Absmeier of New York. He did nothing with it. But in 1965 the Press Herald told of plans to put in an air strip, a summer theater, a hotel complex . . . part of a scheme for big money development of Little Chebeague and part of Jewell Island, farther out in Casco Bay. But, thank heaven, nothing came of it.

"After John Absmeier died, his estate sold the island in 1972 for $155,000, making about $149,000 profit. Guess who bought it? The State of Maine, which had refused it 20 years earlier when the price was one dollar. John Absmeier of New York was smarter than Mainers. He bought it for $6,250 when no Maine resident thought a 200-acre island, 10 minutes from Portland, with a magnificent beach, was worth $31 an acre!

"But now this beauty of an island is a Maine State Park for everyone to enjoy."

Maine woke up very late to the value of our precious islands. From the time Maine became a state in 1820 until the 1960s, the State of Maine and the towns along the coast hardly gave a damn about the islands. Often nobody knew who owned them. Often when the state or town had title, they were eager to be rid of them and sold them for a song.

In Casco Bay alone there are plenty such instances.

The same John Absmeier who bought Little Chebeague also bought 160 acres of Jewell Island, further out in Casco Bay. Again he bought it from the federal government after the State of Maine and various Maine towns had refused it as a gift. Absmeier paid $10,240 at auction for these 160 gorgeous island acres ($64 an acre). His estate sold his 160 acres on Jewell in 1972 to the State of Maine for $200,000; and they are now part of the Jewell Island State Park.

On Great Diamond Island, David L. Lukens of New Jersey and Michael Montalbano, also of New Jersey, bought 200 acres and 50 buildings at auction from the federal government for about $40,000. The same David Lukens in 1956 bought 125 acres of Cushing Island, once the site of Fort Levett, for $33,750, complete with 15 brick army buildings. Another little eight-acre island, called Overset, close to

Portland, was offered to the City of Portland for just $500 by the federal government. By a vote of 5 to 3, the City Council refused it. In 1965 a private buyer got the island at auction for $3,300.

The State of Maine and the City of Portland both turned down the chance to take for one dollar the spectacular, spacious military reservation on close-in Peak's Island. So in 1958 Peter Cioffi of Massachusetts bought it for $14,671 at auction and later sold it off as subdivisions for cottage colonies. Today one small oceanfront lot costs more than Cioffi paid for the entire parcel.

Why did the state and the city turn their backs on these bargain-priced islands? Of course, it's fun to blame the bureaucrats for lacking foresight. But private Maine people had no more foresight than the bureaucrats. No Maine residents made winning bids at the public auctions. The fact is islands in Casco Bay were unwanted Cinderellas as late as 1960.

Casco Bay has been unappreciated until recently. When city, state or federal funds were available, they went for the development of the Portland airport, not to the Port of Portland or the islands. Millions for air, not a penny for harbor and sea.

Why? One reason may be that in the years from World War II until the 1970s Casco Bay meant little to most people. More than 100,000 people live near Casco Bay today; yet perhaps not more than five in a hundred have had a chance to set foot on the islands from which Portland sprung. We have cared little about these precious islands because we have known little about them.

I was lucky that my job as a Portland newspaper reporter put me in working contact with the bay and the islands.

For 17 years I've been looking at Casco Bay from the windows of my newspaper office. I've looked up from the typewriter to glance with joy at sunsets, storms, fog, sea smoke; seen the passage of ships winter and summer, spring and fall, night and day. Over the years, I've been out on the bay on rescue stories with Coast Guard boats; in pilot boats in storms; on an ocean tug, towing an oil barge 678 feet long behind it; in my own small boat, spending days and nights on and among the islands; in a racing yacht on the Monhegan

race; have ridden the Portland-Yarmouth cruise ferry with
its dance bands and gambling salons; flown in helicopters to
hover over the islands where Indians feasted and the first settlers fought for a tochold; seen them from the bridge of a
supertanker arriving in port from the Persian Gulf. But the
more I learn about Casco Bay, the less I feel I know. These
islands are so filled with history, romance, adventure, with
terror and hardship, scullduggery and kindliness; and each is
so different from the next, that no man in a lifetime could
know more than half there is to know about them. This next
chapter gives only part of what there is to tell.

Freighter passing Cushings Is.

9.

Casco Bay Islands:
Part Two

There's a catchy story that there are 365 islands in Casco
Bay, which are sometimes therefore called "the calendar islands." Untrue. The man to blame for this neat exaggeration
is Colonel W. Romer, His Majesty's Chief Engineer for the
Colonies. In 1700 the colonel made a quick inspection trip of
Casco Bay and reported to his bosses: "Said Bay has a multitude of islands, these being reported as many islands as there
are days in the year." However, that more mundane bible,
The United States Coastal Pilot, gives the number as 136, including ledges. Some island-counters say they can see 200
islands from the tower of Portland Head Light. But the view
from that handsome, historic light, built by order of George
Washington in 1791, is so gorgeous that it can make a man or
woman see double.

Biggest of the islands is Great Chebeague, over 2,800 acres;
the most heavily populated is Peak's Island, 720 acres, close
to the city and linked to Portland by commuter ferries. But
Peak's is no modern day suburb of an island. Peak's was first
settled over 350 years ago by the Palmers and Bracketts,
whose families were massacred in a bloody Indian raid in
October, 1689. The name changed as ownership changed, from
Munjoy's Island to Mitton's to Michael's; finally the name of
Peak's Island stuck, although Samuel Peak's greatest claim to
fame may have been that he married the widow of the previous owner, George Munjoy (whose name stuck to Munjoy
Hill). Some of the small islands with such grand names as
Pound of Tea and Junk of Pork, and Pumpkin Knob were prob-
ably christened to commemorate the price paid for them.

Casco Bay is huge, more than 200 square miles. The entrance is 18 miles wide; the average width is 12 miles; and the tides run 12 feet or more. The depth in the channel is deeper than the shipping channels of Boston, New York, Philadelphia and Baltimore. The harbor is unobstructed by bridges. Anchorages in Hussey and Luckse Sounds are sheltered and spacious enough to hold half a hundred ocean-going vessels. When the Navy in World War II operated a refueling depot on Long Island, as many as 60 warships waited with room to spare to take on bunker oil. In 1891 half a million passengers sailed through Casco Bay. Freight trains a mile long used to bring wheat from the Canadian praries to be shipped out of Casco Bay to Europe. In the 1970s, 438 big tankers from the Persian Gulf and Venezuela unloaded six billion gallons of crude oil at Portland, making this just about the biggest oil port in the East.

In 1623, young Christopher Levett, age 27, became the first permanent white settler in the Casco Bay islands. For his anchorage he chose the protection of four islands, now called Cushing, Peaks, Diamond and House. Three years after the Mayflower reached Plymouth, Levett and his 10 men went ashore at House, and built a stone home there, the first permanent white settlement in Casco Bay. In his journal, Levett described his chosen spot:

"It lyeth about two leagues to the east of Cape Elizabeth. . . . There are foure Ilands which make one good harbor, there is very good fishing, much fowle, and the mayne as good ground as any could desire. On the mayne I found one good river wherein the Savages say there is much salmon. . . . The river I made bold to call by my owne name Levetts river, being the first that discover it." (Poor Levett! it is now called Fore River).

Island buffs today still argue over which island Levett settled on; some say House, some say Cushing, some say York. Levett, like the Indians, himself called his settlement Quack (the Indian word "Maquack" means the red colored earth. On these islands there is still plenty of "Maquack"). But in his written reports he called it York, after Yorkshire in England, his home county there.

Levett had earned the favor of King James through his earlier work as His Majesty's forester. As a reward, King James gave Levett membership in the Council of New England and a land grant of 6,000 acres in Maine. Levett sailed the coast from the Isles of Shoals to Cape Small, making friends with the Indian chieftains and examining sites where he might settle. In the winter of 1623, he chose the sheltered island harbor in Casco Bay. Levett was the first settler to take pains to get along well with the Indian tribes, to write about their way of life, to stay with them and invite them to eat and visit at his settlement. Levett wrote extensively about the Indians he knew and liked in his book "Voyage into New England," published in London in 1628.

"I find them generally to be marvellous quick of apprehension and full of subtlety; they will quickly find any man's disposition and flatter him and humor him, if they hope to get anything of him. And yet they will count him a fool if he do not show a dislike of it . . . They are slow of speech, and if they hear a man speak much, they will laugh at him and call him 'mechecum,' a fool.

"They have no apparel but skins. In winter, they wear the hair side inwards, in summer outwards. Sometimes you will not know the men from the women but by their breasts, the men having no hair on their faces.

"When their children are born, they bind them on a board and set it upright against a tree. They keep them thus bound until they are three months. You will see them take their children and bury them many times in the snow, all but their faces, for a time, to make them the better to endure cold. And when they are above two years old they will cast them into the sea, to teach them to swim. Their houses are built in half an hour's time, being only a few poles stuck in the ground and covered with the bark of trees.

"I find they have two gods; one they love and one they hate. The god they love they call Squanto; and to him they ascribe all their good fortunes. The god they hate, they call Tanto, and to him they ascribe all their eveil fortunes.

"Thus when anyone is killed, hurt or sick or when it is evil weather, they say Tanto is angry. They say that no one can see Squanto or Tanto except their "paw-waws," or medicine men, and then only when they dream. Every sagamore or chief has a 'pawwaw' in his company and is altogether directed by him. One time I was at a sagamore's house and saw a martin's skin, and asked if he would sell it. The sagamore told me no; the pawwaw used to lay that under his head when he dreamed, and if he was without that he could do nothing. Thus we may perceive how the devil deludes these poor people and keeps them in blindness. I have had much conferences with these savages about our one and only true God and have done my best to bring them to know and acknowledge Him. But I fear all that labor will be lost and no good will be done, except it be among the younger sort.

"The sagamores will scarce speak to an ordinary man, but will point to their men and say: "Sanops must speak to sanops, and sagamores to sagamores."

"They are very bloody-minded and treacherous among themselves. One will kill another for his wives; and he that hath the most wives is the bravest fellow. Therefore I would wish no man to trust them, whatever they say or do, but always to keep a strict hand over them, and yet to use them kindly and deal uprightly with them."

Because of his friendship with Indian chiefs Levett was able to get Indian help in making many trips in small boats up the rivers around Casco Bay and to report in detail on the natural wealth of fish, timber, game and fresh water. Enthused about the possibilities of turning his 6,000-acre land grant into a flourishing colony, Levett returned to England in the spring of 1624, to spread the word and drum up new backers and new settlers to establish a new colony on the mainland, which he hoped to develop as the town of York, close to where Portland now stands.

Levett left ten men behind on his island when he sailed home to recruit new settlers in England. He never returned. He died at age 45, in 1631, probably drowned at sea. His men and his headquarters were abandoned. Had Levett come back with the support from the Crown and the Church which he sought, this able, educated leader, who got along unusually well with the Indians, might have begun the diocese and the City of York, which he envisioned where Portland is today.

Today people driving in and out of Portland and its suburbs cast a passing glance out to the islands of Casco Bay, seeing them as scenic but unimportant appendages of the city and the mainland.

When the nation began, it was the other way around. Three hundred years ago, Cushing and Peak's, Chebeague, Diamond, Long and Jewell islands were the hub of living, of trade, of work; the islands were the population centers, and the Portland mainland was the rough and dangerous land.

If you put yourself in the shoes of those first settlers of Maine, it is easy to see why they chose the islands for their homes and farms. First, they were safer from Indian raids. Second, an island seemed far more tamable than the vast forests of the unknown mainland. The job of clearing land, building a house, keeping sheep or cows from straying, seemed easier to a settler if he had the shore line as natural boundaries. The first, most plentiful food supply was, of course, fish from the ocean; and it was handy to have that at your door and your boat only a short walk from your cabin. The ocean was the road, far safer than woods trails on the mainland, where it was easy to get lost or get attacked, and hard to travel on foot or horse.

At first, when the settlers were few, each island was the fiefdom of one family. But they were not isolated. They visited back and forth; they helped each other in "raisings," the building of houses and barns, exchanged seeds for planting, swapped vegetables, and the men and boys teamed up to go on fishing and hunting trips together. In disasters, such as the loss of boats or men at sea, or in defense against Indians, or in

dealing with the courts and the government of the Massachusetts Bay Colony, the island families worked together. Natu-
rally they inter-married. The same family names crop up on
many different islands. And the names of the islands changed
often in the early days, since they were generally called by the
name of the principal family settled there. The mainland developed through families who decided to move off islands
which were getting crowded. As island families grew in numbers, there was not always space enough for more farms and
fish houses, or enough trees suitable for turning into new
homes, outbuildings, boats, firewood, wharves and barrels,
without disputes and quarrels.

Disputes and quarrels over land titles on the islands, and
then the mainland, pockmarked the first 150 years of settlements in Maine. Little wonder. For in England, different companies kept being formed to milk the wealth from the New
World. They obtained land grants to ill-defined areas throughout New England, marked upon maps which differed from each
other and which had little accuracy when it came to "marking
the bounds" on the actual territory. In New England itself,
some jurisdiction over land lay with the governors and deputy
governors, sometimes in Plymouth, sometimes in Boston. Sir
Ferdinando Gorges and others gave away or sold off parts of
their original land grants to settlers, whom they sent out to
colonize the region. The story of who owned which island, and
when, is tortuous. But a few thumbnail sketches of these islands give an idea of the changes in ownership.

Cushing Island

Christopher Levett, after he'd sailed home to England and
never returned to his little colony in Casco Bay, sold his 6,000
acres of land grants, which he had obtained from Sir Ferdinando Gorges. He sold to a number of different buyers. A
merchant in Plymouth, a Mr. Wright, got title to some of the
Casco Bay land, including Cushing. He never set foot on it. In
turn Wright sold Cushing Island to George Cleaves. Cleaves,
a wheeler-dealer of prominence and persistence in the early
days of Casco Bay, gave the island to his daughter, Elizabeth.
Elizabeth married a boy from nearby Peak's Island, Michael
Mitton. And it became known as Mitton's Island. They in turn

gave Cushing to their daughter, Sarah, who took it as her dowry when she married James Andrews. Andrews kept the island from 1667 to 1698, and it was known as Andrews Island. But even during these 31 years, the island had three different names; Andrews, Portland and Fort Island. Andrews built a small fort there when he first married Sarah. When Indians attacked the islands, which happened often in the 1670s, many settlers on nearby islands fled to Andrews' fort. The men, working together, expanded its defenses and their families hunkered down in safety on Fort Island (Cushing) when they saw war canoes heading their way. They built a fine protective fort. But they had too little food for all the families to eat while they kept out of the way of the Indians for prolonged periods. After living on berries and fish for three weeks, George Felt, one of the men who'd fled to the island fort from Indians, recruited six other men and they rowed over to nearby Peak's Island. There they planned to round up and bring back the sheep that had been left behind when George Palmer's family and other frightened Peak's islanders fled for safety to far off Boston. But the Indians who had earlier attacked and laid waste to Peak's were still on that island. They let Felt and his party land, let them round up the sheep; then the Indians attacked, killing them all.

The murders took place in earshot of the hungry men, women and children waiting on Cushing for their meal of mutton.

Andrews' fort must have been large and well-built, for traces of it existed until the Civil War; 800 soldiers were stationed on the island as Indian fighters in 1754, more than 80 years after Felt's party was murdered.

After 31 years on the island, Andrews sold to John Rouse of Marshfield, Massachusetts; who in turn sold to his neighbor, John Brown; who in turn sold it to John Robinson of Newbury, Massachusetts; who in turn sold to Nathaniel Jones; and by 1735 Jones sold the island to Captain Joshua Bangs. Again, the name of the island changed. For the next 100 years, it was called Bangs Island. But Bangs himself did not stick long. Soon after he got ownership, Bangs sold to another Massachusetts man, Ezekiel Cushing. Cushing paid $2,300 for the island in 1762, more money than some of the Casco Bay Islands were sold for in the 1960s.

Ezekiel Cushing, like many a minister's son after him, grew up to be a money-making, fast-trading, luxury-loving business man. He made a sizeable fortune in trade with the West Indies, largely from rum. He spent money lavishly on the island, building himself a big home which he called "The Homestead in the Willows." There he entertained in grand style and his guests drank from the finest wine cellar in Maine. (In the War of 1812, this house was used as a hospital). Cushing, who held the high rank of colonel, and became selectman of Falmouth (as Portland was called then) tired of this island; sold it back to Joshua Bangs, and bought nearby Long Island. There he built another, even grander "Homestead in the Willows," and lived a life of fabled luxury as a feudal overlord until he died. He left Long Island, Overset Island and Marsh Island to his children.

This time, when Joshua Bangs came back to Bangs Island he lived there until his death. His daughter meanwhile married an island-raised man, Brigadier Jedediah Preble, who had once owned Richmond Island; and Preble became owner of Bangs Island. His son, the famous Commodore Edward Preble, father of the U.S. Navy, inherited it. The Commodore's heirs split and sold off much of the property. By 1812 Simon Skillings had moved into "The Homestead in the Willows" and set about acquiring as many of the island parcels as he could buy. In 1856 Skillings and the last of the Preble heirs left on Bangs Island agreed to sell the whole island to Lemuel Cushing, a distant cousin of Ezekiel. Once again, the name of the island changed.

Bangs Island now became Cushing Island. And this Lemuel Cushing, who came from Canada, went into the resort hotel business, perhaps the first man to try it in the Casco Islands. He made a success of it, too. First he built a large brick hotel for a mere $10,000 in 1858, on a high granite cliff overlooking the bay. He named it "The Ottawa," and wealthy Canadians came in great numbers to spend their summers there, traveling on the newly completed railroad from Montreal to Portland. But fire burned the hotel in 1886; and Lemuel Cushing spent $75,000 to build a new one. This, too, burned, in 1917; but was never rebuilt.

Military men instead of vacationers took over Cushing. The fort, first begun by Andrews in the 1670s, was rebuilt at the

time of the Spanish American war; was expanded again in
World War I and yet again in World War II, when it was
equipped with 12-inch and 16-inch guns. This fort was named
Fort Levett to honor Christopher Levett, who'd built his stone
house in 1623.

To buy the land, construct Fort Levett, dig underground
tunnels hundreds of feet long, to build 15 brick residences and
barracks, to install and maintain the great guns, the federal
government spent untold millions of dollars.

Then in 1956, the federal government put it all up for sale —
buildings, docks, fort, roads, tunnels and 125 acres of island
close to Portland. A New Jersey man, David Lukens, bought
it all for $33,750. A few years later, at the time of the Cuban
missile crisis, Lukens sold his part of historic Cushing to the
United States Safekeeping Corporation, supposedly for $90,000.
This outfit plainned to modernize the huge underground tunnels into a vast vault and rent out sections of it as safekeeping havens for the precious documents of banks and corporations in the big cities which felt insecure in the face of possible missile attack. At the time it was reported that $100,000
were spent in pursuit of the idea, which, with the ending to the
Cuban missile crisis, died a quick death. The precious, historic
island finally came back into Maine ownership, bought by a
group called The Cushing Island Associates, Maine residents
with strong ties to summer homes on Cushing. Sidney Thaxter
of Cape Elizabeth led the group, which included Farrars,
Meachams, Hammonds, Quinns, Coles, Hitchcocks, Hales and
Gignouxes.

In 1970, Cushing underwent another milestone change. Four
men from the Portland area, Martin Johnson, Peter Murray,
Richard Balser and Howard Dana organized Whitehead Associates and bought the old fort and 50 acres around it for
$25,000 from Cushing Island Associates. Buyer and seller
agreed to deed an additional 75 acres to The Nature Conservancy, thus insuring the scenic land would remain unspoiled and
undeveloped. Further, Whitehead Associates agreed to limit-
ing the buildings on their 50 acres to 18 units, including the 12
buildings already there and built by the military; barracks,
NCO and officers houses, a hospital, jail and messhall. Each
of the original six partners (Peter Colli of New Jersey and
Peter Lincoln of New York City joined the original four Maine

partners) took one house each and sold the five other original buildings to friends, who agreed to renovate their properties within two years. This has been done. Even the six-cell jail has been turned into a summer cottage, with bars on the windows left in place. The only vehicle now permitted on the island is a service truck belonging to the year-round caretaker. A daily ferry serves the island in summer. so the Portland people can commute to work.

Great Diamond Island

Bangs Island got its name changed to Cushing, an improvement in connotation caused by change in owners.

Hog Island got changed to Great Diamond — a still bigger change in connotation for a smaller reason.

Great Hog Island earned its name because originally the island was used as a 230 acre hog pen. Tons of hay were later harvested on the island farm, cut and shipped to Portland stables in the horse and buggy era. Horses gave way to autos; hogs gave way to summer residents on the island; and the summer people — wanting a more mellifluous address — changed the name from Great Hog to Great Diamond Island. They justified the new name because of the way the sun glinted on pockets of quartz, mica and crystal in the rock ledges. Great Diamond is one of half a dozen islands within Portland City limits. City tax records show Great Diamond in 1981 had 68 homes on its 230 acres, with its land valued at $570,000.

The first land transaction known regarding Hog Island was in 1635. Then Sir Ferdinando Gorges (a man of long vision) gave a 2,000-year lease to George Cleaves and Richard Tucker for "one island known by the name of Hogg Island." Thereafter the land transfers came fast and frequent. Cleaves sold Hog to Thomas Kimball of Boston in 1658; and Kimball sold it five years later, in 1663, to Edward Tyng of Boston for 25 English pounds. In the next 100 years it changed hands many times until in 1756 Deacon James Milk, who lived on Exchange Street in Falmouth (Portland) bought it. The island soon became ideal housing for the big family he was to acquire. In 1762, Deacon Milk married his second wife, the widow Deering of Kittery. She came to the marriage bed with 11 children, he with five; and the 18 people in the Milk family moved out to live on Hog Island. The property passed through parents to children, to granddaughter Mary, who married the famous Commodore Edward Preble; and the Preble family, which also had an interest in Cushing Island and Richmond Island, kept possession of Hog or Great Diamond for a century.

By 1882, this island was a rather exclusive resort. A Great Diamond Island Association bought 97 acres of land by raising $7,679.55 overnight, paying it over immediately to Francis and J. D. Fessenden who needed to raise that specific amount within 36 hours. Seven years later, in 1889, the Association reported 57 cottages (only 11 fewer than in 1981) and a population of 300 people. Great Diamond had become a summer resort for Portland's upper crust. The Portland Club built a summer clubhouse on the high knoll. Steamboats and ferries landed at three sides of the island, even then shuttling commuters back and forth to work in Portland. The trappings of urban life quickly developed: roads, lit by kerosene streetlights; a 140,000-gallon reservoir; an acetylene gas plant for home lighting.

The smell of real estate development began to permeate the island air. The firm of Ilsley and Cummings surveyed the island and presented a plan which showed room for 506 cottage lots covering 126 acres, to be served by 30 avenues and streets; some 76 acres of the most desirable water view lots were earmarked as the property of the Great Diamond Island Association. Members built and operated a nine-hole golf course, two tennis courts, their own steamboat, Isis, to carry them back and forth to Portland. The harbor blossomed with moorings for their pleasure craft. The threat of World War however, put a crimp in the idylls of summer life on Great Diamond.

The government built Fort McKinley, as part of the Portland Harbor Defense System, and the exclusiveness of the resort declined. The War Department took the northeastern part of the island by eminent domain, paying $149,850 in damages for it. Soon there was a year-round military population of over 1,000 men, dwarfing the summer colony of 350. The former summer island became the site of a great building program of massive gun emplacements, barracks, roads, ammunition dumps, warehouses, stables and hospitals. Target practice for the 12 and 16 inch guns ruined the island's quiet. Cottages were sold or rented to the military.

But Portland Harbor was never attacked in either World War I or II. By the 1950s, the mliitary decided it had no further use for the multi-million installation on Great Diamond. The great brick buildings, wharves and warehouses stood empty. In 1961, it was all put up to auction. The once powerful association sent a representative to the auction, but without money or authority to bid. Michael Montalbano, a developer from New Jersey, and David L. Lukens (who had bought 125 acres and military installations at Cushing Island for $33,750) made the winning bid. They bought 200 acres of Great Diamond plus Fort McKinley's hospital, theater, barracks, brick homes, paved roads, sewer systems, power and water plants for $42,350. In 1970, they sold it for a reported $225,000 to King Resources, an oil company which had bought the Navy Oil Depot on nearby Long Island. King Resources, however, went into bankruptcy in 1972; Fort McKinley and 200 acres of Great Diamond Island went into the hands of the receivers.

What you see depends on where you sit. First time I saw Great Diamond up close was from Steer Clear when cruising for a few days and nights with photographer Donald Johnson and the perspective then was different. I turn back to the log of Steer Clear to recapture a night in Diamond Cove.

"Near seven o'clock on this July night, we dropped anchor in Diamond Cove. We have the cove to ourselves, except for one unoccupied power boat tied to the wharf on Great Diamond Island. We decide to cook a steak on a nearby island, a precipitous hump of rock and scrub brush, inhabited only by nesting gulls and an automatic navigation light.

"At the water's edge we watched the summer sun go down, cooked an epicurean steak and fed scraps to angry gulls, as payment for disturbing them when Don photographed their nests. Through a cut between Crow Island and a tip of Great Diamond we see cars darting between Falmouth and Portland on the mainland. The world ashore seems 1,000 miles away from our peace and isolation. Etched against the evening sky out here are unlikely telephone poles and drooping, broken wires, strung and abandoned long ago by the military along the ridge of nearby Crow Island's 14 acres. A rotted military wharf lies twisted and broken, drooping into the quiet sea.

"We douse the embers from the hibachi and stretch out, warming our backs on the ledge which has baked all day in the splendid sun. I wonder how many Indians, how many explorers, how many early settlers, how many G.I.s have lain warming their backs on these same rocks, watching the same sun go down. No Mainer lives on Crow Island now to relish its island beauty, so close-in to Portland. John A. Richardson of Brookfield, Massachusetts, was smart enough to buy the 14-acre island in 1958 for the sum of $2,656.

"The night is balmy. We stay on the ledge until the moon is high and the water turns velvet black. Then row back to Steer Clear, and read old books about the Indians, the first settlers, the fishermen-farmers, the pirates and the treasure-seekers who once roamed the islands we have seen and loved today. Feel a kinship with that ghostly company."

Little Diamond Island

Ted Rand has been making little Diamond Island run since 1954. He was 25 then and bought the old Coast Guard buoy station atop the hill for $2,500 and came to live here winter and summer. A University of Maine graduate and one-time teacher, Ted Rand has fathered two boys and three girls on this island. He is busy. He has been island policeman and fireman, lobsterman (450 traps), runs the wharf and has built up a flourishing boat storage and marine gas and waterfront store business. Between times, he has served as president of the Casco Bay Island Association.

He knows the islands must change with the times. He is a realist. But his goal is to see that development of them benefits all; that the islands are neither raped to enrich a few nor held back, unnaturally keeping the clock standing still, to make a special sanctuary for those rich enough to maintain summer retreats here. He knows the past and present of these islands and intends to safeguard their future as best he can.

When the tide is out, you can cross the sand bar from Great Diamond and walk over here to Little Diamond. Yet in feeling, the two islands are many miles apart. There are 40 or so houses on Little Diamond now. But until 1900 this little, lovely island was one working farm. Then it began to change, in the footsteps of Great Diamond, into a summer colony, until by 1910 the open farm land was dotted with 25 cottages on the south side. The north side was owned by the Catholic Diocese of Portland, which ran a summer camp for girls from the St. Elizabeth's Orphanage in Portland. Busiest cottage on the island in those days was the Nissen cottage, run as a boarding house. Charges were four dollars week, all meals included. This Nissen family later become the prosperous and famous bakers of Maine and New England.

George W. Brown bought 40 acres of Little Diamond in 1908 with the idea of making it into a fancy summer colony. He put in a water system, roads, even promoted sun-heated salt water baths and began an attractive restaurant. But within four years his company ran out of money, and the members of the Little Diamond Association took over. General Frederick Keating, British vice-consul in Portland, bought the restaurant and under his management it flourished until he left Portland after World War I. He sold the restaurant, casino and bathing beach facilities to the Association and in 1924 the old Keating cottage was turned into the new Casino. (Nothing so exotic as gambling! "Casino" is what the Little Diamond Island Association called its prim and proper clubhouse.) Two years later electricity came to Little Diamond, and drove out "Old Charlie" the lamplighter, and his pet pig who accompanied him on his nightly rounds.

Peak's Island

Peak's is the only island in Casco Bay which has developed into a bedroom suburb of Portland. There are more than a thousand homes here built on less than 700 acres. Morning and evening ferries are filled with commuters who go daily to jobs in the city; and with youngsters who go to school in Portland. Peak's is only a 15-minute boat ride from the city.

The Casco Bay Lines ferry is a focal point in the lives of Peak Islanders; its fares and schedules are issues which bind all Peak's Islanders together in a running battle with the ferry line. In frustration, they often threaten to operate their own private line.

Peak's Island, so close to the mainland, was settled 350 years ago by the Bracketts and the Palmers, and later the Sterlings, Trefethens, Mittons, Munjoys and Trotts. The name of the island changed often, depending upon who was living here. The busy hand of George Cleaves is imprinted in its history. Cleaves held title, then gave it to his son-in-law, Michael Mitton. Two Brackett brothers married two daughters of Michael Mitton and sold out to B. Trott.

Peak's problem was that it was in easy striking distance of the Indians. They raided in 1689, and wiped out many of the settlers. Only the presence of Major Benjamin Church and his soldiers, stationed there to help guard Falmouth (Portland), kept that fight from becoming a total massacre. The next year, a second battle drove the brave souls remaining from the island. Yet soon a few settlers came back; the island was too handy, too big and too lovely to leave totally empty. But even 100 years later, at the time of the Revolution, only three major houses stood on Peak's Island named after Samuel Peak.

By 1850 William Jones had begun to turn Peak's into a tourist island for day visitors from Portland. Jones turned his boarding house into a restaurant specializing in shore dinners. Canadian visitors coming into Portland on the Grand Trunk Railway would take the boat out to Peak's and eat lobster, clams and corn at Jones' restaurant. By 1851, the tourist traffic was big enough for Horace G. Cook to put a fast steamer, Antelope, into service out to Peak's Island.

In the next 30 years Peak's became Casco Bay's great summer attraction. Amusement parks, boarding houses, hotels, skating rinks, and theaters dotted the island. A huge building, first used as the Forest City Skating Rink, became the Gem Theater, run by a Portland entrepreneur named Bart MacCullum. He staged musical comedies and Broadway tryouts on this Maine island. A kind of Coney Island amusement park, called Greenwood Park, attracted thousands of families on a day's outing. A famed balloonist named Prince Leo was a top drawing card. The Prince would climb into his balloon, ascend hundreds of feet into the air, then parachute down to Peak's Island. A Professor Oldwie astonished visitors by walking on water. He wore two outsize floats as shoes, and plowed across the water rather like a cross country skier over snow.

A fleet of steamers, able to carry several hundred passengers each, plied in summer between the island and Portland.

The day's outing was offered at a bargain; only 25 cents, which included the boat ride, plus a chance to see the open air vaudeville shows.

That great figure of Broadway, George M. Cohan, produced some of his first hits at the Gem Theater on Peak's Island. John Ford, the Portland boy who became one of America's greatest film directors, started on his theatrical career by being an usher at the old Gem.

Peak's Island enjoyed fame as the supposed site of Longfellow's "Wreck of the Hesperus." It wasn't. Longfellow wrote "The Wreck of the Hesperus" in Portland, in the year 1839. But the shipwreck of the Helen Eliza on Peak's Island, on which the poem was supposedly based, did not happen until 30 years later, on September 8th, 1869.

The Helen Eliza was wrecked off Peak's Island, with 11 persons aboard, ten of whom drowned. Here is the story, told by the sole survivor, Charles Jordan. But first, a word of caution. Jordan was a colorful character, prone to embroidering facts; he'd been taken prisoner in the south in the Civil War, supposedly the sole survivor of a company of 80 men. At war's end, Jordan was released from Libby Prison and boarded a schooner headed north. That schooner was wrecked off Cape Cod — and Jordan was, supposedly, the sole survivor of that, too. He then took passage aboard the Helen Eliza, and became the sole survivor again, when she met her end at Peak's Island.

Now, for Jordan' account of the wreck of the Helen Eliza at Peak's Island.

"During the afternoon of September 8, 1869, thick fog set in, followed by a perfect deluge of rain, and wind increased till it blew a regular hurricane . . . Both anchors were let go, but the cables parted . . . there was little doubt the vessel would go aground on Peak's Island. Capt. Miller at the helm probably received his death blow from the main boom . . . The vessel struck heavily, killing instantly five persons with me in the forecastle . . . I was swept into the raging water . . . Seeing an empty barrel floating by, I was fortunate enough to secure it . . . The waves ran fearfully high. I was swept by George W. Clark and Benjamin Lurvey who were clinging to a plank . . . I decided I must not make myself known to them, for the chances of three clinging in safety to my barrel were slim . . . The undertow was very powerful, but I managed to get to a ledge of rocks. I heard Clark, hailing. I answered the call, enjoining him to hold on to his plank and get to the ledge. I did not hear him again and probably the two men were swallowed up in the undertow . . . I soon found the ledge did not form part of an island, but would be covered at high water. I plunged again into the seething waters. Another terrible contest with surf followed . . . Moments seemed like hours . . . My strength was fast failing . . . Making one last desperate effort, I neared a shore and made a landing . . . Now it was nine in the evening and the past two hours of exertion told on me. I could scarcely lift one foot before the other, but I persevered and came to the house of Mr. Smith Hadlock . . . When rested, I joined the men of the island in a search for my shipmates. Mr. Jones, landlord of the hotel, secured me a free passage home. The inhabitants of the island, mostly poor fishermen, made me up a purse of $18."

Jordan swore he'd never come close to water again. So he went inland, and took up farming in New Hampshire, far from the sea. There he slipped on a log crossing a stream. And drowned.

Jewell, Stave and Outer Islands

The many islands of Casco Bay can be grouped into three rings, inner, middle and outer. Here is an account of a visit to Stave Island, one of the smaller, unspoiled islands in the Outer Ring.

"Seal pups," says Elmore Wallace, as he slips Steer Clear between sea covered ledges and creeps into the sheltered cove at Stave Island.

At first glance the baby seals look like silvered logs of driftwood, floating atop the blue water. Now they lift their heads in curiosity, twitching their long hard whiskers, gazing at us with their bulbous eyes. While they are pups, their hide is white and furry. The approach of Steer Clear rouses them from lazy sunbaths on a ledge barely above water.

With a splash a dozen seals that had looked like silver logs now move, slide into the water and vanish.

"We'll tie to this mooring," decides Elmore. He has been cruising these waters for 50 years, 14 of them as a marine warden. "You don't want to miss going ashore on Stave. Go for an hour. I'll stay with the boat. Then we'll move over to Jewell before you head out of the Bay and home to New Harbor."

Thousands of years ago, when the Ice Age created the islands of Casco Bay, it left three tiers of islands; the Inner Ring of Mackworth, Clapboard, Cousins, Bibber and others closest to the mainland; the Middle Ring of Cushing, Peak's, Long Island, Great and Little Diamond, Great and Little Chebeague and others, a little further out into the Bay; and the Outer Ring of Cliff, Stave, Jewell and others to seaward.

Stave Island is as pretty and unspoiled as any. Not as large and magnificent as Jewell; not as close to Portland as Little Chebeague; not as wild as Whaleboat;

not as flat and barren as Bangs or Stockman or Minis-
terial Islands. But little Stave has every kind of island
beauty mingled in a smaller scale.

Our safe cove is peppered with black rocks for surf to
foam upon; there's a small white sand beach for a man
to stretch out on and snooze in the sun; there are cliffs
to climb and, breathless after racing to the top, to watch
the sea and nearby islands from; ripe, salt-savored berries to eat, sweet-smelling bright-colored wildflowers
and fresh fern to smell; there are green spruce for the
winds to whistle through and birds to nest in and men
and girls to lie under.

Abner Harris, founder of The Harris Company, ship
chandlers on the Portland waterfront, once owned
Stave. The weir and lobster pound he built still stand,
tumbled and punished by 50 years of storms. Scores of
Casco Bay fishermen sold Abner thousands upon thousands of lobster here, and he held them in these pounds.
Now the old lobster pound is a grand place to skinny-
dip, far out to sea; Abner's old fish house stands by
the water and the house he built atop the hill amid
sweet ferns is still there. The doors are open; and inside are a few survival essentials for a man caught out
here in a storm.

Austin Harris, Abner's grandson, says Abner sold the
island in the 1940s to Charles Olsen, a Cape Elizabeth
fisherman. Now, according to tax records of the town
of Cumberland, six people own Stave; and they are all
from Maine. "I haven't been back in 30 years," mourns
Austin Harris. "My grandfather took me out often
when I was a little boy. Those memories come flooding
back whenever I hear the name 'Stave.'"

From atop Stave we see a huge, immaculate lodge on nearby
Hope Island. Well-to-do Philadelphians, with an eye for beauty
at a bargain price, bought Hope Island and have kept it as a
private club, complete with private power plant, private water
supply and private boat service. Beyond Hope is the Singing
Beach of Long Island, the beach where the undertow of the
Atlantic rolls stones to create a wild and eerie song. On the

far side of Long Island is water 100 feet deep, and the piers where in the early 1970s an oil company, King Resources, planned to dock supertankers, 1,200 feet long, and unload over two million barrels of oil from each. That incredible juxtaposition to the wild loveliness of Stave never happened: King Resources went into bankruptcy. But it is a good time to look at Long Island, part of the Middle Ring.

Back in 1640 John Sears of Boston owned Long Island. According to a 1703 map in London, it was called Smith's Island, after the Boston merchant to whom Sears sold it. By 1763 Col. Ezekiel Cushing was the big landowner, and he sent his brother Ignatius to live on it. By 1830, Maine, a state only ten years, took its first census; and Long Island had a population of 146, largest of any island in Casco Bay. The Godes and the Doughtys, experts in swordfishing, prospered and multiplied here. Then tourism almost swamped fishing as Long Island's primary business. Hotels such as Dirigo House, 100 rooms; Casco Bay House, 60 rooms; and the grand Granite Springs Hotel with 150 rooms, offered accommodations from $1 a day to $17 a week. Only Peak's Island, crowded with 21 hotels and boarding houses, was a busier tourist center a hundred years ago. Long Island staged the biggest clambake in Maine history. In 1886, more than 2,500 people came out to Long Island by steamers to celebrate Portland's bicentennial. Records show 16 cords of wood were needed for the fires, and 500 bushels of clams were eaten that day.

Last in the Outer Ring of Casco Bay is Jewell, 221 acres of history-packed and heavenly beauty. It was our last stop in a week spent in Casco Bay Islands. If God was in his Heaven on that July day, He was missing a lot by not being on Jewell Island.

George Jewell, of Saco, bought this island gem from the Indians in 1637 for one powderhorn, 12 fishhooks and a barrel or two of rum. The unlucky man fell overboard in Boston Harbor a few years later and drowned. But his name, a good one for this island beauty, has stuck for almost 350 years. Henry

Donnell of York owned the island after Jewell and was lucky enough to live on it for 30 years.

Today Jewell Island is a Maine State Park. The State paid $290,000 for it in 1976. About $200,000 went to the estate of John B. Ahsmeier for his 130 acres (he had paid $33,000 for them 20 years earlier, buying from the federal government). For the remaining 90 acres, the State paid $90,000 to the heirs of the McKeen family, direct descendants of the McKeen who had been the first president of Bowdoin College. McKeen had bought his part of Jewell in 1894. His whole family enjoyed summers there; some of them spent several winters on the island; and three children were born on Jewell. The McKeen cottage was horribly vandalized in the 1960s and 70s and was in total collapse by the time the State bought Jewell. Where it once stood, there now grow wild roses, wild peas, sweet-smelling honeysuckle vines and a bold banner of white daisies.

From the new State wharf on Jewell, it is a half-hour walk to Knife-Edge Rock, which towers above a cove where Capt. Kidd is supposed to have buried treasure. The Army in World War II installed 70-foot-high watch towers here, great coastal gun emplacements, together with underground tunnels and bunkers. Forty years later, they stand, scarred, rusty, decrepit. But for those who will climb the steep, winding, concrete stairs to the top, the views will remain a spectacular, lifelong memory. The walls are scrawled with graffiti, marks of a moment of beer, or love. One — strange echo of a London scandal in the 1960s — reads "Dr. Stephen Ward loves Mandy Rice-Davies . . . P.S. So does John Profumo."

Deep in the ground beneath the watch-towers are sweating, dark tunnels, eight feet wide, winding for hundreds of yards. Massive iron doors hang precariously from broken hinges, doors which once guarded eight-inch shells which never were fired in anger.

The blood of Indians and early settlers once wet this island soil. Settlers fled here for safety from the atrocities on Harpswell Neck and closer-in islands. They believed no Indians would paddle out to Jewell, exposing themselves to fire from its high point. The settlers built a fort on Jewell and felt secure. On the second day of September 1676, fine weather blessed Jewell. Richard Potts and all the other men, women and children who had fled here for safety from Harpswell, sailed over to cut corn on nearby Green Island, where the corn stood high and rich, thanks to regular fertilization by gulls.

Left alone on lookout at the fort on Jewell was nine-year-old Thomas Potts, well-trained to load and fire his father's musket. Suddenly young Thomas spied eight canoes, each carrying four Indians. They were less than half a mile away, paddling fast from Cliff toward Jewell. The boy raised his musket and fired the alarm. At the signal, men cutting corn on Green Island, and women washing clothes in the stream, rushed back to defend Jewell. By the time the Indians reached shore the settlers were in place, ready and able to fight them off.

It is not known how many settlers or Indians died that day. But the whites were scared enough to leave. Earlier that summer, 35 whites had been murdered near Back Cove in Portland. Others had been killed on Casco Neck. Settlements all along the coast were being attacked. So the families on Jewell Island fled that September afternoon, aboard sloops which John Damarell from Richmond Island had led to their rescue. At Richmond, they were safer; but during that long, bloody autumn of 1676, Indians destroyed almost every white man's building between the Piscataqua and the Kennebec rivers. In fear, the Potts family fled to faraway Pennsylvania. Young Thomas Potts, when he inherited the family farm on Potts Point at Merryconeag Neck, never returned to live on it. He sold it without a qualm to Benjamin Marston.

Today, walking the wild meadows of Jewell Island, looking to sea from Knife-Edge Rock, time plays strange games. Despite gun emplacements and watch towers from World War II at my back, I feel closer to the Potts family of 1672 than to the G.I.s of 1944. The roots of the old McKeen family cottage seem closer than the new docks installed by the State of Maine in 1976.

Out among these Casco Bay islands there is a strange kinship of feeling which pays no heed to time. From Jewell I can look at Eagle, and feel close to Admiral Peary, as he sat there, planning voyages to the North Pole; to Edna St. Vincent Millay, writing her poems on Ragged Island off to the east . . . to the 32 men wrecked on the Oakey L. Alexander in 80-mph winds and 40-foot seas near Cape Elizabeth, across the bay, on March 3, 1947 . . . to the holiday crowds who swarmed to see the fireworks on Peak's in the 1880s; and to the men aboard the dragger now heading out to fish on the Banks.

This wondrous bay, with its hundred and more islands, may sometimes look empty. But stand on an island alone and listen. Casco Bay fills with the ghosts of explorers, Indians, first settlers, men manning forts and massive guns in many wars; and fishermen, farmers, land-grabbers, pirates, holiday crowds, convoys heading out for Murmansk, tankers heading in from the Persian Gulf.

Portland Head Light, first built under President George Washington

10.

Lighthouses:
Sentinels Of The Coast

I admire the beauty, the toughness, and the duty of Maine's 66 lighthouses. Their flashing beams at night can be more welcome than a letter from home. The heroic lighthouse keepers, men and women, who've kept their light burning in the foulest storms are splendid badges of courage, emblazoned into the saga of the Maine coast. Yet when it comes to downright gratitude, mine goes mostly to foghorns and the whistle buoys. After hours of tension when fog, vapor or lashing rain blot out even the bow of the boat, the sound of that deep-throated hoarse moan is like the sound of a friend's voice.

The easternmost light in the United States is at Mt. Desert Rock. Far to sea and brutally exposed to the North Atlantic, the light is anchored to a barren half acre of volcanic rock rising out of the Bay of Fundy. It is now automated. But a special breed of men and women operated this forsaken outpost for 145 years from 1832 to 1977. Just before Christmas 1977 a helicopter landed on the wave-swept rock and took off the last men to man this light. They were two young Coast Guardsmen — Robin Runnels, 22, from Hyannis, Massachusetts, and Douglas Nute, 20, from inland St. Louis, Missouri.

From Grand Manaan to Mt. Desert to the Isles of Shoals on the New Hampshire border, 66 lighthouses stand along the coast of Maine and her rivers.

Oldest is the Portland Head Light, begun before our Independence and finished by order of George Washington and first lighted January 10, 1791. Only four lighthouses ordered by the first president still stand today. Portland Head Light is one of them. In 1981, it was featured on a new postage stamp.

Two Lights at Cape Elizabeth was the first lighthouse ever featured on an American stamp. This light was built in 1828 at a cost of $4,250. The stamp was issued in 1970 and bore the famous Two Lights painting by Edward Hopper, which now hangs in New York's Metropolitan Museum. Only one of the famed Two Lights shines now. Actor Gary Merrill bought the West Light for $30,000 in 1971. He planned to make living quarters on the six floors with an all glass living room with a 360 degree view in the tower, but his plans never became reality.

The names of Maine's lighthouses unlock a torrent of history, hardship, heroism, and loneliness. The names alone flash vivid pictures across the mind's eye . . . Boon Island Light, where, in 1710, survivors of the wreck Nottingham Galley kept from starving by eating one of their mates . . . Matinicus Rock Light, where 17-year-old Abbie Burgess kept the light burning through a month of horrendous storms while her father was marooned on the mainland and her mother was a bedridden invalid below in the keeper's house; Seguin Light, on the great island rock, where the first colonists in December 1607 headed in to land at Popham; Monhegan Light, run by a woman for 18 years; Petit Manan Light at the foggiest spot in the nation . . . The lights at Goose Rocks, Eagle Island, Burnt Coat, Great Duck, Heron Neck, Isle au Haut, Whitehead, The Cuckolds, Whaleback, Pemaquid. The roll call evokes all the perils of the sea.

Lighthouses are as ancient as the times men first ventured far to sea. The first lighthouse of the world was built by King Ptolemy Philadelphus on the island of Pharos near Alexandria. Built 250 years before Christ was born, the light was a marvel of size and beauty. Made of marble, it stood 600 feet tall. At the 400-foot level was a meat and vegetable market. At the 500-foot level was a terrace from which tourists could see the great lamp itself. The wonder of the world endured for 1600 years and its light guided the ships of Caesar and Cleopatra.

By comparison, the Colossus of Rhodes was a pygmy. It stood a mere 160 feet high and lasted a mere 56 years, until felled by an earthquake in 224 B.C. While it stood, the fire was kept burning in its eyes, as a beacon to ships of the Mediterranean.

Lighthouses were slow to come to North America, though our nation was founded by seamen. More than 100 years went by after the first colonists came here before the first lighthouse was built in 1716, in Boston Harbor. Throughout the whole 18th century, only 24 lighthouses were built along our entire Atlantic coast. However, once our nation had broken ties with England and knew that its destiny lay in the sea, the pace quickened. In the first 50 years after Independence 66 lighthouses were built from Maine to Florida and round the Keys to the Gulf Coast to Louisiana, compared to only ten built while we were an English colony.

The ninth bill passed by the First Congress, enacted August 7, 1789, authorized lighthouse construction. So important were lighthouses that Presidents themselves appointed the lighthouse keepers. Washington personally chose Joseph Greenleaf to be the first keeper of the Portland Head Lighthouse on the 7th of January, 1791.

Portland Head Light

Captain Greenleaf's job carried more honor than money. He received no pay for more than two years, though the government did supply him a house. In July 1793 he got cash, too — a federal salary of $160 a year. He didn't collect it long, for two years later he died of a stroke while crossing the Fore River in a skiff. He was succeeded by a Portland blacksmith, Barzillai Delano, who died on the job in 1821 and was succeeded by his son.

Politics perhaps crept into the appointment of John F. Watts. When the new Board of Lighthouse Commissioners made an inspection of Portland Head Light on July 5, 1852, Watts surprised them all. He said that when he had taken the job his predecessor refused to tell him how to operate the light. He had to hire a man for two days to show him how to run it. The inspectors also found that Watts blew his foghorn only for special steamers, with whom he made private arrangements, in cash, in advance.

The two best known keepers of the Portland Head Light were the father and son team of Joshua and Joseph Strout, who between them kept the light almost 60 years, from 1869 until 1928.

The year Captain Joshua Strout became keeper, at a salary of $620 a year, one of Maine's infamous September gales smashed 20 ships in Casco Bay and took scores of lives. Rogue waves tore loose the huge fog bell and tossed it like a tennis ball into a cut in the rocks below the lighthouse. The replacement lasted only three years; then the stronger, louder Daboll trumpet was brought from Monhegan and Portland Head got its first real foghorn. This lasted but two years. The light tower was raised and lowered several times over the years; lowered in response to budget cuts; raised in response to protests from ship captains who could not see it soon enough.

On Christmas Eve, 1886, the Annie C. Maguire met disaster at Portland Head. She was a 34-year-old, three-masted bark, British registered, with 15 in crew, headed from Buenos Aires to Quebec. In command was Capt. Thomas O'Neil, with his wife and young son aboard. Some accounts say a blizzard and a windstorm were blowing and that the Annie Maguire turned off course for Quebec to seek shelter in Portland Harbor. But Weather Bureau records show the weather on Christmas Eve that year was a balmy 49 degrees; seas were moderate; visibility was excellent; that a light rain and a southerly breeze were coming off the sea. Whatever the conditions, the Annie Maguire hit the ledges by Portland Head Light so hard that the impact shook the lighthouse like an earthquake. Strout and his son, Joseph, raced from the family Christmas tree, rigged lights and shone them on the still-filled sails and frantic crew of the Annie Maguire. The Strouts hurled a line aboard, which the crew fastened to the cross trees, while the Strouts made their end fast to the base of the lighthouse tower. They quickly rigged a bo'sun's chair and snatch block between wreck and light and the Strouts hauled the entire crew, the captain, his wife and son safely ashore. At daylight on Christmas morning everyone could see that the gaping hole in the Annie Maguire was so huge that the ship was a total loss. The tides poured into her holds; waves tore asunder her broken frame. So little was left of her that she was put up to auction on December 29 and fetched only $177.50. Before even those remnants could be salvaged another storm on New Year's Day hit her again and her wreckage was strewn for miles.

There is an odd ending to the wreck of the Maguire. Days before she hit the ledge the sheriff had told Strout to keep an eye out for Annie Maguire because American creditors were trying to attach the vessel for bad debts before she reached Quebec. So on Christmas morning the sheriff arrived to serve attachment papers. He searched the sea chest for the ship's papers. The captain then discovered the satchel with all his and the ship's money was missing. He whispered his loss to his wife in frantic undertones. She calmed him and told him to shut up and pretend it had been lost in the wreck. She had the money and the papers, well hidden. Just before going overboard she had ransacked the strong box, taken the cash, and put it inside her hat box. When she climbed into the bo'sun's chair her hat box was in her lap.

In the winter storm of February 22, 1864, the almost new iron steamship, The Bohemian, out of Liverpool, hit Alden Rock near the Portland Head Light, slid off and began to sink with 313 souls aboard. The captain called for "full ahead," hoping to ground her out, but he was too late. Seas poured in. The captain ordered his 218 passengers and 95 crewmen into the lifeboats. All boats were launched well except for No. 2 lifeboat. A huge wave hit it, turned it turtle and drowned nearly fifty people. Among the survivors was a little boy named John F. Fitzgerald. For years people said this boy grew up to become the popular leader of the Boston Irish, and his offspring became President John Fitzgerald Kennedy. It's a good story; the dates and ages fit, but it is untrue.

In 1914 the Boston to Portland steamer hit rocks near Portland Head Light in thick summer fog and blew her distress whistles full blast immediately. The revenue cutter Androscoggin rushed out from Portland Harbor and hauled her off on the flood tide. Still another wreck at Portland Head Light involved a local fishing boat. In the fog on Tuesday evening, October 4, 1932, the schooner Lochinvar, with 40,000 pounds of fish aboard, owned by the Willard-Daggett Fish Co. of Portland, and skippered by Captain Frank Doughty, a veteran of 28 years experience, hit hard only 100 feet from where the Annie Maguire had met her end. She sank fast. Her 13 crewmen leaped into dories, but they had a hard time getting Capt. Doughty to abandon ship and climb into his dory before Lochinvar sank. For several days thereafter the tops of her masts and sails showed above water until a new storm demolished her.

The beacon on the Portland Head Light went out on June 27, 1942, in World War II, lest it be a marker for German submarines, and the fog signal went silent July 5. The 200,000 candlepower beacon went out again just after midnight March 22, 1977, in a storm which devastated the Portland area.

Lights of Casco Bay

At night over Casco Bay and Portland Harbor you may see half a dozen lighthouses flashing their signals to the sea . . . Portland Head Light, Two Lights at Cape Elizabeth, Halfway Rock Light, Spring Point Ledge Light, Ram Island Ledge Light and perhaps the Portland Breakwater Light, though it is no longer a navigation aid.

A lot of Portland's story lies in those lights.

President John Quincy Adams appointed the first keeper of the Cape Elizabeth Light. When Elisha Jordan got the job in October 1828, he received a salary of $450 a year, along with strict instructions that it was a full-time job and that he "must make it a habit to be at home."

The monster storm of November 22, 1831, devastated Portland Harbor, carrying away boats, wharves, buildings, flooding the city. Result was the construction of the Portland Breakwater, begun in 1836, but not finished until 1855. A light 25 feet high was illuminated August 1, 1855, by the first keeper, W. A. Dyer, who was paid $400 a year. Next to be built was Halfway Rock, put into operation by Captain John T. Stirling, August 15, 1871. He often rowed 11 miles back and forth to Portland for supplies. A quarter century passed before work was started on Spring Point Ledge Light, activated May 24, 1897, with William A. Lane as keeper.

Last light to be built in Portland Harbor was the Ram Island Ledge Light, where William C. Tapley first lit the kerosene lamp an hour before sunset April 10, 1905.

Disaster and death and shipwreck, not forethought, triggered the building of each light. Portland was a shipping center for the big lumbering and rum trade, during the 1780s, but it had no light and no way of paying for one, since all such funds were funneled through the Massachusetts Legislature. In 1784, 74 owners and masters of vessels around Portland went to Boston seeking a lighthouse. They got nothing. The next year they tried again and got nothing. But in 1787 disaster spoke louder than reason. On February 4, a Sunday, a 90-ton sloop bound for Massachusetts was wrecked on Bangs Island. Captain Moses Crane and a boy called John Deane were drowned; five others in crew clung to pieces of wreckage and saved themselves.

The Cumberland Gazette, Portland's only paper then, ran editorials asking, "Does not this unhappy accident evince the necessity of having a Lighthouse at the entrance of our harbor?" Portland citizens signed petitions demanding a light, but English officials of the Massachusetts Legislature responded with a mere $750. However, two months later George Washington became president the first Congress in New York City provided Portland with $1,500 to resume construction of Portland Head Light.

At Cape Elizabeth, where Two Lights stand, a rubble stone day marker was built. Mariners said it was not much help, but politicians thought it was quite enough — until disaster hit. The lumber sloop Resolution was wrecked there October 24, 1811. Over the next 15 years more wrecks raised more public outcry for better lights. They were built, but wrecks kept on happening almost in the shadow of the lights. The 386-ton Tasmania was lost in 1857; the Abigail met her end the next year. Then the little schooner, Susan; then the Catharine Beals; followed by the Kate Aubrey and next the coal schooner, Australia, in 1885. Many men and ships had to die first, but by 1900 Two Lights was finally well-equipped.

Before Halfway Rock Light was finished, the Bath-built brig, Samuel, was wrecked there in 1835. So many more followed her onto those treacherous hidden ledges that by 1837 Captain John Smith of the U.S. Revenue Cutter Service urged his superiors in Washington to spend $300 to erect a marker. His plea fell on deaf bureaucratic ears. Over the next 31 years, uncounted wrecks followed. Then in 1861, after a

February storm, a ship's wreckage washed up on Jewell and Inner Green Islands. The water was crowded with flotsam, but no survivors were found. The only clues were the letters on a medicine chest "Boadicea" . . . a British bark which had cleared New Orleans December 2, 1860, bound for Glasgow and has never been heard of since. Congress appropriated $50,000 in 1869, but the Halfway Rock Light did not get into operation until August 15, 1891.

Even by the time the Spring Point Ledge Light was built in 1897, it took shipwreck, death and disaster to pry funds for lighthouses. The schooner Nancy hit this ledge in 1832, shattered her hull and the sea poured in over her dangerous cargo of lime. The water and lime mixture caused fire and explosion. She burned to a hulk. The government responded by installing an inadequate spar buoy. It was of little help. The Mazaltan, Seguin, Solomon Poole, Smith, and untold others hit Halfway Rock.

Then came the savage gale of the equinox, March 20-21 in 1876, which destroyed dozens of vessels, among them the fine new bark Harriet S. Jackson, 393 tons. After six days of trying with numerous tugs, she was hauled off for rebuilding at the Dyer Yard in South Portland.

Wrecks and groundings continued. In 1891 seven steamship companies banded together and presented a joint petition to the Lighthouse Board in Washington. All seven lines served Portland. They said that between them they carried more than half a million passengers every year past Spring Point Ledge. They urged that a light and fog bell be installed without delay, but for years Congress refused to appropriate the needed $45,000. By 1895 money was earmarked and the Spring Ledge Light shone at last on May 24, 1897.

Even after all this, it took more disasters to get a light for Ram Island Ledge. This danger was marked only by a wooden triangle, which storms washed away on at least three occasions. When the 400-ton steamer California pulled out from Grand Trunk Wharf in Portland just before midnight, February 24, 1900, she had 21 passengers and $300,000 worth of freight aboard. She hit Ram Island Ledge and it was six weeks before the damaged vessel was pulled off. Her accident made headline news, and demands for a light became so strong that Congress earmarked $166,000. However, since the ledge on which the light tower was to be built was under water 70 percent of the time, work was slow to start. Disaster struck again when the three-masted Glenrosa, heavily laden with 850 tons of coal for the S. D. Warren Co., tried to enter Portland Harbor in dense fog. She was stripped by scavengers, then broke to pieces where she lay. Shortly thereafter a fishing schooner, Cora & Lillian, met the same fate on the same ledge. After construction was begun, another disaster struck. This time the lime carrier Leona, out of Rockland, hit the ledge. The crew abandoned ship in a brutally cold January storm at 3 a.m. Visibility was nil. They rowed for four hours in the dory, not knowing where they were headed, in freezing, stormy darkness. They fired flares. At dawn the Ram Island work crew, sheltered within their shack nearby, spotted the signal and rescued the exhausted rowers. Three months later, an hour before sunset April 10, 1905, the Ram Island Light was officially lighted.

The famous mark, the Portland Lightship, now an inhuman automated buoy anchored off the entrance to Portland harbor, went on station on March 7, 1903, during the administration of President Theodore Roosevelt. Her name was then "Cape Elizabeth," and did not change to Portland for several years. In the early days there was no communication with land, and the only news came when a passing fisherman would draw alongside and throw an old newspaper on deck. Mail arrived only when the tenders would come out to bring water or coal for the lightship.

Edward L. Eaton, who served 15 years on the old lightship, reported "she was a terrible roller" who would shiver and shake in a storm. The ship was anchored in 150 feet of water and pitched and rolled, fighting the cables. "We broke away twice — once on February 14, 1912. The big combers hit us like a ton of bricks. One sea swept the vessel from stem to stern and took everything with it. We steamed ahead all the time and took what pressure we could off the chain; but she was dancing around so and surging back and forth that somehow the anchor chain shackles unshipped. We worked her into Portland and they were some surprised to see us come sailing up the harbor. We got a new anchor and chain and went back again.

"Next time we went adrift was in a fog mull. The old 12-inch fog whistle had been hammering away for 24 hours. I was asleep when I was awakened by a motion, and, by johnny, we were adrift. We made soundings and decided we had plenty of water under us and anchored. When daylight came and the fog lifted, scores of fishing vessels were all around us. We were anchored near Cashes Ledge.

"Well, to see a lightship anchored on Cashes with the name 'Portland' on her sides had the old skippers guessing. One old feller in a vessel out of Gloucester stood down to us and shouted, 'Where in the hell am I?' We had 25 vessels all around us. I saw one man run below, come back on deck with a chart, lay it on top of the cabin, look at the chart, look up at the lightship."

Thirteen men lived aboard the old lightship, but the pounding of the giant seas took their toll and the old wooden ship had to go. She was replaced with a steel-hulled vessel. She, too, had to go and was replaced by an unmanned light buoy.

In recent years, with almost all the state, city and federal money spent on highways and airports, it is easy to forget what a busy port Portland has been during the past hundred years. Here are a few figures to put a surprising perspective on Casco Bay, and to suggest that this huge harbor, in the present fuel crunch, may again become a hub of coastal and international trade.

In 1872, 65 trains a day were arriving and departing from the waterfront in Portland. Twice a week steamers left for New York, and more often for Boston. Ships came and went to Europe regularly. In 1874 six million feet of lumber left Portland for the West Indies alone; and on return they brought sugar and molasses for Portland's huge rum industry. Along Commercial Street alone, 30 lumber companies flourished. For five months a year Portland was the winter port for Montreal. The grain elevator on the waterfront had a capacity of 200,000 bushels, and the adjacent warehouses could store more than 450,000 bushels of wheat. In 1899, 22 million bushels of Canadian and Midwest wheat poured into Portland, and 13 million of them left by ship for Europe. Portland was a human gateway to America. In 1913 over

26,400 aliens came through immigration on the Portland waterfront. As recently as the mid-1970s almost 500 oil tankers a year unloaded here.

While this vital water commerce was going on, Portland harbor became the third most heavily fortified harbor in the United States, dotted with island forts and thousands of troops traveling back and forth to the islands from the waterfront. The lovely islands of Casco Bay were in their heyday summer resorts, with scores of hotels and boarding houses catering to tens of thousands of waterborne visitors each month.

Lighthouses in Casco Bay were as essential as traffic lights are to a city today.

How The Lights Burn

Automation and electricity run most lights today, and therefore the human bond between ship and lighthouse, seaman and lightkeeper is gone. But how did those men and women, frequently far beyond middle age, keep the lights burning before automation and electric power? Ships without loran, radio, radar or telephones, often without an engine, depended more than we can realize today on lightkeepers and their lamps.

At the beginning, the lighthouse lamp was simply a fire of wood or pitch, blazing in a brazier atop a tower. Later the fire was fueled by coal, coal which had to be hauled by hand in small buckets from ground to tower top. When the first light on the New England coast was lit in 1716, in Boston Harbor, the keeper lit tallow candles. Fifty years later keepers were using spider lamps fueled with whale oil or fish oil, later with lard. Groups of lamps hung together in the tower and the stench was strong.

Maine lightkeepers used these oils at Portland Head (1791), Seguin (1795), Whitehead (1807), Franklin Light (1807), West Quoddy Head (1808), Boone Island (1812). About 1812, sperm oil in an Argand lamp, newly equipped with magnifiers and parabolic reflectors, began to come into use, but such labor-savers were a long time reaching the Maine coast.

The French were far ahead of us. In France Augustin Fresnel had invented and the French government had installed Fresnel lenses and prisms which brought new brilliancy and more distance to the beam. They were not installed

in all U. S. lighthouses until 1859, 30 years after France; but
the basic fuel for the light stayed sperm oil (until the price
got too high because of the scarcity of whales), then lard
and various fish oils were tried, and finally, by 1880, kerosene.
A few lights soon after 1900 got electric power, but not until
the 1930s was electricity universal among lighthouses in
Maine. After World War II the automation of Maine lighthouses slowly spread, often opposed by coastal seamen, because when men no longer manned the light, there was no
longer a lifesaving service. Today only a dozen lights in Maine
are manned.

Fog Signals

In fog no light could be seen and sound became the guide
for seamen. The first fog signal, like the first light, was installed in Boston Harbor. In 1719 cannons were fired to alert
the shore that a ship was creeping into the harbor. Bells
were rung by hand to reply. Their sound was feeble even when
bells weighing 4,000 pounds were struck by primitive machinery. By 1851, trumpets, sounded by compressed air, were
tried. They were somewhat better than bells, but mariners
complained they were too hard to hear. Steam whistles were
tried at West Quoddy Head Light and at Cape Elizabeth Light
in 1855, the first installations of this kind in the U.S. The
sound was louder, but it took time to generate the steam, and
there might be no signal until hours after fog filled a harbor
approach. Finally, the air diaphone horn, powered by compressed air, electricity or steam, was developed and refined
until foghorns, too, were automated, triggered into action by
the approach of fog, and governed by timing devices, so that
horns, like lights, had their own identifiable characteristics.

11.

Favorite Lights:
Heroic Keepers

Behind every lighthouse along the coast there is a story. Almost every seaman has his personal favorites. I have chosen a few of mine. Some because the stories involve a breed of men and women gone forever from our coast; some because I have developed a special love for particular lights that have proved special friends in need to me. I marvel at their beauty or solitude or plain ability to stand there, take punishment and render service against the worst the wind and ocean can mete out.

Boon Island Light

For 27 long years, stretching from the 1880s to World War I, Capt. William W. Williams was the keeper of Boon Island Light, nine miles out from York Beach. A light has stood here since 1799, on one of the smallest but most battered ledges off Maine, just 700 feet long and not 14 feet above sea level.

For 55 stormy years, until 1854, the early keepers had nothing but a hole in the hard ground to crawl into for safety in storms. None could stand the duty for 27 years as Williams did. He was past 90 in 1934, when he told some of his memories to a younger light keeper, Robert L. Sterling. "There were days when I first went on station," said Williams, "that I could not get away from the idea I was locked up in a cell. All we had was a little stone house and a rubblestone tower. When rough weather came seas swept the ledge clean. I was always thinking what I would do to save my life should the whole station be washed away."

Carrier pigeons carried news and messages to the mainland. The ledge had no natural soil. Williams brought out dirt in buckets to grow a few vegetables and flowers. His wife shared the hard life with him. Together they rescued shipwrecked crews from December storms. When six men and a 14-year-old Negro boy were encased in ice, frozen to the thwarts, Mrs. Williams nursed them back to life. "Boon Island derived its name," said Williams, "from a 'boon,' or barrel of provisions placed on the rock for over 50 years, from 1800 to 1854, by fishermen from York, for the use of shipwrecked sailors."

No such "boon" awaited the shipwrecked crew of the Nottingham Galley, which broke up here in 1710. As storms raged over the ledge for weeks, the crew was dying of exposure and starvation. When one died, the others to keep alive, fell to cannibalism and ate their shipmate. Kenneth Roberts wrote a gripping and gruesome novel about the incident.

An heroic and tragic legend persists about one keeper of the Boon Island light in the middle of the last century and his bride of just a few months. The keeper fell ill and died. That night a great storm lashed the ledge. The frantic young widow, alone with the body of her dead husband, climbed the tower and kept the lights shining. In free moments she'd climb down to stand watch over her dead lover. Night after night the storm continued and the widow climbed between lights and lover. The young widow finally lost her reason and the light failed. Next day the storm abated and fishermen came out to see why the light had gone out. They found the demented, mad girl grieving, wandering the rocks, and took her ashore to York.

Seguin Light

Highest light in the State of Maine, the beacon at Seguin flashes into the night at 180 feet above sea level. This is not because the tower itself is so high, but because Seguin, a giant 22-acre rock, rises 150 feet out of the sea at the mouth of the Kennebec River.

According to one of the endless "pidgin English" Indian stories, Seguin got its name from the words an early Indian guide spoke to an early settler as he piloted him to the mouth of the Kennebec, "Sea-go-in here," said the Indian, supposedly — from which "Seguin" derives.

A more likely story to those who've sailed off Seguin in foul weather is that it derives from the Indian word "sutquin," which means "sea vomits." This is an accurate description when the current from the Kennebec crosses the incoming tide and wind from the ocean. Seguin can be a violent passage, made more disturbing by a magnetic phenomenon which sends a ship's compass spinning.

In 1796 the first keeper of Seguin Light came onto the rock. He was an unusual man and before long an unhappy one. He was Count John Polerecsky, whose first home had been in Alsace. He voyaged to the New World, fought in the American Revolution, became Major John Polersky of Pownalboro, Maine. As a reward for his military service, he was named the first keeper of Seguin. A bitter reward it turned out to be. Soon Polersky was writing letters of complaint to his supervisors, detailing his desperate living conditions and abysmal pay, and the fact that he was marooned on the island for months at a time. Death relieved him of his troubles before his earthly superiors did.

Three Seguin Lights were demolished by weather before Congress in 1857 authorized a 53-foot stone tower at a cost of $35,000. Improved and automated, it stands now.

Frank E. Bracey, who'd endured five years rolling and pitching aboard the old Portland Lightship in the 1920s, became keeper of Seguin in 1926. He spent five years on the rock before transfer to the quieter life at the Eagle Island Light in Penobscot Bay. But Bracey never could get the sound of Seguin's foghorn out of his head.

"That Seguin is the foggiest spot in America, I swear. The horn blew weeks, even months, on end, and it's among the most powerful along the coast. I've seen seagulls flying by get knocked down by the concussion of the sound waves."

Bracey boasted that the Seguin Light had been seen 42 miles away by the Boston to Maine boat, and that the blast of its fog horn had been heard in Bath, 14 miles away.

Pemaquid Light

This is my home light and so my favorite. Once we have Pemaquid Light in sight, Steer Clear can sense her mooring nearby in New Harbor and heads to her stable.

Pemaquid Light is on the mainland, a sweet and luxurious post compared to Seguin or Boon Island lights. And it is newer, built in 1827 for $4,000. Isaac Dunham from Bath, the first keeper, even took up farming on the side. His successor, Nathaniel Gamage, paid Dunham over $1,000 — a big sum then — for his barns. Politics cost Gamage his job in 1841, when newly elected President Benjamin Harrison gave the Pemaquid job and the farm to J. P. Means. Poor Gamage could never collect from Means, despite appeals to President Harrison, then after Harrison's death to President Tyler. In desperation Gamage tried to get back his job at the light so he could reclaim the farms which went with it. He never got either.

Fourteen men lost their lives by Pemaquid Light September 16, 1903, aboard the fishing schooner George F. Edmunds, Capt. Willard Poole, skipper.

The light is automated now. The handsome farm is a parking lot. The keeper's house was rented to strangers. In recent years friends of ours have lived in and painted from the keeper's house. Now it has been turned into a fine Fishermen's Museum, project of local fishing families and filled with the gear used by local fishermen in generations past.

Monhegan Light

Thomas B. Seavey lit the Monhegan Light for the first time on July 2, 1824, and more males succeeded him. Keeping the light is thought of as a man's job — but not always on Monhegan. A woman, Betty Morrow Humphrey, kept the Monhegan Light burning for 18 years, including the years of the Civil War when raiders were sinking ships close to Monhegan.

Betty Humphrey's husband, John F. Humphrey, became keeper in March 1861, two weeks before the outbreak of the Civil War. His two sons immediately enlisted and Humphrey took ill and died in December. From Christmas of 1861 until 1880 the dauntless Betty served as official keeper of Monhegan

Light. During her tenure the government cut her pay from $820 a year down to $700.

Besides running the light, Betty Humphrey also took over operation of the fog signal, separately housed on Manana Island, almost half a mile distant across the harbor. The first fog signal was installed in 1854 but on a breezy day nobody at sea could hear it, so in 1870 a Daboll trumpet was tried, without success. Then a steam whistle was tried, and it, too, could not be heard. Finally a first class, very loud, new Daboll trumpet was relocated over on Manana Island and a telegraph line was run across the harbor. When Betty Humphrey, high in her lighthouse atop Monhegan, saw fog rolling in far at sea, she pushed a button. That rang a loud electric gong in the bedroom of Fog Signal Keeper Frank Adams on Manana, who would leap from bed and start his trumpet sounding.

When Betty Humphrey retired, men again took over the job; first Sidney Studley, then William Stanley, who ran the light for 19 years, from 1883 to 1902.

The early keepers burned sperm oil from whales to keep the Monhegan light burning. When that grew too expensive, the switch was made to lard oil. Did the smell permeate the tower? Did the keepers grow accustomed to the reek? How often did they curse as they hauled heavy containers up the endless circular stairs? In 1912 the great modernization was made — a change to incandescent oil vapor. The early fog signal over on Manana was huge — a 2,500-pound bell that was struck by hand in foul weather, until in 1870 an engine was installed to operate the first 10-inch Daboll trumpet. And in the same year of 1912 that the light got incandescent oil vapor, the fog trumpet was replaced by an air siren. Keeper followed keeper — Pierce, Wallace, Orne, Handley, Dyer, Woodward, Hutchins, Robinson, Foss and Wilson B. Carter.

Today the automated light sends out a 170,000 candlepower beam. The diaphragm horn explodes with two terrific blasts every minute. Despite automation, the indispensable Monhegan Light can still fail. It did, just after midnight during an icy gale on February 2, 1981. Coast Guardsmen William Spencer and Mark Wilson, on duty across the harbor on Manana, got the bad news. They launched their 16-foot pea pod and outboard into the teeth of the gale and set off to repair the light. Halfway across their outboard quit, their boat capsized, and the 40 knot winds lashed waves pouring through the narrow harbor and swept the little boat and two men crew into the ledges at Smuttynose. They scrambled through the storm, drenched and bitter cold. The tide was rising and could submerge Smuttynose. On their portable VHF radio they called the Coast Guardsmen back at the fog station, who relayed their plea for help to the Coast Guard in Boothbay Harbor, 15 miles away — a risky, many-hour trip to Smuttynose in a February gale. On Monhegan Sherman Stanley and harbor master Steve Rollins were awakened from sleep about 3 a.m. by a call from the Coast Guard asking if they could rescue the stranded men. Stanley and Rollins went out into the black, storming night, with winds reaching 50 mph. The seas were too rough for an outboard so Stanley and Rollins rowed 300 yards in a small skiff to Smuttynose and took off the half-frozen Coast Guardsmen.

Owls Head Light

Heading east after passing through Muscle Ridge Shoals, the Owls Head Light signals the entrance to one of Maine's best cruising grounds — Penobscot Bay.

Owls Head is one of the most handsome of all Maine lights. Rising 100 feet above the water from atop a tree-studded high cliff, it is a joyful landmark. Its horn has been our guide poking through dense fog across West Penobscot Bay. After saluting the light with a toot of our horn for many years, we finally went ashore, met the keeper and admired the immaculate house, light and surroundings.

The Thomaston-Rockland lime trade triggered the building of Owls Head Light. When Rockland lime sold for a dollar a barrel, after the Revolutionary War, schooners began carrying lime to Europe and returned laden with salt for Maine fishing boats. Fog and storm wrecked many when they were within only a few miles of home. The need for a light became more urgent when the steamer Maine began making Owls Head a regular stop. The light was built and in September 1825 Keeper Isaac Stearns lit the light for the first time.

In the more than 156 years since Stearns lit the light, Owls Head has saved scores of ships from disaster. But not all.

Dozens of dire wrecks have marked the rugged ledges of the outlying islands and there are many tales of shipwrecks.

One of the weirdest occurred in the terrible gale of December 22, 1850, when five ships were lost along the eight-mile stretch between Owls Head and Spruce Head. One of those was a small coasting schooner at anchor in nearby Rockland harbor, with the mate, his bride-to-be and one deckhand aboard, all asleep. Near midnight the raging storm snapped her anchor lines and the schooner blew out of Rockland toward Owls Head, was smashed on ledges, but did not sink. Water poured into the hold, but the vessel held fast to the ledges. The mate, his bride-to-be and the deckhand pulled heavy blankets on deck and sought shelter under them; but coats of ice built up as each wave swept across them. Ice soon encased the three. The deckhand used a knife and his fists to keep open a breathing hole. By 6 a.m. he decided he could get ashore for help. He struggled across the wave-lashed, iced ledges and got half way to the lights shining from the Keeper's house and collapsed on the dirt road. His body was seen from the kitchen. He was rushed to the warm house where he told the Keeper, William Masters, of the ice-enclosed bodies still on deck. A rescue party brought the bodies back to the house thinking they were frozen dead; but Masters poured water over the ice, slowly increasing the water temperature. First the ice fell off from the hands and legs of the man and girl. As it melted from their bodies the rescue party massaged the frozen limbs. After an hour both the girl and the mate revived to consciousness. Weeks later they were able to walk. Six months later, in June, they were married, but the deckhand never fully recovered.

Brutality laid its early scar on Owls Head, too. The high ground near the light had been fought over by settlers and Indians for many years. On June 7, 1757, 30 Indian war canoes landed. In the battle which followed, Captain Joseph Cox reversed the usual story; he scalped two of the Penobscot Indians.

Mt. Desert Rock Light

It can be a long, long haul from Owls Head to Mt. Desert Rock, most remote of all Maine lighthouses. Between the two are dozens of lighthouses, each with its own beauty, romance and — above all — usefulness, to boats at sea. There is not room here to tell all their stories. For lighthouse buffs who want more, I suggest "The Lighthouses of New England" by Edward Rowe Snow and "Lighthouses of Maine" by Robert T. Sterling, as good starters; and "Lighthouses of Casco Bay" by Peter Dow Bachelder. Town libraries often have local histories giving great detail on the lights of their slice of coast.

Mount Desert Rock Light is a hard, remote lonesome world, and is not easy to come to. It lies, a speck in the fierce Atlantic, 26 miles out from the mainland. The might of the ocean hitting this rock for thousands of years is difficult to conceive. According to federal records, a mammoth stone 18 feet long, 14 feet wide and 6 feet thick, weighing 57 tons was hurled from its place in a storm of 1842. In another storm a 75-ton boulder was moved 60 feet by the gigantic waves. This is not a place keepers stayed long and today the light runs by remote control.

The first known white man sailed by here in late May 1524, the Italian, Giovanni da Verrazano. The light was built over 300 years later in 1830. A more difficult, dangerous construction job is hard to name. Men and materials not only had to be hauled 26 miles from the nearest mainland, but once here, getting the men and materials ashore was a terrible challenge. The rock is barely a half acre; its high point is barely 11 feet above the waves on a calm day and awash or submerged in bad weather, yet for almost 150 years men (and for a while women) lived here; kept the light; saved lives in peril.

In 1880, the Helen and Mary, out of Halifax, with a deckload of timber and a cargo hold of granite, foundered off here. Captain Jared Parker, after putting his wife, baby and crew into the first lifeboat, climbed into the second boat with First Mate Nelson White. It capsized in the wake of the sinking schooner. When White surfaced, he saw the first boat floating, bottom up, and no sign of any human. White reached some floating wreckage, and climbed on it. Then he spotted a bundle of yellow oilskins, and grabbed it. Inside was the infant baby of the captain's wife, who was White's sister. White and the infant lasted the day and the night in violent surf. By the next morning the wild ocean had calmed. The gale had carried the wreckage to which White clung with the infant in oilskins strapped to his chest, to within 10 miles of the coast. At noon they were sighted and rescued by the lighthouse tender Iris, No others survived.

An ocean tug, Astral, towing a big barge, met a strange fate here in a dreadful storm of December 9, 1902. The Astral hit hard at five in the morning. Her frantic signal on her whistles was heard by an assistant keeper; but until the tide went down there was no possible way the lighthouse keepers could rescue the crew because mountainous, icy seas forbade the launching of any boat. At low tide the keepers dragged rescue lines to the outer point. From there they hurled a line aboard and brought 17 men ashore one by one. The eighteenth man froze to death. For six days the keepers and their wives nursed the 17 injured back to life.

But the barge they towed was still out there. The crew aboard the barge had no idea what had happened to their tug. They could not see it. Ice more than a foot thick blocked the windows of their pilothouse. Sea vapor was so dense that visibility was less than 25 feet. The crew thought the tug had anchored to weather it out. So they lay on the barge from Tuesday to Thursday, held from drifting by a hawser over 2400 feet long, still tied to the wrecked tug. The length of the hawser allowed the barge to be blown into the lee of Mt. Desert Rock, giving them a little protection from the worst of the storm.

By Thursday the wind shifted to the south. The barge crew cut the cable, hoisted sail and were picked up 40 miles down the coast, off Rockland. Once ashore the captain of the barge called his home office at Standard Oil Co. in New York, which sent a wrecking crew to tow off the remnants of the tug and take ashore the 17 crew members.

Matinicus Rock Light

Today the Audubon Society on calm summer days runs special boat trips for members to see the spectacular puffins on Matinicus Rock Light. The trip is memorable and unforgettable for birdwatchers who can see the colorful, parrot-like puffins strutting and nesting in the volcanic rock, and marvel at the huge colonies of Arctic terns, guillemots and gulls which call this outpost home.

But the Rock carries its tales of tragedy, violent storms, heroism and amazing human endurance through fearful isolation and terror.

The Rock is a 32-acre volcanic outcrop, barren and vulnerable, 25 miles out to sea from Rockland. The nearest human habitation is six miles away on Matinicus Island. In a running sea there is no safe way to land a boat here.

Over 154 years ago, on June 26, 1827, John A. Shaw got the job of first keeper of Matinicus Rock Light by appointment of President John Quincy Adams, at a salary of $450 a year. Shaw and his wife moved into the wooden structures which were to serve them, perilously, as home and lighthouse. The North Atlantic seas and gales made short work of those wooden buildings. All that remains to tell of what they endured are the laconic one-line entries from a logbook kept by Shaw, now in the Federal archives:

"31 Oct. 1829 - a savere gail Broak over Rock

9 Nov 1829 - a bad storme

24 Nov - a man of war pased hear to Day

25 Jan 1830 - A vilant Snow Storm

9 Feb - trim and set up All night

23 May - The keeper very sick

June - The keeper is Beter and he aught to be."

Keeper Shaw first lit the light on this godforsaken rock when he was 65. He died of sickness in 1831, aged 69.

Abbie Burgess will forever be one of the great heroines of seafaring Maine. She came to the Rock as a 14-year-old girl in the springtime of 1853, when her father, Samuel Burgess, was named keeper. Abbie was later to marry on the Rock; bear children on the Rock; bury one infant there; and tend the light in the direst of times. Half a century after she died in 1892, sea coast historian, Edward Rowe Snow, found a note she had written: "I wonder if the care of the lighthouse will follow my soul after it has left this worn out body. If ever I have a gravestone, I would like it to be in the form of a lighthouse or beacon." In 1946 historian Snow arranged for a replica of the Matinicus Rock Light to be placed on the grave of Abbie Burgess at Spruce Head, Maine, where she had been buried in 1892.

Here in brief is the story of Abbie Burgess and her courage and tenacity in single-handedly keeping the light burning on this barren rock 600 yards long, 200 yards wide, 25 miles at sea.

At 14 Abbie became her father's helper. Mrs. Burgess was an invalid, mostly bed-ridden. Abbie had two younger sisters and took care of them too. Her father also taught Abbie how to care for the light. She spent her free hours reading the old logbooks of earlier keepers and their stories of the storms they had endured. When she was 17, Abbie got her first test. In January 1856 her father took Abbie aside and told her that he had to make an emergency trip to Rockland for food and supplies to last through the winter. The supply boat, he said, had failed to come with replenishments in September as scheduled. So while the weather was good, he would leave the light and the family in her care, while he sailed 26 miles to Rockland and 26 miles back for supplies. But storms stopped him from getting back for almost four weeks.

I quote now from Abbie's story:

"For a month no landing could be effected on the Rock . . . we were without the assistance of any male of our family. Though at times greatly exhausted from my labors, not once did the lights fail. Under God I was able to perform all my accustomed duties as well as my father's . . . The waves destroyed the old dwelling and swept over the Rock . . . The sea is never still and its roar shuts out every other sound, even drowning our voices."

The next winter her father was on another trip to Rockland and again was cut off for 21 days by storms. Again Abbie was alone on the Rock, feeding herself, her invalid mother and her young sisters on a diet of one cup of corn meal a day. In addition the teen age girl had kept the 23 wicks in the lights burning, feeding them with thinned-out lard oil through the wild storms.

Almost 35 years later she wrote; "Many nights I tended the lights and then could not sleep the rest of the night, thinking nervously what might happen if the lights should fail . . . When I dream of the old lamps on Matinicus Rock, I am always hurrying to light the lamps before sunset . . ."

Burgess lost his job. It was a political appointment. In 1861, after Abraham Lincoln was elected president, Burgess was fired and John Grant was named to replace him; but Abbie stayed on the Rock with the Grant family to show them the ropes of running the station. The son of the keeper was attracted to the 22-year-old Abbie. Later that year Isaac H. Grant and Abbie were married, and four children were born to them on the Rock.

An infant, two-year-old Bessie Grant, is buried on the Rock, the only person ever buried there. The little grave was discovered almost 20 years ago by Harriet Buchheister, wife of the president of the National Audubon Society, who went often to the Rock to see the puffin colony there.

Little Bessie died suddenly, almost 120 years ago. The weather was too severe to take her body to the mainland, so the Grants scraped together buckets of scarce soil on the Rock, lugged the dirt to the top of a cliff, away from the waves, and between two sheltering slabs of weathered granite, made a grave. Remnants of a small wooden cross were found by Mrs. Buchheister. Coast Guardsmen stationed on the rock 20 years ago helped shore up the grave with brick and mortar to stop further erosion. George R. Perry of Rockland carved a little headstone marker which was taken out to the Rock.

Abbie Burgess Grant, and her husband and their children left the Rock in 1875, but the Grants were not finished with lighthouses. Abbie and Isaac went as keepers of the White Head Light, near Spruce Head, and over 20 miles closer to shore than Matinicus; but old Capt. John Grant stayed on the Rock until 1890. The man who succeeded him as keeper was his grandson, William G. Grant.

Today helicopters land on the Rock. There is a microwave phone to the mainland, and a central power plant to power the light, the radio beacon and horn. Storms lash still at this barren volcanic rock. During the 1970s lobstermen six miles distant on Matinicus Island sent over a Christmas tree to the men on the treeless Rock. At Christmas Albert Bunker and his wife organized "bakes" to supply pies, breads, cookies, candies to the men on the Rock who all year long kept a weather eye on lobstermen. One year the seas were too rough to land a Christmas tree so the boat fired off a line from a rescue gun. The men on the Rock grabbed the line and hauled ashore their Christmas tree through the towering seas.

These stories of a few Maine lighthouse keepers have recounted the highlights of storm, disaster and shipwreck. But a keeper's job has long stretches of routine work, days of gorgeous weather, moments of supreme happiness and long hours of boredom. Keepers turned often to time-passing hobbies; to reading, writing, music, and attempts at gardening, even farming.

A journalist, Gustav Kobbe, writing in the 1890s in "The Century Magazine," told of a visit to Matinicus Rock Light and the cow he found there.

"The keeper owns the only quadruped on the rock — a cow. This valuable beast is called Daisy. She was brought over from Matinicus Island on a small boat and a short distance from the shore, the boat was tipped so far over to one side that Daisy lost her balance and fell into the water where she was left to swim ashore. I have often seen her standing upon that mass of barren granite, the only living thing in view, the wind furrowing up her hide. She would gaze out at the waste of wild waters with a driven, lonely look, the pathos of which was almost human. . . Often the cow looks over in the direction of Matinicus Island and moos pathetically . . . She formerly found some companionship in a rabbit, with which she was accustomed to play at dusk; but the rabbit died."

The bane of every keeper's life was polishing the brasswork; and the cussedness of having it all shined, only to have the fog roll in and spoil it.

Fred Morong, born down east in Lubec in 1883, became a keeper and hated the brasswork with a vengeance. He wrote a poem about this hated chore of keepers. Here are a few verses from it:

O what is the bane of a lightkeeper's life
That causes him worry, struggle and strife,
That makes him use cuss words, and beat at his wife?
   It's Brasswork.

What makes him look ghastly, consumptive and thin,
What robs him of health, vigor and vim,
And causes despair and drives him to sin?
   It's Brasswork.

The devil himself could never invent
A material causing more world-wide lament
And in Uncle Sam's service about ninety percent
   Is Brasswork.

The lamp in the tower, reflector and shade,
The tools and accessories pass in parade.
As a matter of fact the whole outfit is made
   Of Brasswork

The machinery, clockwork, fog-signal bell,
The coal hods, the dustpans, the pump in the well.
Now I'll leave it to you, mates, if this isn't-well
   Brasswork

I dig, scrub and polish, and work with a might,
And just when I get it all shining and bright,
In comes the fog, like a thief in the night;
   Good-by Brasswork

And when I have polished until I am cold
And I'm taken aloft to the Heavenly fold
Will my harp and my crown be made of pure gold?
   No, Brasswork."

View of old Portland Harbor

This etching depicts Portland Harbor as the artist saw it over 100 years ago. (Maine Historical Society)

Monhegan Island
View across the harbor from Manana Island. (Gannett file photo)

Cod fishery on Georges Bank

This is one of hundreds of excellent illustrations from a huge docu-
mentary volume issued by Bureau of Fisheries in the 19th century.

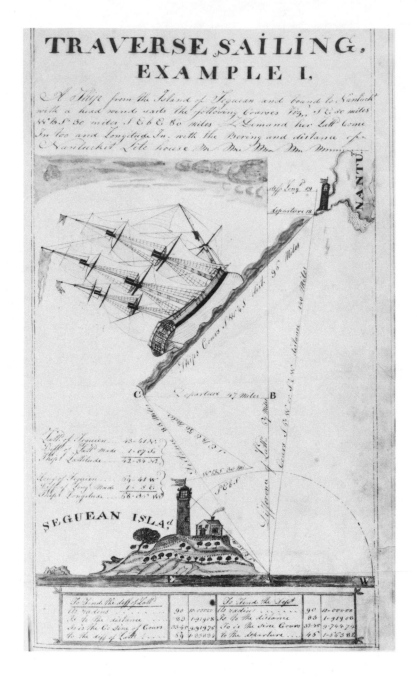

Course and Distance from Seguin
Another painted page from the Navigation book of Capt. Francis Rittal,
1805, showing his elaborate calculations. (Courtesy Bath Marine Museum)

Packing fish on a Maine wharf
Maine fishing harbors had dozens of packing plants, where women and children canned the fish their menfolk caught. (Bureau of Fisheries, 1887)

Miss Lizzie Rich, postmaster, Isle au Haut
Miss Lizzie ran the island post office for over half a century on Isle au Haut, jewel of Penobscot Bay. (Gannett file photo)

Beloved island doctor
Dr. Ralph Earle devoted his important lifetime as the one doctor on Vinalhaven, established the island clinic and documented and controlled hereditary diabetes. (Gannett file photo)

Jug and fish lines
The indispensable properties of a man who harvested the silver mines
of Maine. (Illustration by Burns, Harper's New Monthly, 1880)

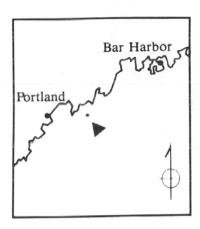

12.

Damariscove Island:
Shelter And Sanctuary

If you enjoy going to extremes, leaping quickly from Vacationland 1981 to frontier Maine 1581, spend a day in Boothbay Harbor at the peak of summer; and at nightfall sail out to Damariscove Island and anchor there. The contrast is superb, with the best of opposite worlds only an hour apart.

In summertime Boothbay Harbor, not a parking spot is empty. Traffic creeps as drivers hunt for 20 empty feet in which to leave their car. Summer business booms in this hilly, handsome harbor town. Since early morning tourists have been swarming from cars and buses; some headed for salt breezes on the decks of sightseeing boats, some went off to fish from party boats, some prowled the shops. All day sidewalks have overflowed with vacationers licking ice cream cones, snapping pictures of fishing boats, nursing sunburns, buying souvenirs and postcards with lobster motifs. Now with darkness falling, Fisherman's Wharf, Jordan's, Rocktide, The Tugboat Inn, The Thistle, dozens of restaurants, bars and pizza parlors shine bright with neon lights. The sounds of music throb across the harbor.

Out in the harbor, cabin lights shine from cruising boats, resting here for a night or two on their way down east. Dinghies visit back and forth. Voices from sailors relaxing on decks come loud and clear across the water. Youngsters in outboards kick up an unwanted and illegal wake as they speed on missions of love or party. The Catholic church shines serene and handsome, bathed in floodlights on the eastern shore. The scene is happy, lively, noisy, frenetic, the essence of a Maine summer resort in the happy throes of tourism.

Leave all this behind. Sail out as I often do, slow and easy on the night breeze, past Tumbler and Mouse and Squirrel Islands, leave Ram Island Light to the east and the Cuckolds to the west, sail by Fisherman's Island, and six miles from downtown Boothbay, slip past the swells of The Motions and drop anchor in the darkness of deserted Damariscove.

This is where America began 400 years ago. Long before the famed early colonists set foot at Popham, Jamestown or Plymouth, nameless seamen from England and Europe anchored in this cove, dried and salted fish on this island, cooked supper and passed the rum on this rocky shore.

But on this night not a soul lives on Damariscove except perhaps the ghost of a headless man and his barking dog, walking the lonely shore. Their legend lives, and will be told. On a lucky night, yours may be the only craft here; but 400 years ago scores of fishing boats and crews from England, France, Spain and Holland sheltered here. Their shouts, their motley of languages, echoed between these lonely ledges. On one night when we anchored in the snug harbor at Damariscove Island, I wrote in the ship's log:

"Black night has fallen, the wind has dropped. The sea is so flat calm that the stars shine back up from the ocean as well as down from heaven. The only night noises are the laugh of a loon, eerie and primeval in the darkness of a deserted island, and the sound of small waves lapping on the shore and the tide gurgling among the boulders. It is warm. I lean over the side of the boat and run a hand through the black sea. The water comes alive with flashes of fire, the miracle of phosphorescence. Thousands of years ago, thousands of miles away, the Romans gave a beautiful name to these tiny creatures of the sea who cause this light to shine. The name is notilucci — lights of the night."

The Mayflower sailed into this harbor of Damariscove. Long before she, or her namesake, carried 102 pilgrims into Plymouth, Mayflower was a fish boat and this harbor is where she loaded cod. The log of the Mayflower during her pilgrims' voyage records that she stopped here, "to take some coddes before sailing on to Maffachufects Bay" in 1620.

The second winter after they landed at Plymouth, the pilgrim fathers were threatened with starvation. Edward Winslow sailed from Plymouth to Damariscove to seek food from this flourishing colony of fishermen on this little known island.

"It was about the end of May 1622," Winslow wrote, "at which time our store of victuals was wholly spent, having lived long before with bare and short allowance." So Winslow sailed here, set his anchor and asked for food at Damariscove. He wrote: "I found kind entertainment and good respect, with a willingness to supply our wants; and they would not take any bills for same, but did what they could for us freely." Winslow reported in 1622, "there were thirty ships of sail" in the harbor when he came in to Damariscove, all taking on loads of dried fish for markets in Europe.

Damariscove Island proved a safe haven from Indian attacks. In 1675 the Indians staged widespread attacks on white settlements all along the Maine coast. Over 200 settlers from Sheepscot, Damariscotta, Arrowsic, Pemaquid and Newagen fled their burning homes, took to their boats and sought safety and refuge on Damariscove Island, six miles at sea.

The island is only two miles long, not more than a quarter mile wide, and pinched to a narrow waist in the middle, yet 300 refugees, fleeing without provisions of any kind, were able to find food and shelter enough from the little colony that had been long established here.

Now, centuries later, we were alone out here, refugees of a kind from the midsummer invasion of Boothbay Harbor. We went below on Steer Clear and slept in our bunks with a feeling of being strange intruders into a heroic past. We'd sailed only six miles out from vacationing America, and dropped our 20th century Danforth high-tensile anchor deep in the same mud where killick stone anchors had held fishing boats of early settlers almost 400 years before. But we slept soundly. Soon after daybreak we loaded the dog into the dinghy and went ashore to explore.

The remnants of an old Coast Guard station, built in 1897

and abandoned in 1959, stand dilapidated and vandalized. During its time as a lifesaving station they averaged 25 rescues a year. In World War II they installed listening devices to detect German submarines when they surfaced to recharge their batteries at night. When the lonely Coast Guardsmen heard such sounds they radioed Brunswick Naval Air Station to send out attack planes.

Far up the little harbor are a couple of rough shacks used by lobstermen to store gear or to shelter in overnight during a storm. John W. Sargent was the last man to live and fish full time out here. He spent many years on Damariscove, but they ended in tragedy. His child drowned here 30 years ago; and 25 years later, in 1976, Sargent's own body was found washed up on the shore near the spot where he kept his boat. Someone found his hat later and nailed it over the door of his one-room camp.

On high ground further inland are cellar holes of granite; in fields beyond, the rusted relics of plows and farm tools. Lovely-hued wild flowers grow among them, in soil those plows once had tilled. Obscured and overgrown by salt grass are traces of stone walls, built long ago to keep sheep and cattle out of the planted fields. The only sounds today are the calls of meadowlarks roused by our dog, and the mew of gulls following a dragger.

This island land has been farmed and timbered for centuries. Standing on the high ground you can look back to the harbor and envisage it as a fishing station. Historian Charles K. Bolton, in his book, "The Real Founders of New England," wrote about Damariscove.

"Here was the chief maritime port of New England. Here was the rendezvous for English, French and Dutch ships crossing the Atlantic. Here men bartered with one another and with Indians, drank, gambled, quarreled and sold indentured servants." Then, hundreds of years back, this empty shore had been busy. Wharves, salting houses, sheds, boatyards, makeshift taverns and perhaps a bawdy house or two for sailors ashore after a long Atlantic crossing, must have lined this empty harbor.

Humphrey Damarill was the first kingpin here, the first major businessman in residence. By 1608 Damarill was operating a busy trading post on Damariscove, catering to the ships and crews, and soon he owned the nearby islands — Fisherman's, Outer and Inner Heron. The harbor was called "Damarill's Cove," and through usage became Damariscove. His influence may have spread further. In some early records the Damariscotta River is called "Damariscove River." Linguists are confounded in their efforts to decide whether the name, Damariscotta, is related to Damarill, or whether it stems from the Indian words meaning "river of alewives." In any case, Damarill flourished on his island for close to 40 years, then with money in his pocket, headed to Boston to enjoy the fruits of his labor. There he died in 1650.

Captain Richard Patishall owned the island after Damarill. His headless body is said to haunt the island still. He met his bloody end when Indians captured him aboard his boat at Pemaquid on August 2, 1689. His body was beheaded and thrown into the sea — an Indian tribute to a brave enemy. His dog jumped in after him. Both bodies were later washed up on the shores of Damariscove Island where the two had long lived together. Legend has it that the headless Patishall and his dog can be seen today wandering the island shores on moonlit nights.

The headless man and his dog were seen, according to local historian Harold W. Castner, by one of the work crew building the first Coast Guard station on Damariscove almost 85 years ago. The petrified man rushed back into camp, trembling, ashen white and dripping with perspiration and spewed out his tale of terror to his workmates. Next morning the entire work crew hurriedly left the island. Months passed before other men could be persuaded to go back. Later a highly respected fisherman, Captain Chase, saw the headless man and his dog. Chase refused to set foot on Damariscove again. "Now, living men," says Castner, "tell tales of ghostly barking across the treeless island." Today a visiting dog will suddenly stop, cock its ears in surprise, and excitedly return the barks which humans cannot hear.

Pirates and smugglers have had their fling here, too. Captain Kidd, that peripatetic pirate, is supposed to have sunk a cable across the harbor mouth and then buried treasure on its shores. The notorious Dixy Bull, who pillaged Pemaquid 350 years ago, is said to have buried treasure in the bottomless pond of Damariscove.

Sweet smelling roses with an unusual flower bloom in profusion in a few sheltered spots beside the shore. The story is that the seeds were brought here from France by a French trader 365 years ago. On the fresh-water pond, two hundred yards from the head of the harbor, yellow cow lilies make a dazzling display. But all the trees of Damariscove, once used for ship repairs, for barrel staves, shelters and firewood, are gone. The northern half of the island is still called Wood End; but there is barely a tree left where thousands once grew. Fires destroyed great stands of lumber; and herds of sheep chewed all vegetation down to the roots.

Certain of those early sheep served a traitorous cause, just before the Revolution. The British Captain Henry Mowatt, in October 1775, put into Damariscove and requisitioned sheep from a farmer there. That night, on the eve of battle, he served his men a great meal of roast mutton. The next day Mowatt bombarded and burned Portland, or Falmouth as it was then called.

Damariscove enjoyed a touch of revenge some years later. In early September 1813, Boxer, a British brig of 18 guns and 104 men, and the American brig, Enterprise, with 16 guns and 102 men, met and fought within sight of Damariscove. For 35 minutes the firing of their guns was incessant. Then Boxer, having lost her masts, her captain and 46 of her crew, struck her colors. A spar from Boxer washed ashore on Damariscove. The islanders promptly made it into their flagpole.

Island families farmed and fished on Damariscove from the 1600s into the 1930s. In 1918 a tutor was teaching 14 young island children. In 1937 five families were still living year-round on the island, but at the bottom of the Great Depression the last of the year-round fisherman-farmers came ashore. The brothers, Isaac and Chester Poole, and their 13 children packed up and sold out. Later, summer folk came to enjoy Damariscove. The last of them, the Kenneth L. Parkers of Cornwall Bridge, Connecticut, grew discouraged by repeated vandalism. In 1966 they gave the island to The Nature Conservancy, which holds Damariscove in trust today.

The greatest single-handed sailor in the world went aground coming into Damariscove. Joshua Slocum and his 15-year-old son, in the famous boat Spray, in which Slocum circumnavigated the world alone, got off the ledge on a rising tide.

On one large rock is a strange carving, very faint today, after untold years of salt and sea and wind. Some think it may have been drawn by Phoenician voyagers 10,000 years ago. That is wholly unsubstantiated, but it is certain that almost 400 years ago, long before white men settled in the now famous places of Plymouth, Popham and Jamestown, this 300-acre island of Damariscove was home and haven to hundreds of English and European seamen and fishermen. Some of those hardy men were the first white men to inhabit North America.

Heading to Monhegan

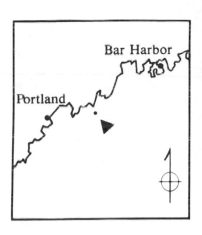

13.

Monhegan:
Shaped Like A Whale

Fog swirls in on the night wind. Its wet white blanket blots out brilliant stars which an hour ago canopied the sky, helping to light the narrow dirt road from Deadman's Cove, past the creaking pines of Cathedral Woods. We walk past Dr. Alta Ashley's house, called The Pill Box, past the little white school, past Don Cundy's big grey home and its swimming pool, past the summertime store, Island Spa, down to the island wharf.

Chris, the Winnie N., Phalarope and the 12 other boats which make up Monhegan's 15-vessel lobster fleet in winter, are barely visible on their moorings. Gone from sight because of the fog are all Monhegan's giant lobster cars, each of which may hold from 1,000 to 3,000 live lobsters. They have strong moorings of their own, for they hold Monhegan's wealth till the buyer from Port Clyde comes 11 miles out or till lobstermen sell direct to mainland dealers.

The beam of Monhegan Light flashes yellow in the fog. A light from Monhegan has been warning men at sea on nights like this since 1824. Across the harbor where the fog horn now wails on Manana, a giant bell stood, cast in Boston in 1832, and a man stood by it on foggy nights; sounding its clapper by hand to warn ships off the death-trap rocks below.

Monhegan is historic ground. Some believe the runes near today's Coast Guard station on Manana were carved into the rock there by Viking sailors about 1000 A.D. Six hundred years after the Vikings, English fishermen salted shiploads of cod on these shores. Hundreds of years ago men and ships perished here, not far from the Washerwoman Ledge. These Monhegan shores are where Captain John Smith of Pocahontas fame came ashore in May of 1614 and where, for centuries before him, Indians encamped and harvested the sea.

Now, 367 years later, on this stormy night in January, nearly 100 people sleep on Monhegan.

This island, 11 miles out to sea, high, rocky, unprotected, alone and beautiful, is a unique and almost foreign land.

For example, here are a few everyday matters on Monhegan that are perhaps unique to the wonderful island.

Monhegan may have the only doctor in the United States who was the town clerk, director of civil defense, collector of taxes, registrar of voters, school physician and newspaper correspondent. She is Dr. Alta Ashley, who is proud to be the oldest winter resident on Monhegan and is the medical examiner, island historian and local correspondent for Maine newspapers.

Monhegan may have had the only road worker, David Boynton, who was a nuclear scientist at MIT, and the only two Maine lobstermen, Bill and Duggie Boynton, who graduated from Wesleyan University, in political science, and from Trinity College, in Chinese studies.

Monhegan may be the only community which has just 10 kids going to the island school, but which has its own truant officer, Alfred Stanley, highliner, lobsterman and third generation islander.

Crime rate on Monhegan is a marvel to gladden most hearts. The big crime of summer was when a young man was caught putting slugs instead of coins into the pay phones. He caught the next boat back to the mainland.

There is no town water on Monhegan in the winter. When you want water, you go to the kitchen and pump it, and when you want light you use a kerosene lamp. If you must have power, to watch television for example, you go out and start up your own generator. There is no central source of power on Monhegan. Two homes use solar power.

Just getting out to Monhegan in winter is not easy. The only public transport is by the mail boat Laura B, which runs out of Port Clyde on Monday, Wednesday and Friday. The trip takes just over an hour, and the necessities of life on

Monhegan from milk to stovepipes travel with you as deck cargo.

In summer, when up to 1000 people instead of under 100 may inhabit Monhegan, the Laura B makes two round trips a day, and excursion boats make daily trips from Boothbay Harbor and weekend trips from New Harbor.

It is January on Monhegan Island, a special kingdom.

In the schoolhouse on the hill four big days of Monhegan's winter are written on the blackboard — Thanksgiving, Christmas, New Year — and Trap Day.

Trap Day is unique to this island, the January day Monhegan lobstermen set out their traps. Lobstermen of Monhegan long ago made their own rules, rules that are rigid and excellent, but which no other lobstermen in Maine have been able to establish.

Maine law now prohibits catching of lobsters within two miles in any direction of Monhegan shores from sundown on the 25th of June till dawn of the 1st of January. Monhegan is the only spot in Maine with a closed season on lobstering. The men out here go lobstering in the coldest, roughest winter weather. When other lobstermen on the mainland quit, the Monhegan men begin.

Sherman Stanley, whose family has lived on Monhegan and fished these waters for three generations, explained how Trap Day began.

"Back about 1907 Monhegan lobstermen made their own closed season. No lobstering between late June and New Year. Then two years later they petitioned the State Legislature and got the rules made into law in 1909. My father spearheaded that effort."

Monhegan Island and the ocean around it are special territory. No fisherman from the mainland or other islands in the bay is fool enough to set traps within Monhegan waters, winter or summer. The outsider may be deterred more by Monhegan lobstermen than by the Maine law. The ocean within two miles of Monhegan is off-limits for fishing to all outsiders, and wise outsiders stay away when it comes to setting traps.

Not many men choose to go lobstering in winter out here, living on this high, windswept, high-cliffed island which measures 1.75 miles long and .75 across. Less than 15 lobster boats fish from here in the winter Atlantic. But precisely because the Monhegan tradition for 74 years has been to let the lobsters breed and live in peace from July till January, the lobsters they get are likely to be fat, plentiful and fetch high prices in the winter when other lobsters are scarce on the market. The lobsters are kept alive and fresh in storage cars, securely anchored in the cold harbor.

On a day of good hauling in January or February a Monhegan lobster boat may bring in $500 or more worth of lobsters. When the season ends June 25, the bank accounts are often fat. Winter lobstering in these far offshore waters is not for many men, yet in recent years, there has been a fine resurgence of new young blood into the island's year-round community. Sometimes men from distant places get bitten by the love of Monhegan, through Coast Guard duty here or through a summer job in an island hotel, and come back here to live and work year-rounnd.

"Can a new fisherman move onto Monhegan and be welcome?" I asked Sherman Stanley, Sr., an island power.

I was a bit surprised when he answered: "We'd welcome a new fisherman — provided he showed good intent to live here year-round, and proved himself to be an honest individual. He'd be welcomed more than hindered by us; but it would be a different story if a fellow tried to move onto Monhegan, fish our six months, and then move off — or if he couldn't keep to our Monhegan standards of honesty and fair play."

I asked Stanley what he meant by "Monhegan honesty." He said; "If I go off on vacation, or get sick and can't get out hauling traps, on Monhegan I know for sure that no one will touch my gear or my traps or my house. That's Monhegan honesty." I didn't need to ask him what "Monhegan fair play" meant. I had seen "Monhegan fair play" in action one night at the island store in a Fisherman's Meeting.

Soon after Christmas each year the fishermen get together to talk, vote and then decide the date for Trap Day, usually close to January 1. The men swap news, then slowly creep up on the subject of Trap Day. This time they voted to put off Trap Day for a week or so.

That meant they'd all miss some $500 days. Why did they

vote to postpone? Because one man's engine was out; another was on shore visiting a mother near death. So all the other fishermen voted to put off Trap Day until the engine was fixed and the man with a sick mother was back. That way, they said, everyone got an equal chance.

Monhegan is one community where the dollar is not king, and where "dog eat dog and the devil take the hindmost" is not the business code. Instead they live by Monhegan fair play.

Just before Trap Day the wharf gets piled high with traps, ready to go. To get to the boats you walk through a forest of traps, higher than a man's head, piled on all sides. When first light of Trap Day dawns, wives, friends and helpers load the boats high with traps, the engines roar, and the fleet is off, each boat racing out to set traps where the skipper thinks the most lobsters will be. After setting one load, the boats race back to harbor for the next. Wives send down replenishments of food. It takes each boat two or three days of work to set out over 1,000 traps each.

From January till June 25 the men lobster, often in high seas and sub-zero weather. Boats that work in this water are built big and strong, and men seldom go out single-handed. For safety, and to share the work and the money, there is almost always a helper aboard every boat. In fine weather or foul the younger wives are often out with their husbands. In 1981, three husband and wife teams were lobstering, and on Dan Cundy's boat a father-daughter-son team were seen fishing.

On the island, weather dominates everyone's mind, around the clock. Storms at night can damage boats or the precious lobster car, full of the island wealth; or drag away traps by the hundreds from the ocean bottom. In lost traps alone a storm can cost thousands of dollars because each trap represents about $30. Storms sometimes isolate the island by knocking out Monhegan's tenuous telephone link to the mainland. Storms prevent the Laura B., the supply boat in Port Clyde, from delivering essential bottled gas or food, spare parts for boats, or mail.

One January, when I was on Monhegan for Trap Day, I stayed with June and Henley Day. That year Henley, at 65 was the oldest working fisherman there. June Day is an island-born girl. "My great grandfather came out here, and my

family, the Bracketts, have been on the island ever since."
June's mother owned the Monhegan House, a hotel which
housed 65 guests in summer. Henley used to be the postmaster, the lighthouse keeper and for a while lived in the fog-
signal keeper's house across the harbor on Manana.

Soon after dark in winter, the anxious eyes of women begin
to look out the windows to scan the harbor, checking which
boats are back in. The women light the kerosene lamps, begin
supper, and wait. June Henley, while she was still wintering
on the island, could look out her windows and in a flash glance
at the moorings she'd know which boats were back. "Unless
the weather is real bad, I didn't worry. But no matter how
good the weather, I felt better when I looked out and saw
everyone back in on their mooring." By the light of kerosene
lamps June knitted bait bags. "Having extra bait bags filled
and ready saves time when a man is out hauling."

That winter Doug and Harry Odom, inseparable bachelor
brothers, were still keeping the only store on the island. In
winter, the brothers would go fishing for six or eight hours
in the morning, then at two in the afternoon Odom's store
would open and stay open till six at night to serve the needs
of the few people on the island that winter. In summer, of
course, when 800 people are on the island, the store does a
roaring business all day long.

Doug and Harry Odom sold out to Bud and Sally Murdock
in 1979, after keeping the island store for 49 years.

Come October and November, the summer people have gone.
The island men overhaul their boats, traps and gear, getting
ready for Trap Day. Between Thanksgiving and Christmas
most years, Doug and Harry, like many islanders, take a
holiday. The brothers may spend it luxuriating in the Bar-
bados, with a stopover in New York City, where their friend,
Zero Mostel, who lived, loved and painted here, used to get
them good theater seats and throw a party in their honor.
Sometimes they'd go to Chadd's Ford to visit their friend,
Jamie Wyeth, another Monhegan neighbor. (A painting by
Jamie Wyeth hangs in the Odoms' living room, above the
stove — young Wyeth's birthday present to Harry one year).

The Manana hermit, Ray Phillips, was alive that winter and
came into the store. He'd row his skiff over from Manana,
where he had lived alone with his sheep on the hillside in a

ramshackle set of shanties for 40 years. His brown eyes were merry and his long beard and hair were, to say the least, off-white. He wore an incongruous, bright, hand-knit beanie, made for him by Pat Ellis, one of the young Monhegan summer girls. He wore two pairs of baggy wool pants and two belts. He bought a pound of sugar, a bottle of red wine, three packs of tobacco, then pulled over an empty crate and sat down.

Ray Phillips sailed his sloop into Monhegan harbor about 1930. He originally came from Newport, near Bangor, but once here, he never left. In time he became famous as the Hermit of Manana, and the most photographed man out here, but not above taking a dollar or two from summer tourists when he posed for their cameras. Over the years he posed for thousands of pictures.

Ray was a beguiling, wise and college educated man, despite his awful smelling clothes and the hovel he shared with his sheep. "I laughed at the income tax man," he told me. "He came all the way out here to question me. Said he knew I had about 30 sheep, and knew I sheared 'em. And got nosey because I had not reported income from selling my wool. Never struck him that I might have sheared the sheep but never sold the wool. I told him I couldn't get the right bags to ship the wool in. Off he went on the next boat with a funny look in his eye."

Pretty Pat Ellis stopped in for her groceries that day and greeted her friend Ray gaily. "He is a very, very nice man indeed," she told me. Pat offered to wash Ray's long-worn longjohns. He turned the offer down, saying she didn't have any soap strong enough.

Toward six o'clock the young fishermen, home from hauling, came by the store to pick up their cartons of groceries. Almost all business was done on the cuff — except for wine sales, for which cash had to be paid. Most of the wine sold was California wine, but a few very fine French wines were left on the shelves, some with price tags as high as $60 a bottle. They were left over from the summer trade, and it was odd to see them in January on Monhegan.

In summer Monhegan is a vastly different world. Fewer than 100 winter residents multiply to 800. Summer houses fill with families and friends, who've been coming here for years, often for generations. The two or three hotels are filled. Tourist boats from Boothbay, Port Clyde and New Harbor disgorge visitors by the hundreds, on day excursions. Visiting yachts try, often in vain, to find a sheltered anchorage. The winter lobstermen either turn to building work on the island or go off dragging on other boats in other waters. But despite the summertime invasion, Monhegan's rugged character cannot be changed. It remains a remote and enchanted place.

Artists have always found joy working here. Robert Henri came here to paint as early as 1903. He told his young pupil, Rockwell Kent, about the island and in 1905 Rockwell Kent, just turned 23, came, loved it and stayed. He was broke, of course, and turned to house-building, at first for others and then for himself. He was a strong, able man and a daring and experienced sailor. He worked as stern man in lobster boats, and became accepted by the islanders, as much as the stormy, womanizing, rebellious Kent was ever accepted anywhere. He spent several winters here. Some of the best paintings ever done of the island were done by Kent. His clarity, his concentration on the stark forms of the island cliffs, his relish of the great expanses of wild sea and northern sky all fused together to make Kent's paintings on Monhegan among his most moving work.

Henri sent another pupil to Monhegan, the brilliant and prolific George Bellows, who worked here in 1911, 1913 and 1914. His major work "Fisherman's Family," first done in small scale while on Monhegan, was redone and enlarged 10 years later in 1923 as a tribute to his happy life with his wife and first child during their Monhegan summer of 1913.

Jay Connaway and Andrew Winter lived and painted on Monhegan, winter and summer. They were followed by Ernest Fiene, Joseph de Martini, Leo Meissner and Ernest Hekking. They in turn have been followed by Reuben Tam, with his original interpretations of the breaking sea; and, of course, by Jamie Wyeth, whose recent work on Monhegan is a fine culmination of almost 80 years of continuous great paintings on Monhegan by many artists.

Brilliant flowers are a special, surprisingly gentle hallmark of Monhegan. Most homes have flower gardens. Botanists say there are more than 600 varieties of wildflowers on thousand-acre Monhegan. Bird watchers have logged over 200 bird species here. On the stormy eastern side of the island, where the surf boils and the waves never cease to pound and fume, stand the dangerous cliffs of Burnt Head, Black Head and White Head. They rise 80 to 165 feet straight from the tormented sea at their base. Several lives have been lost here, usually the lives of visitors who climb on rocks too close to the sea. Once a wave snatches a body wandering too far on a ledge, there is no way to render help. The Monhegan Library is a memorial to Jacqueline Stewart Barstow, 10 years old and Edward Winslow Vaughn, 14, who were swept off the rocks to their early deaths on August 10, 1926. The book plates in each juvenile book reads "Jackie and Edward's library to the children of Monhegan."

Cathedral Woods are the gentlest, quietest part of this wonderful island. High, quiet as a church, the trees gentle the sound of wind and sea. Birds sing, hidden in the branches, and the air is aromatic with a heady mixture of balsam and sea. In here you feel remote and safe from storm, but even as you stand deep in the woods, you can feel the rote of the pull and the booming strength of the ocean, out of view; and you can begin to feel that special island bond which links you closely to all those who stood centuries ago on this same island.

Magnet that Monhegan is and will always be to island lovers, much future growth in homes or hotels is unlikely here. First, water supply is limited. The Plantation of Monhegan has set limits on the number of people who can be served by the available fresh water and those limits are close to being filled. Building permits therefore are hard to get. Second, in 1956, a group of people on the island, spearheaded by the Edison family of Thomas Edison, inventor, years ago formed a trust called Monhegan Associates, Inc. and together they bought or were given most of the eastern part of the island. The Association wisely wrote restrictions into the deed which, in effect, prohibits building and development on this land.

Monhegan is the boldest outpost of the New World. For a thousand years Monhegan has been a landfall for seamen from the Old World. To understand why, it is necessary to see Monhegan by approaching it from far at sea, rather than from the Maine coast. From 40 miles — some say 60 miles — out in the Atlantic, it is possible to see the outline of tree-crested Monhegan rising over 200 feet high from the sea. Add to this the fact that the coast of Maine is 300 miles closer to Europe than any other part of the United States, and it becomes easier to realize why the great whale shape of Monhegan has been such a vital landfall to sailors exploring the New World.

Who came here first?

There is a legend that about 565 A.D., Brendan, an Irish monk, came to Monhegan. The story is that Brendan heard of an Isle of Saints across the ocean, and with a band of 17 followers set sail in a reed boat covered with well-greased tanned hides. In 40 days Brendan came to an island with steep cliffs. Carried by winds and tides, the monks came next to an island with countless sheep. They took a lamb and went to a nearby, barren island rock to set up an altar and celebrate Easter. On this barren rock they started a fire to roast the lamb. Then to their consternation, the island began to move. They leaped back into their boat and watched the island slowly swim away. They realized then that they had set up their altar and begun to roast their lamb on the back of a giant whale ("Jasconius is his name"). Thereafter, for six years St. Brendan and his band sailed among the islands, searching for the Isle of Saints. Finally an angel appeared to Brendan and told him to take his monks back to their own country.

Some think that the Vikings were the first white men to come to Monhegan. They contend that about the year 1000 A.D., Leif and Thorwold, sons of Eric the Red, sailed this coast on a trip from Iceland and put ashore on Monhegan and Manana to cut long timber. Advocates of this story point to the strange inscriptions found on rocks on Manana Island and say they are old Norse writings.

John Cabot in his explorations of 1494 made his first landfall at Monhegan, according to some, but others deny this and say Cabot's landfall was Newfoundland.

The evidence is strong, however, that Verrazano in 1524 inspected Monhegan. The records of his ship La Dauphine (told in Chapter 3) describe Monhegan and position these mid-coast islands accurately.

The first recorded English description of Monhegan came

from David Ingram, who said he saw the island in 1569.
Ingram is that remarkable sailor, described also in Chapter 3,
who was marooned on the Gulf of Mexico while he was a crew
member of Capt. John Hawkins' famous expedition. Ingram
told the world he walked from the Gulf of Mexico to Canada.
When Ingram finally got home to England, part of the testimony he gave before a law court contained this description of
Monhegan, which has lasted 400 years:

"Taking me into his canoe, the Indian paddled from
the place he called Sabino to a peninsula he called Pem-
cuit (Pemaquid), where we rested over that night.
When the morning broke, I saw not far to seaward, a
great island that was backed like a whale. . . . The Sag-
amo said it was an island, and that the people who lived
on it were the subjects of Bashaba."

(Bashaba was the Indian chief of this region and his title
crops up often in the writings of Sir Ferdinando Gorges and
Capt. John Smith).

Martin Pring, with his two ships Discovery and Speedwell,
dropped anchor in Monhegan harbor in 1603. His log describes
the island and plots its exact latitude, 43½ degrees north.

But it was the irrepressible Capt. John Smith who put Monhegan truly on the map. Here is Smith's description:

"In the moneth of Aprill, 1614, with two ships from
London, I chanced to arive in New Englande, a parte of
Ameryca, at the Ile of Monahigan in the 43½ of Northerly latitude; our plot was there to take Whales and
make tryalls of a Myne of Gold and Copper . . . We
found this Whale-fishing a costly conclusion; we saw
many, and spent much time in chasing them, but could
not kill any . . . For our Golde, it was more the Master's
device to get a voyage that projected it, than any
knowledge he had at all of any such matter. Fish and
Furres are now our gold . . . Of dry fish we made
about 4000. Of cor fish about 7000. Whilst our sailors

fished, myselfe with nine others ranging the coast in
a small boat, got for trifles neer 1100 Beaver skinnes,
100 Martine and near as many Otters . . . With these
furres and the cor fish I returned to England in the
Bark; where within six months of our departure we
arrived safe back. The best of the fishe was solde for
five pounds the hundredth, the rest by ill visage betwixt
three and four pounds. The other ship staied to fit her-
selfe for Spaine with the dry fish."

That other ship was captained by Thomas Hunt, who kidnapped 27 Indians at Cape Cod, put them in the hold and
carried them to Spain, where he tried to sell them for slaves.

Smith's enthusiasm for Monhegan led quickly to the island
becoming the first port of call and a fishing center. In March
of the next year, 1615, three more London ships sailed into
Monhegan and fished there. In 1616 the Plymouth company
sent out four ships, and London sent out two more; and "eight
voluntaire" ships also showed up in Monhegan harbor that
year. By 1618 Monhegan had a year-round settlement.

The prosperity attracted a new investor. Ownership of the
island changed from Gorges to Abraham Jennens or Jennings.
Jennens, a merchant who owned many fishing vessels, was a
member of the North Virginia colony headed by Gorges.
Jennens expanded Monhegan's trade in furs and fish and attracted more settlers. Governor Bradford of the Plymouth
colony reports buying supplies worth 400 pounds sterling from
Monhegan in 1626. Then the Jennens sold Monhegan to two
merchants of Bristol, England, named Abraham Aldworth and
Gyles Elbridge. The price was fifty pounds, and the new
owners sent over their trusted agent, Abraham Shurt, to
negotiate the sale.

Soon after, turbulent changes in England led to troubled
times on Monhegan. In England, King James died suddenly in
March, 1625, and Charles I came to the throne. Charles, as
prince, had been forced by his father to become engaged to
marry Maria, sister of the King of Spain. But once Charles
became king, he dumped Maria of Spain for Princess Henrietta
of France. The repercussions were felt along the Maine coast.
England and France, so long at war in the New World, now

became friendly. England gave back to France the contested title to lands in Acadia and Nova Scotia. The French immediately expanded their land and trading ambitions there, and began to ravage English trading outposts along the Maine coast, including Monhegan. Shurt had to evacuate the settlers on his Monhegan island, and move them to greater safety in the fort at Pemaquid, on the mainland.

By 1635 no one lived on Monhegan. During the next 20 years Monhegan was used only as a summertime fishing post. Meanwhile, in England, Charles I was beheaded; the crown was deposed, and Cromwell took over the country, establishing a short-lived Republic.

By 1657 Monhegan changed hands again. The new owner was Nicholas Davidson, merchant, of Charlestown, Massachusetts. Davidson and his heirs owned the island till 1747. During the next 90 years Monhegan grew, was ravaged, and finally resettled again.

Soon after Davidson became the owner settlers moved back onto the island, and the records of the time reveal human weaknesses went with them, weaknesses often blamed on sailors from visiting boats. For instance, the first murder case from Monhegan to come before the Massachusetts Court.

A fishing boat from Boston, skippered by a Mathew Keninge, came to Monhegan for a season's fishing. In the young five-man crew was a Gregory Castle, a hard-drinking fellow, quarrelsome in his cups, according to the records, who picked fights with his captain. One day as Capt. Keninge sat outside his Monhegan home mending a pair of shoes, sailor Castle came staggering along; bitter words were exchanged, and Castle picked up the hammer which the captain was was using to mend his shoes, and whacked him on the head, inflicting injuries from which Capt. Keninge died. Castle was arrested and hauled off to Boston to stand trial.

Then there was a lawsuit filed by Francis Johnson of Marblehead against Richard Bedford in 1672 for "damage done on a fishing voyage at Monhegan." Johnson charged that Bedford was so drunk he "caused injury to the fish to the extent of thirty English pounds." The evidence given in Court says "Beford would make himself drunk . . . would lie under flakes upon which fish were drying, or in one house of another, and let the fish rot in the sun until spoiled." He would also get others in the crew to drink with him, "from the bottle hidden in the knee of his breeches."

The Monhegan settlers, and other settlers on the mainland, were having a hard time from "vagabonds," drunken sailors and "riff-raff from shippes." In desperation six settlements joined together and sent a petition to the Governor and Deputies of the Massachusetts General Court, asking "that you please take us under your government and protection that we may have benefit of laws." The document contained 21 signatures from Kennebec, 15 from Sheepscot, 16 from Cape Newagen, 11 from Pemaquid, 15 from Damariscove and 20 from Monhegan Island. The number of signatures from Monhegan indicates it was close to the largest settlement in the area.

The petition was granted and each town was taxed for the new protection. Monhegan was assessed five pounds, ten shillings — more by far than any other settlement, indicating it was the most prosperous.

Law and civic officers were appointed. Among the senior officers for the County Court of "Devon," held at Pemaquid July 22, 1674, were various Monhegan men, among them Richard Olliver, named "Clarke of Writs"; John Palmer, named as magistrate, who could also perform marriages; and John Dolling as constable; while George Bickford and Reynold Kelly were named 'grand jurymen.' One Monhegan man held an interesting combination of offices. Constable John Dolling was also "licensed to keep a house of public entertainment and was given a license to retail beer, wine and liquor" on the island.

Far worse trouble lay ahead — war with the French and Indians. Again the major cause lay in political turbulence in faraway England. There, in 1688, another revolution had taken place. King James II was forced to abdicate and flee for his life to France. The Protestant William of Orange sat on the English throne and ruled with his Queen as the William and Mary team till 1702. The news shook Boston. The populace there grabbed the chance to seize the hated Governor Andros, appointed by King James, and threw him and his top men into the Boston jail. The deposed and exiled King James took his revenge by stirring up the French, who had given him refuge, urging them to make war on the English colonies in North America. This was all the encouragement needed by the French Baron Castine. He emerged from his fort at Castine and his first target was Pemaquid. Baron Castine had a special score to settle with Pemaquid and Monhegan, for John Palmer there had seized a ship with a cargo of wine belonging to the Baron. The cargo consisted of 70 pipes of Malaga, one of brandy, two of oil, plus 17 barrels of fruit. (A "pipe" of wine equals 126 gallons, so Baron Castine had lost a lot of precious liquor).

Baron Castine used the Indians to do most of his dirty work. He had special influence with the Indians because he had married an Indian princess and fathered a family of half-breed children. He sent a frigate, plus a land force of Indians, to attack the fort at Pemaquid on August 5, 1689, and then to go on to destroy the flourishing settlement at Monhegan Island, stronghold of the fishing fleet. The destruction of Monhegan took place that October.

The islanders, forewarned by the attack on Pemaquid, fled to save their lives before the attack came. But the Indians destroyed the island by fire. No records of the attack, written from Monhegan, exist; but records from Charlestown show the arrival there of island families who fled from Monhegan.

The ruination of the island is a sad chapter in the nation's early history. The sadness was well expressed by Ida Sedgwick Proper in her fine, detailed book, "Monhegan, Cradle of New England," published in 1930. In it she wrote:

"There is immeasurable pathos in the destruction of this island, the oldest English settlement . . . which had sheltered fishing boats for more than 200 years. Many of the inhabitants may well have been descendants of the men sent over by Gorges, when he planted the Island in 1608 or 1609. All the labor that they so joyously expended on building their homes, and clearing out fields, was wasted. The stone fences and cellars are all that remain of their heroic efforts to establish themselves in the new and free world. An occasional spoon, button, bricks, pieces of broken clay pipes, an axe head . . . are mute evidences of their occupations and habits."

Indian attacks and devastation could not change the strategic geography of Monhegan, or deplete the rich fishing grounds. Though settlers were scared to return, the Royal Navy began using strategic Monhegan as a rendezvous point in the wars against the French; and fishermen from the mainland still ventured out to fish from the island in summer, though they never lived here during these perilous years.

In the face of all these troubles, the heirs of the Davidson family of Boston, who had owned Monhegan for 90 years, decided to sell out. In 1749 Shem Drowne, a Boston tinsmith, bought the splendid island for a mere ten pounds, 13 shillings. Tinsmith Drowne was the artist who made the grasshopper weather vane still to be seen atop Faneuil Hall in Boston, and he made the gilt-bronze figure of an Indian with drawn bow and arrow atop the Province House of Boston.

Drowne's son, Thomas, sold the island at a handsome profit to the Bickford family of Salem and Beverly, Massachusetts, in 1770 for 160 pounds. But the Bickfords, too, sold at almost a 100 percent profit seven years later, to Henry Trefethren, a cabinet maker from Kittery. Trefethren paid 300 pounds for Monhegan. He never came to the island. But his son, Henry Trefethren and his married daughters Mary Starling and Sarah Horn moved to Monhegan. They had to buy the island all over again in 1823. The cause of this double purchase was the fact that when Maine separated in 1820 from Massachusetts, the government of Massachusetts chose to keep Monhegan. But when offered 200 pounds, they sold it back again.

The population was far smaller then than it had been a hundred years earlier. Records show that in 1810 there were 43 inhabitants, and by 1820 the number was up to only 68. But the importance of of the island as a landfall was reaffirmed by the building of the Monhegan Lighthouse in 1824, four years after Maine won statehood.

That light is still a landfall for ships at sea. Monhegan, so highly praised by Captain John Smith in the early 1600s, is still praised as perhaps the most beautiful of Maine Islands.

Monhegan, the island where the first fishing fleets gathered hundreds of years ago, is still the gathering place for thousands of visitors each summer in the 1980s. Its magnetism and its majesty are as strong as ever.

14.

The Fox Islands:
North Haven
And Vinalhaven

There is probably more blue blood and old money along the Fox Islands Thorofare than can be found along any other short stretch of salt water in the United States. On North Haven and Vinalhaven both are subdued instead of flaunted.

Here, a dozen miles out to sea from Rockland, are clans of Cabots, tribes of Lamonts and Saltonstalls, roomfuls of Rockefellers, Reynolds and Rhinelanders, a punch card of IBM Watsons, a rich strike of Standard Oil Jennings; coveys of college presidents; judges and lawyers enough to pack a Supreme Court; surgeons enough to staff the most prestigious hospital, and a battery of bishops big enough to talk all Maine past St. Peter's Gate.

But seldom does one hear the crass clink of money or see the muscle of power on these islands. Yet here, from July to September, U.S. senators in tattered shorts sail North Haven dinghies their grandfathers sailed and ambassadors in sweatshirts barbecue hamburgers at cookouts; here Supreme Court Justices patiently lick ice cream cones while their wives buy groceries at Waterman's or Carver's store; here college presidents in filthy sneakers clean fish their grandchildren just caught; bankers from Wall Street and Back Bay borrow dimes to buy licorice shoelaces; dowagers with diamonds shining on wrinkled fingers go raspberrying; and Episcopalian bishops cuss like stevedores at outboards which won't start.

For a hundred years the islands of North Haven and Vinalhaven have been summer havens for blood that is very blue and money that is very old, very quiet and very plentiful.

These "first families" of America do not impress the island people. One reason is that the islanders are wholly competent in island living, in self-sufficiency, and the summer folk are not. Another reason is that the island people are, very often, the true First Families. For instance, when I pulled into Calderwood's dock at Carver's Harbor, Vinalhaven, for the first time in 1968, the man who gassed my boat was James Calderwood. Back in 1785 another James Calderwood, and his brother John, were already important men in Vinalhaven. Those Calderwoods signed a petition from the 800 Fox Islanders living here then to the General Court of Massachusetts. The petition asked that their land titles, issued by the English before the American Revolution, be reconfirmed. The Court granted new legal titles to all who had settled land on the islands prior to 1784, provided the islanders agreed to set aside 200 acres to supply funds for a minister and church and another 200 acres to fund a grammar school, and that the islanders agree to pay the cost of surveying their 10,000 acres.

The same day Calderwood gassed my boat, I walked from the dock to the Town Hall and met First Selectman Wyman Philbrook, and found that his ancestor, Joel Philbrook, had also signed that 1785 petition. In the store I drank a soda with John Carver and found that he was part of the family Thaddeus Carver started here before the Revolution and for whom the harbor was named. On this close-knit island almost everyone's roots run long and deep into the beginnings of this nation.

The first white man to name these islands was Martin Pring, from Bristol, England. He sailed down this Thorofare in 1603, long before any colonist landed at Jamestown. Pring, in his 50-ton vessel Speedwell, with a crew of thirty men and boys, and accompanied by the smaller vessel Discoverer, 26 tons with thirteen men and one boy aboard, anchored here. Pring admired the high, sheltering shores full of good woods and the excellent fish his crew caught. He was especially impressed by the sight of many handsome silver grey foxes, and gave the name "Fox Islands" to what we now call North Haven and Vinalhaven.

How did Pring's Fox Islands get their names changed to

Vinalhaven and North Haven? The answer is by the persuasion of a lobbyist — one of the first political lobbyists, John Vinal, of Boston. Soon after Calderwood, Philbrook, Carver and others signed that land title petition mentioned above, the islanders spent the rather large sum of thirty-six pounds to hire John Vinal as their lobbyist at the Massachusetts legislature in Boston. He did the job they wanted and the islanders acknowledged this by marking their payment to him with the words "for obtaining legislation in our favor." But Vinal did himself a lasting favor, too. The law he lobbied through the Massachusetts legislature June 25, 1789, 'incorporates the islands commonly called the North and South Fox Islands, in the County of Lincoln, into the town by the name of Vinal Haven." Later his son William Vinal came to settle on the island bearing his name. Soon Arthur Vinal was appointed assessor. Next move of the newly incorporated town of Vinalhaven was to build roads. At the first town meeting it was voted that "for labor on the roads, men should be paid three shillings a day, plus one shilling and six-pence for oxen and that the roads should be 18 feet wide."

The new town grew rapidly and prospered. By 1790 the population was 855. By 1880, when granite quarrying on Vinalhaven was at its peak, there were 3,380 residents; and today, the population of Vinalhaven is just over 1,000 and North Haven numbers about 400.

Carver's Harbor at Vinalhaven, became the hub for business and pleasure for 60 islands in Penobscot Bay. Matinicus Island paid taxes to the Fox Islands till 1801; Hurricane Island was part of the township till 1878, when at the height of the granite quarrying boom, it was set off. Sawmills, gristmills, plants for salting abounded, located at Indian Creek, Arey's Harbor, Coomb's Neck, Bartlett's Harbor, Crockett's Cove, Leadbetter's Island and Lane's Island. The islanders made their own salt — a tedious process which required boiling 400 gallons of sea water to get one bushel of salt.

Lobstering was very big business. Firms from Boston and New York ran canning plants at Carver's Harbor from 1846 until the Civil War temporarily hindered the operation. Another big canning plant in The Reach operated till 1900. In 1884 a Boston firm, Johnson and Young, set up a massive fresh lobster pound in The Basin, a rockbound salt water lake, in which they kept up to 150,000 live lobsters. They made a handsome profit by shipping them to Boston when the price there for fresh Maine lobster reached a dime a pound!

Thaddeus Carver, for whom Carver's Harbor is named, was 15 years old when he set foot on the Fox Islands, brought here by his father from Marshfield, Massachusetts. When Thaddeus Carver died in 1832 he was a wealthy patriarch of 81 years, living in his big house on the hill overlooking Carver's Harbor.

Young Thaddeus Carver got his first job in the sawmill owned by Francis Coggswell. In short order Carver bought the sawmill and 700 acres of land from Coggswell and married an island girl — Hannah Hall, of Matinicus Island, daughter of Ebenezer Hall, first settler on Matinicus, who was slain by Indians. Thaddeus and Hannah began married life in a rough log house he built; they prospered and raised 10 children. Thaddeus endured raids from the British at Castine, lived through the American Revolution, got new titles to his land as the result of that 1785 petition he signed, lived to see Maine win independence from Massachusetts in 1820, and to see his Carver's Harbor grow into an important fishing port.

By 1826, his son, Reuben Carver, was building the first vessels for the new granite trade. His first boat, Plymouth Rock, hauled granite quarried on Vinalhaven to build a prison in Massachusetts. Reuben went on to build eleven more boats for the growing granite trade.

The Carvers were an inventive, industrious clan. At the other end of Carver's Harbor, John Carver launched a new kind of enterprise in 1852 — the business of knitting horse nets, which seems a strange trade on an island 16 miles to sea from Rockland. But the nation had millions of horses then and each horse was plagued by flies in summer. And so the horse net business thrived at Carver's Harbor. John Carver passed the horse net business on to his son and daughter, Thaddeus and Josephine, who enlarged it. By 1900 they passed it along to Edwin R. Roberts, a modern merchant who mechanized the business and eventually had 1000 people making horse nets for him, not only on Vinalhaven, but at Port Clyde and on Deer Isle. They produced horse nets in 140 different designs. As cars came in, the demand for horse nets dropped and the business begun by the Carvers passed into oblivion.

But the memory lives; the rise at the east end of Main Street is still called Net Factory Hill.

Carver's Harbor boomed. By 1878 the islands were curing 22 million pounds of fish a year. The Vinalhaven Fish Company by 1899 had a 50,000 square foot factory, a 350 foot long granite wharf and five big vessels, each carrying 145,000 pounds of fish.

Many of the old island families who were here before the American Revolution are here still. Their homes are mostly clustered near Carver's Harbor. The softer folk, the families of the summer estates, live on the ocean rims of the island. That ocean front once sold cheaply. Take the choice area called Arey's Harbor. Isaac Arey, a native of Cape Cod, saw it and loved it in 1770, while sailing to Mount Desert with his wife and one child. He liked the harbor so well, he bought 700 acres of land around it; paid the sum of thirty pounds to a man named Wheeler for it. Isaac Arey met a tragic end. He drowned while crossing in a small boat to Isle au Haut, where his wife, a skilled midwife, had gone to deliver a baby. Today a dozen Arey families are listed on the Vinalhaven tax rolls. Back in Isaac Arey's day, taxes were modest. In 1785, when 42 taxpayers lived on Vinalhaven's 10,000 acres, the total town tax amounted to thirty-two pounds and two pence. Today shorefront property cost is $150 up a front foot, and the town taxes top three million dollars. A new fish freezing and packing plant on the harbor began operation in 1981.

Walk five fascinating minutes up the hill from Carver's Harbor and you come to an extraordinary story of island sickness and health — The Vinalhaven Community Clinic, the only diagnostic and treatment center built in Maine under the Hill-Burton Act. It was opened in 1962, paid for with $60,000 raised in Vinalhaven and $60,000 from the federal government.

Inside I met an amazing man and a wonderful doctor, Dr. Ralph Earle. Dr. Earle is dead now, but he will not and should not ever be forgotten. When I first met him in 1971 and spent an afternoon and night talking with him in his remarkable clinic, he had already been the island doctor for 35 years. The name of Ralph Earle, M.D. is on the birth certificate of every child born on this island from the mid-1930s to the mid-1970s, except those who sneaked into the world while Dr. Earle was away in the military during World War II.

Ralph Earle came to Vinalhaven as a boy, on vacation with his father. After graduating from Hahneman Medical School, he returned to the island as its only active physician, although in the 1890s three doctors had made a living here, caring for the islanders with 50-cent office visits and 75-cent house calls.

"When I arrived in 1937," Dr. Earle told me, "it was the Depression. Almost all island men were on WPA at $11 a week. They ate off the land and sea; grew potatoes, dug clams, jigged mackerel, cut spruce for fuel. No one had cash to spare for a doctor."

Strangely, out of this came some of the finest preventive medicine in Maine, a doctor the islanders loved, and an amazing probe into hereditary diabetes.

Here is that story. It began, almost by accident, in 1965.

In 1965, after being the island doctor for 28 years, Dr. Earle became concerned about a major gap in his work with his island patients. "I knew too little about the adult males, medically. We had 138 men on the island, aged between 40 and 60, and most every one of them shied away from the annual physical checkups which I had persuaded the island women and children to get. So I wrote letters to all 138 men. I spoke to every fishermen's group and firemen's group and civic group, about how checkups and preventive medicine could keep them healthy. Result was that 40 per cent, 53 out of the 138 men, volunteered to take part in a medical survey. For $15 every man got a three-hour checkup, a careful review of his own and his family's medical history, an electrocardiogram, a chest X-ray, a battery of lab tests, including blood, urine and stool examinations, as well as a glucose tolerance test."

Then Dr. Earle made his discovery. Out of 53 adult males examined, 17 tested positive for diabetes and 4 more were questionable.

Islanders showed a diabetes rate 20 times higher than the general population of the U.S. On a national basis, about two percent of all Americans have diabetes and half of them do not know it. But tests on Vinalhaven indicated that 50 percent of the adult male population might have diabetes.

Dr. Earle asked, "Why?"

Since heredity can play a part in diabetes, Earle began digging into all available marriage, birth and death records on the island. Marriage records had been kept since 1790, but because Maine did not require birth and death certificates until 1892, Dr. Earle had to find another way to discover what had happened in those 100 years between 1790 and 1892 among Vinalhaven families. He spent hours with the town clerk, an expert local genealogist. He scoured records in the state archives at Augusta, the capital. Finally he turned to the family Bible, where rural America has kept the best family records. They proved fruitful ground.

"Vinalhaven is a stable, close-knit island community," Earle explained, showing his charts. "Some 450 of the islanders — about 40 percent — trace their families back on both the mother's and the father's side to the early settlers who landed here before the American Revolution. Most of the other 60 percent trace their ancestry back 200 years through one line of descent, mother or father."

In such ways, Earle was able to trace back 21 suspect cases of diabetes. He found in almost every case hereditary diabetes could have been expected.

The doctor then drew detailed family charts, with small circles, some red, some white, the marks representing male and female, children and grandchildren, diabetic and non-diabetic. He found one woman who had no diabetes, yet gave birth to a diabetic daughter, who in turn gave birth to a diabetic son, whose wife in turn gave birth to a diabetic daughter. He found a diabetic grandmother who had five grandchildren — four of whom were diabetics. Finally he found that he could predict with a high degree of accuracy the chances for diabetes in any native of Vinalhaven.

On the day I was with him, Dr. Earle was studying the records of an island girl, married to an Air Force man serving in Spain. He estimated she had an 80 percent chance of being diabetic. He knew she was far advanced in pregnancy. He telephoned the obstetrician at the air base in Spain, suggesting tests be made. They were. Result—a confirmed case of pre-clinical diabetes, discovered in a patient in Spain on the information provided from Dr. Earle on Vinalhaven.

Earle won financial support for wider diagnostic tests among islanders and for treatment. He then went house to house, lodge meeting to lodge meeting, urging all islanders to come to the clinic for tests. As a result 500 more islanders came to the clinic. Exactly 50 percent of the first 180 tested had indications of diabetes. The National Center for Chronic Disease Control, presented with the facts, said the island population "has one of the highest concentrations of diabetes known."

For the next years Earle's work in treatment, research, early diagnosis and prediction progressed. In 1970 the islanders made over 3,000 visits to the clinic. Dr. Earle made 510 house calls that year.

Before his work was finished to his satisfaction, Earle, the remarkable island doctor, died. Today Dr. Gregory O'Keefe serves the clinic well.

Summer people blend well with island people on North Haven and Vinalhaven, though their lives and backgrounds are poles apart. Of course, each side has had a hundred years of experience since Dr. Weld started the summer colony.

The credit must go largely to the summer people. They bend to the island ways. They have to, for the island ways won't bend. Here on the islands, island ways are better than the ways brought in from Boston, New York, Washington, Pittsburgh, Cleveland or Los Angeles; and the wise off-islander knows it.

Summer people get more satisfaction when an islander calls them by their first names than they do when their broker phones to say their stock has jumped 10 points or their lawyer calls to say a corporate merger has been consummated. Local acceptance hinges wholly on personal qualities, not on bank accounts or family names. Not all summer residents get it, by a long shot.

Actor Robert Montgomery, liked as a North Haven neighbor, but almost ignored as a celebrity, lived for many summers in his lovely white farm house on Little Fox Thorofare. Then in July 1970 Montgomery made it big. He was invited to be guest speaker at the alumni banquet of North Haven School. Those alumni are a select group. The year Montgomery spoke, there were two students in the graduating class.

The field where Charles Lindbergh used to land his plane at the Morrow estate — he married Anne Morrow — is an overgrown, unmarked meadow now. In North Haven no one would dream of erecting a plaque. The lonely, lovely farmhouse where Ambassador Chester Bowles lived, became the retreat where Washington Judge Gerhard Gessel came to recharge his batteries while he was ruling in favor of the Washington Post on the publication of the Pentagon papers.

Behind Pulpit Rock, where ospreys nested for 300 years, the Cabots have a compound of cottages. There is a small sign on the drive which reads "No Lowells are allowed."

By the ferry slip on the Thorofare is Waterman's store, hub of North Haven life for generations. Irma Peters presides there. This brown-eyed cashier knows everyone, their parents and their children. Irma was the first selectwoman elected in over 200 years of town government on the island. Her husband, Gordon, who does the paperwork in a cubbyhole office upstairs, taught cement production in Indonesia and Yugoslavia till stricken with polio. Their North Haven children once went to Chinese schools. Irma and her husband supply the needs of the plain white house by the mill stream, owned by John D. Rockefeller III; and meat and groceries to the big yellow house on the cliff where Mrs. Thomas Lamont, widow of J. P. Morgan's partner, looked out to the Camden Hills at sunset. Watermen's store supplies the long white farm where Thomas Watson of IBM kept a mile-long airstrip for his private jet planes, and where he entertained the Kennedys and that horn-playing jazz musician, the King of Thailand and his beautiful queen.

Jim Brown, thin, spectacled, slow talking, is still building boats and still tending the wharf which his grandfather, J. O. Brown, started in the summer of 1880. Jim and his sons build the same North Haven sailing dinghies his grandfather built for Dr. Weld of Boston 100 years ago, when Dr. Weld began the summer colony on the Fox Thorofare.

Dr. Weld and his sailing friends from Boston dropped anchor here one night in 1880. They rowed ashore and were so captivated by the island they promptly bought land. They gave up their cruise and spent the rest of their vacation on the Thorofare, drawing plans for the summer cottages they wanted. Before they headed back to Boston, Dr. Weld and his friends had made arrangements with local craftsmen to build them by the following summer. The summer colony had begun on North Haven.

Dr. Weld's imprint is still strong on the Thorofare. His

daughter, Mrs. Mary Pingree, lived in the big house at Iron Point, commanding the midpoint of the Thorofare. Almost 70 duplicates of the 15-foot, 4-inch North Haven sailing dinghy first built for Dr. Weld by J. O. Brown, still crowd the Thorofare on race days. Some youngsters proudly sail the same dinghy in which their grandfathers learned to sail.

The most unusual home, architecturally, is the Norwegian Cottage, built for Ambassador Strong after he'd served as U. S. Ambassador to Norway in World War II. The roof, in Norwegian tradition, is of sod a half foot thick with green grass and wildflowers growing out of it. Sometimes a goat is tethered up on the roof there, mowing the grass. A Norwegian sauna bath house stands nearby, complete with a huge bell atop it, for summoning people from outside if anyone is parboiling inside.

The Vinalhaven side of the Fox Thorofare is another Gold Coast of large summer cottages, mostly belonging to the Rhinelanders, the Reynolds, the Saltonstalls, the Lewises and the Brewster Jennings of Standard Oil.

The Saltonstalls were among the early summer people from Massachusetts, who came here 75 years ago. (An earlier Saltonstall, Dudley, had lost most of the American Navy under his command when he got scared off and then defeated by the British at Castine in 1779. His artillery commander, Paul Revere, had to walk home to Boston in a towering rage).

Today, Saltonstalls have summer places all along the Thorofare in a kind of protective family association. There was the mother's place; Richard's place; and Leverett's place. Then a Saltonstall married a Lewis, and now there are newer Lewis places.

Today off-islanders own most of the shorefront and about 75 percent of all North Haven land. The native born islanders have the remaining 25 percent. But there is a sweet irony to all this blue blood, quiet money property.

During the Depression, more than 1,500 acres of the prime land came into the hands of a wonderful junk dealer in Rockland named Isidor Gordon. "They couldn't give away island property in the 1930s and 40s," he told me. "I didn't pay much for the 1,500 acres I bought and I couldn't get much when I sold them. Back in 1929 they wanted to sell me a beautiful waterfront estate with a fine house and 45 acres. I didn't want it at any price. But finally they got me out to take a look. I said I'd buy it for last year's taxes. So I got the house and estate for $700."

The price today would be about $400,000. Even small houses in the village have rocketed in value. One small village house sold for $600 in 1945. It has changed hands six times since then, with the last price topping $60,000.

These Fox Islands are a second home for our boat from May to November. Every year we spend happy days and mystical nights in a dozen different coves and harbors here. Our boat's log is filled each year with pages of notes about friends, new-made, and rediscovered island shores we've walked. Here is one entry:

We are anchored 16 miles out to sea from the mainland, tucked in the shelter of two small islands along the Reach of Hurricane Sound. Just before dawn I climb out of the bunk and go topside, to be there, waiting and looking, when the new day's sun wakens North America The first rays of the new day strike here first. The deck is wet from the night, drenched in dew, so I coil a mooring line into a circle the size of my bottom, sit on it, sip the first cup of coffee and wait alone in a cone of lovely silence for the new day's sun to rise up out of the Atlantic.

The sea is dead calm, leaden, at this hour. No birds sing yet. No gulls fly yet. No breeze stirs yet. The whole world is quiet. At this pre-dawn hour the night animals are back in their homes, finished their prowling hunts.

On shore thin grey light emerges from the night. I can see wet green meadows now, sloping slowly down to the rocky shore, and the shore becomes ledge, and the ledge becomes sea. On the high ground the roof of a house becomes outlined by the dawn. The first sun rays reach and glisten on the dew-wet roof.

Sitting alone on the coiled rope, watching the day be born, time barriers of the 20th century vanish. A man senses a close, strange unison with that old jetty, that wet, granite ledge, that meadow where oxen once plowed, that gaunt old farmhouse. A man feels a link that reaches back 377 years to the first sailors who anchored here, to the first settlers and their successive generations who saw sunrises from this cove.

Were they friends or enemies of the Indians here? When those early settlers watched the sun rising up out of the Atlantic, did their homesick thoughts leap 3,000 miles across the ocean to their roots in coastal England, where the sun was shining at high noon? Did they hope or did they fear that another small boat might be setting sail from Plymouth or Bristol with new settlers who might wind up as neighbors to them on these Fox Islands which Martin Pring had praised in his ship's log of 1603, the year Elizabeth was a dying queen?

Did their offspring, fishing these waters, farming that meadow, stand up at the town meeting of 1811 when it was voted to increase the pay for the road builders on this island "to 12 cents an hour for men, 12 cents for oxen and six cents for carts"; and how did they vote on the warrant which decided these islanders would "not raise any money for support of the gospel"? and the warrant which decided "that William Vinal, Esq. be chosen Representative"; and the warrant which decided "that $400 be allocated to schools?"

Was there a man in the farmhouse near our cove who hid with other fishermen through that night of 1813 so they could surprise and capture the British privateer Fly when she dared anchor off Vinalhaven and fly false American colors from her mast? Was he one of those islanders who recaptured the three American vessels and crews which Fly with her guns had seized?

Were great-grandchildren of the first settlers on that farm working in the Vinalhaven granite quarry that memorable week of August 20-27, 1899, when they cut the unforgettable granite shaft that was 64 feet long and weighed 310 tons, and was bound for New York City, where it would become a spire on the Cathedral of St. John the Divine? Did they sail their boat from here over to Carver's Harbor to watch the first telephone

message go out from Vinalhaven to Rockland at eight
o'clock Monday morning, January 10, 1898?

Now the sun bursts out in full dawn and climbs fast.
Birds wake, sing and fly; gulls cry and swoop on their
morning breakfast mission. The roars of lobster boats
sound across The Reach as they start up and head out to
haul traps. The new day is born. The 20th century is
back. Aboard Steer Clear it is time to up anchor and
head across the bay to Stonington and all the blessed
islands that stretch out from Deer Isle to Isle au Haut.

Goose Rock Light, Fox Island Thorofare.

15.

Granite:
How The Islands Built The Cities

Cruise among the lovely, peaceful islands of Penobscot Bay today and it is hard to realize that these islands were once the hub of Maine's heaviest, noisiest industry . . . granite.

A hundred years ago these quiet Edens were exploding with the violence and noise of thousands of quarry workers and their vast machines, dynamiting and hammering millions of tons of granite out of the bowels of these islands. Men from Maine, Ireland, Spain, Italy, Scandinavia, using oxen and high wheeled galamanders, performed an engineering miracle in moving granite slabs weighing far over 100 tons from quarry to vessels at the wharves. On Vinalhaven in 1878, for example, they moved the largest granite shaft ever quarried until then. It was 60 feet long, weighed 185 tons, and was made into the General Wool Monument in Troy, New York.. This shaft and its seven foundation stones weighed 650 tons when loaded aboard the barge Jemima Leonard on August 16, 1879.

Bright blue galamanders, with wheels high as a man, pulled by teams of oxen and horses, hauled these immense loads over rough and steep Vinalhaven roads. Tremendous brakes were needed to control the massive weight. One weird looking galamander stands as a monument on the Vinalhaven village green.

Granite from Vinalhaven, Hurricane, Crotch, Deer Isle, Swan's Island, Dix and High Islands, off the Muscle Ridge Channel, stands today in distant cities, still performing tasks that seem incompatible to these remote, quiet and lovely islands.

Here are a few buildings and monuments from the astonishing list made from Maine granite: The gravesite of President

John F. Kennedy in Arlington Cemetery; Kennedy sailed among these islands of Penobscot Bay, loved them well, and today when you walk to his gravesite, you walk on pink granite from Penobscot Bay, especially ordered by his family; the Pennsylvania Railroad Station and the Girard Building in Philadelphia; the Board of Trade and the Auditorium in Chicago; the old Waldorf Astoria in New York; Jordan Marsh in Boston; the House of Representatives, the Library of Congress and the Executive Office Building, next to the White House, in Washington, D. C.; the New York Stock Exchange; the Triborough, Brooklyn and George Washington Bridges in New York City; Grant's Tomb; the Tomb of the Unknown Soldier; the U. S. Mint; the U. S. Naval Academy; the New York State Capital in Albany and the State Capital in Indianapolis; the St. Louis Bridge; the first block of the Washington Monument; the Arlington Memorial Bridge; the Cathedral of St. John the Divine in New York; the drydocks at Norfolk, Virginia; the Hibernia Bank of San Francisco; the Hartford Insurance Company in Connecticut; the New York City Post Office; the Washington Post Office; the St. Louis Post Office; the Cleveland Trust; the Andrew Mellon Foundation; the old New York World and New York Herald Tribune buildings; the Pilgrim's Monument in Plymouth; the Frick Building in Pittsburgh, and many more.

Besides granite for huge buildings, between 50 and 100 million paving blocks a year left these Maine islands to be made into the busiest streets of dozens of our biggest cities.

The largest granite shaft in America was cut at Wharff's quarry on Vinalhaven in August 1899. It was four feet longer and many tons heavier than the shaft for the General Wool Monument. But tragedy befell it.

The Bodwell Company of Vinalhaven had been commissioned to quarry and lathe-turn eight immense granite columns for the Cathedral of St. John the Divine in New York City. These soaring columns were to be twice as high as those of the Parthenon in Athens, bigger than any in the world except those of St. Isaac's in Petrograd. The huge shaft, 64 feet long and weighing 310 tons in the rough, was cut at Wharff's quarry in a tense week's work in August 1899. To turn this mammoth piece of granite into soaring, graceful columns, E.R. Cheny of Boston designed and built the largest lathe in the world, and

installed it on Vinalhaven, but the first two monoliths broke
on the lathe. Their vast weight, turning on the centers, could
not endure the vibration and pressure without cracking. Mau-
rice Calderwood, the Vinalhaven-born superintendent of the
project, finally made the columns in two sections, one 90 tons,
the other 40 tons. It took three years of work to complete the
entire contract. One huge monolith, flawed and never used,
lies beside the old Sands Road on Vinalhaven today.

Granite quarrying began here in 1826, when a man named
Tuck, from New Hampshire, quarried stone to build a prison
in Massachusetts. By 1852, Moses Webster, a granite cutter
from Pelham, New Hampshire, came to Vinalhaven and in
partnership with George Bodwell of Maine, began the first
East Boston quarry on Vinalhaven. Twenty years later it had
become the Bodwell Company and was employing 1,500 men.
Other quarries started on Hurricane, operated by General Till-
son, Garrett Coughlin, John Hogan and Patrick McNamara.
Close to a thousand men worked on that island, where today
only the Outward Bound School operates. On Crotch Island,
across from Stonington, was another immense quarry. At
Webb Cove on Deer Isle, the old granite wharf and the giant
cranes still stand, dilapidated and rusted. In the Muscle Ridge
Channel, on Dix and High Islands, you can still see huge machinery, rusted hawsers, giant wharves and cellar holes of the
hotels and boarding houses where another one thousand
quarrymen lived and labored a hundred years ago. The islands
are silent and empty now; but the ghosts are there.

One summer night we slept aboard Steer Clear, anchored between Dix and High Islands, a little boat on a deserted sea. We
had spent the hot summer day ashore, exploring Dix and High.
We had clambered along overgrown traces of road beds where
once hundreds of quarrymen walked, where horse and oxen
teams had strained to pull tons of granite. Through wild grass
and brambles, through thickets of brush, we climbed to abandoned quarry sites. Atop High Island we came suddenly upon
the precipitous cliff walls of an enormous old quarry. A
strange, loud, eerie whirring noise frightened us. Then we saw
hundreds of Canada geese rising in wing-beating panic as they
heard us. They stop on their long journey to rest and feast on
algae-green ponds that lie now in the bottom of the vast quarries. When the geese had flown, silence ebbed back. We looked

in awe at the enormous slabs of perfectly cut granite, each weighing many tons, waiting for shipment. Mountains of paving blocks, perfectly trimmed, are piled, ready to pave the streets of distant cities. Machines, cranes, cables, left to rot where they stood, creaked in the sea breeze. Work seemed to have suddenly stopped, as if pestilence had struck and the men had fled.

On nearby Dix Island we searched for cellar holes of Shamrock and Aberdeen. These were the names of the vast hotel-barracks which housed a thousand quarry workers from Ireland and Scotland. In all, 150 buildings, wharves, stonesheds once crowded this little island.

The empty islands were once a hub of labor unions, strikes, politics, money-making, brawls and murders and ghastly accidents. A great meeting hall to seat 500 men was built on Dix. Music hall singers and dancers entertained packed houses of granite workers. Politicians harangued for election. Union leaders took strike votes.

From the quarries on Dix came the granite for the Treasury Building in Washington, the New York and Philadelphia Post Offices. Now only birds sing and wild flowers bloom here.

That summer afternoon we searched on the northwest high point of Dix Island for remnants of the 26-room mansion where Horace Beals of New York brought his beauteous wife in the 1870s. Despite the sumptuous rooms and marble fireplaces he built for her, the lady hated Dix; and later left the island, and her husband, and became the Duchess of Tomajo. The vivacious beauty married four times. Beals, who had reluctantly taken Dix as payment for a bad debt in 1850, became an even wealthier millionaire. He plowed some of his Dix Island profits into a huge hotel on the banks of the Kennebec River, hoping to create another Saratoga Spa. It flopped, was turned into a National Soldiers' home after the Civil War, called Togus. Today it is a big Veterans' hospital.

The ghosts came that night as we slept aboard Steer Clear. Dreams were loud with the sound of dynamite exploding in the old quarries, with the noise of three 100-foot schooners loading granite at the abandoned wharves, with the singing of quarrymen arriving back in the wee hours from spending like princes in a night of women and drink in Rockland; with

visions of the beauteous Mrs. Beals hating her island life inside her ornate 26-room mansion on the bluff.

Early in the 1900s the great granite boom burst, pricked by
the coming of concrete. One by one, the quarries were abandoned. From time to time, a few contracts trickled in, and a
spurt of the old activity would invigorate the dead quarries.
As recently as 1972, Vinalhaven's quiet was shattered by the
roar of jet torches 500 degrees hot, burning channels into the
granite rock. Maine island granite was needed for the new
Dupont headquarters in Brandywine, Delaware, and the new
Michigan Telephone Building in Detroit. Between March and
October of 1972 they cut 500 massive slabs of Vinalhaven
granite, each weighing up to 24 tons. The operation was puny
compared to the operations of the old Bodwell Granite Company; a dozen men, where 1,500 once worked. Instead of 72
huge oxen, an $80,000 crane hoisted the slabs. The slabs went
onto trucks instead of high-wheeled galamanders. Instead of
loading onto stone sloops from Chebeague, the granite went
ashore on the Rockland ferry (paying $20,000 in fares) and
then was transferred onto multiple-axle trucks. But for the
most part, Maine island granite today is too hard, too heavy,
too durable, too expensive to quarry and move. However, a
hundred years ago granite put more money and more jobs
and trade into these quiet islands than they've seen before
or since.

Fritz Johnson was close to 80 when he talked to me on
Swan's Island one afternoon about his memories as a quarry-
man there.

"I was born in Sweden in 1900," he said with just
a trace of Swedish accent still. "I came to America as
a boy in 1915. My trade was stone cutter. And within a
few years I came to work in the quarries here. I was
the fastest stone cutter in the world in those days,
when we cut stone by hand with a 32-pound hammer
and chisel. My record still stands. I cut 786 paving
blocks for New York City streets in seven hours. Each
block was four and a half inches deep and twelve inches
long, and I cut 'em absolutely straight on all sides."

Fritz went into his house and brought out a lighter hammer,
a mere three-pounder and demonstrated the stonecutter's ver-

sion of Russian roulette. He swung and twisted the hammer
with lightning speed, in a dazzling array of arcs, around his
head until it brushed his lips and he kissed it. "Lotta men
lost a lotta teeth trying to do that trick," he grinned.

Fritz Johnson came to Swan's Island when he was a strap-
ping 21, in 1921. "I worked in the quarry till it closed in 1928.
Usually there were 40 of us top stone cutters here; but in
busy times the crew went up to 75. We lived in John Mc-
Gutherie's boarding house. Cost us $8 a week, room and board.
We got paid about $50 a week, good wage back in the 1920s.
I still remember the amount of rum we drank. The gambling
and the fights were wild in that McGuthrie's boarding house
back then."

Rockland was a boom town, Barbary Coast style, in those
days of the quarry boom. Special boats ran out to the quarry
workers on Hurricane, Swan's, Vinalhaven, Crotch, Dix and
High Islands to bring the big spenders into town for Saturday
night. Several hundreds of lonely men, with lots of money for
a fling, descended on Rockland's waterfront. It was a blazing
place. More than thirty steamships and hundreds of coasting
vessels, plus the ships of Rockland's huge lime trade, crowded
the harbor. Bars, whorehouses, gambling joints, and dance
halls catered to sailors and quarrymen. Fights blazed, and
jails filled. And the money poured in.

Granite worker, Swan's Island
Fritz Johnson, a Swede who came in 1921 to work the quarries on Swan's Island, shows the daring hammer twist and kiss. (Gannett file photo)

Clyde Torrey, Swan's Island
Clyde Torrey was born and lived his lifetime on Swan's Island; was a wizard on the accordion, a great storyteller and a famous island character.
(Gannett file photo)

Island granite
Millions of tons of granite, quarried on Maine islands, built many of America's most famous edifices and monuments. This picture was made on Vinalhaven. (Gannett file photo)

Bar Harbor mansion in ruins
Scores of oceanfront estates on Bar Harbor were gutted in the great
fire of October 1947. (Gannett file photo)

Summer cottage, Fox Island Thorofare
Old money and blue blood abound on North Haven and Vinalhaven since
Dr. Weld of Boston began the cottage colony there 100 years ago.
(Gannett file photo)

Mess of clams
Clam digger's skiff filled with his clam hods. (Gannett file photo)

Steady customer
Island general store, Carver's Harbor, Vinalhaven
(Gannett file photo)

The Camden Hills
Coasting past an uninhabited island, looking at the Camden hills.
(Gannett file photo)

Bathtub and flowers
On Isle au Haut, an old tub rusts in peace. (Gannett file photo)

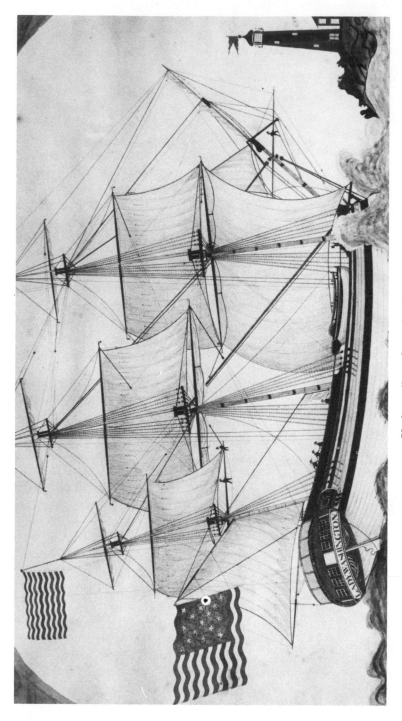

Under sail on the Maine Coast

Shipmaster Francis Rittal drew this beauty in his Navigation book, 1803.
(Courtesy Bath Marine Museum)

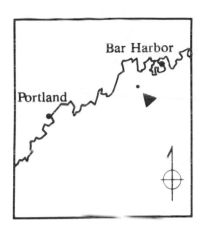

16.

Isle au Haut:
Penobscot Jewel

Italians have always had an eye for beauty and a tongue for compliments. When Giovanni da Verrazano sailed this coast in the early 1520s and first saw Isle au Haut, Mount Desert and Monhegan, he was inspired by their beauty to name them "The Princesses of Navarre." The three teenage daughters of his patron, King Henry of Navarre, were the most beautiful princesses in all Europe. The beauty of Isle au Haut is inspiring still.

One summer morning I moored Steer Clear in Duck Harbor and climbed to the top of the storm-beaten magnificence of Western Head. Climbing the soft moss trail in silence, a man can become intoxicated by ocean air, spiced with bayberry, juniper and spruce. At the peak I stood on a granite ledge and looked out to the Atlantic; and down to the brilliant lobster buoys bouncing below in the green-white surf; and over to Roaring Bull Ledge, where crashing seas foamed.

I was alone, and awestruck. Suddenly I felt the presence of another human nearby and turned. A lady sat motionless, watching the splendor. I walked toward her. She looked up, smiled and said: "This is where I go to church. This is the spot where I am awed by the majesty of Creation."

Isle au Haut, the "High Island," lies six miles to sea from Stonington, Deer Isle. It measures about six miles north to south and two miles east to west, and is thickly wooded, with a long mountainous spine. Its high point thrusts up to a height of 554 feet, and bears the name of the French explorer: Mount Champlain. The island has not, I think, changed very much since his day. There are no hotels, no restaurants, no gift shops, no movie houses. On a fine sparkling day Isle au Haut can be the most peaceful, heavenly spot in all Maine; but in rage of storm or thick of fog, Isle au Haut, and the journey to or from it, can be hellish and terrifying. This is why in most winters these days only about two dozen people live here. But before boats had engines hundreds lived here, because the island was close to the best of fishing grounds. Then the island was almost bare of trees and a thousand sheep grazed here. But winter hardship and economic isolation gradually drove out most people and sheep. In summer, the cottages at Point Look-Out Club fill, boats from Stonington run often, and close to 300 people are here. However, the island is protected from much growth because two-thirds of it is now part of Acadia National Park, thanks to the large gift of land in 1946 from the Bowditch family of Boston. Only about 250 of the island's 7,000 acres remain in the hands of the island's year-round residents.

Captain John Smith in the log of his 1614 voyage along the Maine coast called this island "Sorico," after the Indians he met here. Huge heaps of ancient clamshells are the memories of the feasts and revels the Indians enjoyed here centuries ago. Duck Harbor was a favorite hunting ground of theirs. The tribes drove sea ducks by the thousands into funnel-shaped Duck Harbor, snared them in nets stretched across the narrow head of the harbor, smoked them and took them inland in the fall to eat during winter. In the 1930s and 1940s a few Indians still came to the island from their mainland reservations to gather sweetgrass for basket-making. But they come no more.

The first known white settler came to Isle au Haut in 1772, the unfortunate Seth Webb. His mother-in-law had been scalped by Indians. Seth got a land grant from the crown to Kimball's Island, just across the Thorofare. He made friends with the Indian chief, Orono, either because of or despite the fact his mother-in-law had been scalped. The Indian chief and the white settler hunted together. On such a hunting trip in 1785 the unfortunate Seth Webb was killed by his own musket while climbing ashore from his skiff onto Isle au Haut. His widow was unable to cope with life on Kimball's Island and the stronger Kimball family took possession.

By 1792, a man with a wondrous first name, Peletiah Barter, arrived from Boothbay, with his brothers, William and Henry. Peletiah fathered ten children here and died about 1832. The old cellar hole of his log cabin can still be seen in Thorofare Village. Calvin Turner arrived in 1800 and set up a salt works, an indication there must have been a fair sized population of fishing men and boats here to buy his salt. His son, Asa Turner, grazed 400 sheep here. The Robinsons, Kimballs, Sawyers, Smiths, Kemptons and Lelands soon joined the settlement. By 1801, fifty settlers petitioned the court of Massachusetts to sell and deed to them the land they had settled.

The families seemingly prospered, for by 1820, two dozen men were listed as shipmasters. A survey map of 1824 shows 36 deeded lots of land, varying in size from 32 to 182 acres each. If the families averaged five persons, about 180 people were living year-round here then, compared to 24 or so year-rounders now.

But the "get-rich-quick" bug bit a few, according to a remarkable story from the 1840s. News of gold strikes in the Great California Gold Rush reached this remote Maine island with so much force that a group of islanders decided they, too, would strike it rich in California. They built their own boat in the Thorofare, and sailed her around the Horn to San Francisco. There the islanders joined the "forty-niners" in their wild, frenetic hunt for gold. How they fared the records fail to tell.

A more mundane business enterprise came to the Thorofare in 1860, when a lobster canning factory was built by a Boston firm. More than 24 island women and children worked in it, shipping Isle au Haut canned lobster to Crosse and Blackwell in London. The cannery closed in 1880, but live lobsters were shipped regularly in the island's own fleet of "wet smacks." Each one would carry 1,500 lobsters to market in New York City and make the round trip in a week. By 1880 the island population was up to 274.

Then the first of the summer people arrived. Soon they were to form Isle au Haut into a masculine outpost of proper Bostonians — the Point Look-Out Club. Finally club members gave 4,000 acres of land to be preserved as a national park. That gift has made Isle au Haut among the least spoiled, best preserved islands on the entire coast.

The Point Look-Out Club began this way.

In 1879, Ernest Bowditch, a young landscape artist from Boston, was coming back from Bar Harbor across Penobscot Bay on a small steamer. He recalled the day, 37 years later: "I saw to the southward a bigger island, standing up from the sea and asked how to get there. 'Don't know,' replied the pilot, 'but suppose you get off at the mainland and charter a small boat.'" It was a Friday afternoon and Bowditch had the week-end free, so he got off at Stonington and chartered a small boat to take him through the network of islands out six miles to Isle au Haut. On the way out, Bowditch asked the skipper about a hotel, and was told there were no hotels or boarding houses. The skipper told him to try Captain William Turner, dropped Bowditch off, and left.

Bowditch, years later, recalled what happened next:

> I reached the old lobster factory and found sitting around a stove three or four old fishermen who looked up at me as I were some strange marine animal. I inquired which might be Captain William Turner, at which one spoke up asking what I wanted. I asked if he could keep me over Sunday, which he answered so abruptly in the negative that my vanity was hurt. Then he added, "What's your name?"
>
> "Bowditch," I replied.
>
> "That's a funny name. Any relation to the fellow who wrote the 'Navigator'?"
>
> "He was my grandfather," I replied.
>
> "Your grandfather? Then you go right on over there to that house and tell the old woman you have come to make a visit."

When Bowditch got home to Boston, he told his bachelor friends about the beauties of Isle au Haut. They joined forces, bought land and formed the Point Look-Out Club.

Bowditch, who was an old man when he dictated the above account, said his personal capital at the time amounted to only $3,500, so the original Point Look-Out members were paupers compared to the tycoons beginning to build summer "cottages" on nearby Mount Desert. But land was cheap. Soon Bowditch and his group owned 3,000 acres. By 1945-46 the Bowditch family owned over half the island, and gave it all away to make a National Park.

The club built eight cottages plus a clubhouse for communal eating, and laid down the three cardinal rules: No women, no dogs, no children. Before long, however, the founding bachelors got married. The women came and threw out rules excluding women, children and dogs. The exclusive club grew. In lean years the club even took in a few carefully selected paying guests. Four times the directors unbent enough to place small advertisements in the Junior League Magazine; even stooped, in the interests of solvency, to running one advertisement in Vogue.

The number of club cottages increased to two dozen. Other summer people bought old homes in the village or out on the promontories. Among them was Chief Justice Harlan Stone, who often took his meals at the Turner boarding house. One evening a lady at his table talked too long about how much she loved clams and how many she could eat at a sitting. Justice Stone leaned over and quietly told her, "That reminds me of the story of the woman who ate so many clams that her bosom rose and fell with the tide."

Isle au Haut seemed tough and masculine, but it was women more than men who ran the island that year when I first put ashore for a few days to do research for some newspaper articles.

Isabel B. MacDonald was town clerk. Dorothea Dodge and Mabelle Chapin were two of the three town selectmen. They were also the tax assessor and overseer of the poor. Dorothy R. Barter was the tax collector. Town treasurer was Isabel MacDonald. On the school board three of the five members were women, Donna Tully, Belvia MacDonald and Virginia MacDonald. A lady, Mabelle Chapin, was civil defense chief and Town Registrar; Edna Alley and Virginia MacDonald were the two election clerks. The bus driver and school janitor was a woman, Dorothea Dodge; the senior school teacher was Ann Haynes, helped by her husband, Pat.

But there was no question then, or for decades earlier, about who was the ranking Isle au Haut citizen. She was Miss Lizzie: Miss Elizabeth Rich, postmaster, then aged 79, born at Rich's Cove, on Isle au Haut, 1893, delivered by a midwife who charged three dollars.

"I started working in this post office when I was a 16-year-old girl," Miss Rich told me. "I was named postmaster in 1927. When I got to be 70, I had to retire because the rules said no postmaster can be over 70. So I quit being postmaster and instead became supervising clerk in charge, doing the same job for another 10 years. I've been in this post office over 63 years now."

The Post Office consisted of one corner of her front room, three chairs, one for Miss Lizzie and two for her constant visitors, and a parakeet in a cage.

Miss Lizzie Rich broke both hips just after dark on a March afternoon, when she was 78 years old, and alone.

"They just plumb cracked. I fell to the floor. Inch by inch I crawled and pulled myself across the room till I could reach my walkie-talkie. I called Stanley Dodge. He and some helpers came right over, sat me into my rocker, then lifted me and the rocker into the back of his truck and drove me to the town landing, where a boat was waiting. They carried me in the rocker down the ramp to the boat and strapped me and the rocker tight in the cockpit. Off we went across six miles of open water to Stonington. I'd busted my hips at 5 p.m. By 8 p.m. I was all fixed up in my bed at Blue Hill Hospital. . . . Now that's some service."

Miss Lizzie was soon back at her post office, getting around on two walkers. She managed well on the walkers. Each day she made two trips to the well out back, lugging in a pail of water, sometimes spilling half on the way. Each Sunday she used her walkers to get up the hill in back to the church she had attended over 75 years. "Now I take 15 minutes to get there instead of two minutes. But I get there."

In a storm, Isle au Haut can be a fearsome place. Then the power of the enraged Atlantic bursts upon Boom Beach. The mad ocean foams furiously over the ledges off Eastern Ear, then crashes on Thunder Gulch. Seas of terrifying size smash and fume past Morris' Mistake to pound at the feet of the towering granite Cliffs. Even a mile inland, out of sight and sound of the storming sea, the island ground trembles.

In fog, which can wrap the island for days on end, ghosts of shipwrecked, seablanched sailors drowned centuries before seem to haunt the shore. In hard winters, the ocean freezes over. No boat can move. In the bitter winter of 1935 there were no telephone links to the mainland, and Isle au Haut was cut off from the world for five days.

Coast Guard planes from Boston flew over dropping messages to see if the islanders needed help or rescue. They dropped instructions on how to put a reply on a rope strung between a pole and a rake held aloft by two islanders. On the third flyover the grappling hook from the plane snatched the reply. It read:

"Thank you very much. We have plenty of supplies so far. No one sick. Thank you so much. C. W. Turner."

In the winter of 1857 the bay froze solid for 20 miles out and stayed that way for eight weeks. In 1950 Frank Barton froze to death when he collapsed carrying groceries home. His body lay in the snow, undiscovered for three days.

On the south side, exposed to the Atlantic, lies Head Harbor, once a flourishing fishing community. Recently I found only one herring dory and one blue-hulled sailboat at their moorings. The twelve houses stood empty, their summer occupants gone from September till June. There was a "For Sale" sign on the house by the beach. The owner, Gooden Grant, was giving up and moving to the mainland, grudgingly. He had turned 94 years old. Stone walls which once fenced in cattle on the farms are tumbled down around the unplanted meadows, where only wild flowers bloom, song birds sing and bees gather nectar.

On an island like this everyone is his brother's keeper, especially when fire breaks out, the terror of almost defenseless islands. In the 1870s a huge fire started in the blueberry barrens and burned the entire island. Gooden Grant saw the fire of 1894 at Duck Harbor. He was a boy then, sailing home at night with his father. At age 94, Gooden Grant could still remember the sight he saw 78 years before — sights of burning trees flying into the night air like torches, setting more fires across his island home.

In 1940, a kerosene stove in the Turners' house exploded. Harold Turner was over at Dennis Eaton's house when he heard the church bell ringing the alarm. His wife, Elthea, had fled from the burning house, driven to town and rung the bell. The house burned to the ground. The whole town pitched in to build the Turners a new home. In 1947, Russ Devereux, who runs the work scow in Penobscot Bay, flew over another forest fire on the island. "Most of Maine was burning that summer. It was the year of the great fire at nearby Mount Desert. When the fire broke out in the forest here, I flew, circling low above it, shouting instructions to firefighters on the ground on where it was spreading. The whole island turned out to fight that blaze and got it under control after only 15 acres had been devastated."

Isle au Haut has dwindled in population in the last 150 years, but the special ways of a special island persist. For example, there is one gas pump on the island, not far from the town landing. Island custom is to drive up, fill your tank, and then leave the money on the honor system in a box nearby. It works.

But how long will such things last?

I asked a long-time islander, and she pointed to a prayer tacked on her kitchen door.

"Lord, we thank thee that thy Grace
    Has brought us to this pleasant place,
And most earnestly we pray
    That other folks will stay away."

17.

Lobstering:
Weird Wealth Of Maine

Lobsters, plentiful and cheap in colonial days, were fed twice a day to indentured workers. Weary of too much lobster, they complained so loudly that a new clause in their contracts stated indentured workers should not be fed lobster more than four times a week.

Even 100 years later, in the early 1800s, no boat and no traps were needed on the islands to catch lobster. Island children could go to the shore, turn over a rock and catch lobsters for supper with their bare hands. They were so plentiful that island farmers spread lobsters on their fields and vegetable gardens as fertilizer. Nobody thought of selling lobsters.

Not until the 1840s did lobstering become a way of making a living, and it spread slowly, east to west. In the autumn of 1850 the first lobster carrier, a "wet-smack" from Gloucester, with four men aboard, sailed into Swan's Island. They hired a few islanders to help them catch lobsters, paid cash and left, with their cargo hold swarming with live lobsters. The hold of a "wet-smack" has holes in it, allowing fresh sea water to run in and out, thus keeping live lobsters in prime condition for market. This is the way commercial lobstering began, with dealers sailing into the islands and teaching the islanders how to catch lobsters in quantity with traps, and how to keep them alive until a wet smack arrived to buy them. The dealers, of course, were businessmen interested in building up their sources of supply.

But the dealers didn't pay much. In the 1850s they paid two, sometimes three, cents a lobster. Not per pound, but per lobster; and the lobsters were very big as well as plentiful. Stories can be heard on the islands today about lobsters weighing 20 and 25 pounds. One giant creature of 43 pounds was caught at Friendship, Long Island.

At the start, lobstering was the job of men too old to go on long, hard trips out to the fishing grounds. The older men, with young grandsons along as helpers, went out in a rowing dory or small sailboat and set only thirty to sixty traps close inshore; but they'd catch 200 pounds of lobsters or more. Today young fishermen in big and powerful boats fish 800 to 1,000 traps off the islands, and sometimes come home with less than 200 pounds.

The traps a hundred years ago looked rather like bird cages. They were cumbersome affairs four feet long, two feet high and two feet wide, with slats far enough apart "to afford the proposed victims a clear view of the baits." The baits were codfish heads and cunners, hung on a row of hooks, rather than the bait bags or redfish carcasses used today in smaller metal or wood traps. The traps' ends then were simply tarred rope netting, with a big opening in one end. Lobsters then, as now, would back into the trap through that opening to get at the tempting bait inside. Then, as now, it never occurred to the lobster to back out. Lobsters always try to get out head first and can't do it. The big claws on their forward end are too wide to permit escape.

Lobsters were so plentiful in the 1850s, these traps fished well. The average catch per trap was six or seven lobsters weighing four to six pounds each, for a total of about 25 to 30 pounds per trap. Today a lobsterman often averages less than one lobster of keeping size per trap, and a keeping size lobster weighs only about one pound. But today the price per pound runs from $1.50 to $3.00, compared to a fraction of a cent then.

Canning lobster soon became a big and widespread business. By the 1880s there were canning factories on Swan's Island, Isle au Haut, Deer Isle, Vinalhaven, and all the way along the coast, close to 100 in all, on islands and in mainland harbors. Each year on the islands more and more men, including the younger men, went lobstering, though in midsummer many younger island fishermen would go off to sea for a few months so they could make more money mackerel seining.

The total Maine lobster catch in 1880 was 14 million pounds. Of this almost 9 million pounds went into cans. The canning business opened new jobs for island women and children.

Island lobster canning factories were on the wharf, open at the end so men could bring the catch straight off the boat, carrying loads of live lobsters on a stretcher and dumping them directly into huge copper cauldrons of boiling water. When they were cooked, the lobsters were spread on long tables where the women cut them into various parts. One would punch out the chunky meat from the tail. Another, called a "cracker," would cut off the claws with a cleaver, and still others would pick the meat. Other groups of women did the packing, filling each can with a selection of various parts. One girl weighed the packed cans, adding or subtracting lobster meat till it weighed the specified one or two pounds. Next girl on the assembly line forced the meat down with a special "stamper," made for that job. The next put on a tin cover, banging it down with a hammer, made specifically for that job. A trayload of filled cans went next to the solderer, a man, who sealed them, leaving a tiny hole in the lid. The load then was lowered into a cauldron of boiling water until all the air was expelled from each tin. Then the solderer sealed the tiny hole in the lid and the tins were cooked again.

In the packing room the cans were cleaned with acid, painted to prevent rust, pasted with a bright label showing a scarlet lobster against a blue sea and bearing the words "Maine Lobster" and the town or island where packed. Thousands of such cans were packed daily into pine boxes, which were collected by the canning company's freight vessel and shipped to Boston or New York, usually for export.

In a canning factory, men were paid reasonably well. Solderers got $12 to $15 a week. Other men received $7 to $10 a week; but the women got only $2 to $3 a week. Even that wage was sought after, because at the time women schoolteachers on the islands were paid even less — only $1 a week. Boys from 10 to 14 years old earned 25 cents a day, the same wage paid to boys working in the island granite quarries.

The lobster canning season lasted from April to August. When it was over, the canning of other fish, or corn or vegetables, began.

Most canned Maine lobster was sold abroad, by distributors

in New York and Boston. Perhaps this was because fresh lobster was available in the east; perhaps because housewives were suspicious lest the canned lobster go bad.

There is little evidence of this. Maine indeed was an expert in canning. Eastport led the way. The first lobster cannery was started at Eastport in the 1840s. Eastport also perfected the mass canning of sardines. By 1898 there were 61 sardine canneries producing several million cases of sardines each year. Toward the end of the 1890s the larger islands and most coastal towns had one or more factories canning lobsters, sardines, clams, cod and mackerel.

Island lobstermen sold their smallest lobsters, "shorts" by today's standards, to the cannery and kept the big ones to sell live to the smack buyer, who came weekly in his wet-smack schooner. The island lobstermen would tow their "cars" or crates filled with the big live lobsters over to the smack. They'd agree on a price with the smack-buyer, who would dump the live lobsters out of their cars into the saltwater compartments on his little schooner.

There was more to the exchange than money. There was a visit. The smack-buyer brought news and gossip with him from other islands and the mainland. A good buyer also brought the essential stone jugs, containing rum or whiskey. Island lobstermen, he knew, could not pursue their hard trade fueled only by the spruce beer or dandelion wines made by island women. The island men relied on the smack-buyer to bring them a needed supply of stone jugs. The buyer who arrived at an island with only cash soon learned more was expected of him. "No rum brought, no lobsters sold" was the code of most islands.

On nights after the smack buyer had disbursed cash and stone jugs, islanders would put on a square dance in the canning factory.

Another welcome visitor was the "trader." The trader was essentially a small schooner fitted out as a floating store, which sailed from island to island. The sailor-storekeeper would sail his boat up the harbor and tie up at the lobster wharf or canning factory and do business for a few days. The inside of his boat was filled with shelves stocked with scented soaps for ladies, shaving mugs and razors for men, jackknives and toys for children. He carried shoes and boots, dry goods of all kinds, needles, threads and laces. Below decks was the heavier merchandise; wash tubs, crockery; pots and pans; cans of kerosene; barrels of molasses and apples. The trader would sell his stock for cash or, if necessary, he'd barter. He'd swap his store goods for animal furs, sails, rope, dried fish. There was even a floating cobbler, in a flat-bottomed scow, who in fair weather would call at islands in Penobscot Bay. George S. Wasson, in his book "Sailing Days on the Penobscot," described the odd looking scow as being painted light blue and carrying the words, painted in yellow, "W. Cottle. Boots and Shoes Repaired on the Rolling Deep."

By 1900, lobster canning was on its way out. The Maine legislature passed a law forbidding the canning of lobsters, as a conservation measure. Lobsters too small for the wet-smack buyer were going to the canneries, no matter how small they were. As a result lobsters were being caught before they had a chance to breed, and the lobster shortage was so serious in the 1880s that future stocks were threatened. The commissioners of all New England states met in Boston to establish conservation laws. A hundred years later, in the 1980s, the commissioners were still meeting, discussing the same topic. The trouble is that lobsters are slow developers. A lobster takes five years to reach one pound. It sheds old shells and grows new ones to fit larger bodies many times. It does not reproduce until it is at least five years old. So Maine has minimum and maximum size limits for legal lobsters as a conservation device.

As lobsters became scarcer, the price, of course, went up. Lobsters, which had fetched only two cents each in the 1850s, regardless of weight, were by 1900 bringing nine cents a pound. More islanders were going lobstering. On Swan's Island, for example, where only 10 men were lobstering in 1855, more than 140 men were lobstering by 1900. Today over 8,000 licensed lobstermen all along the Maine coast catch about 30 million dollars worth of lobster a year. The price they get is 100 times greater than the price their forefathers got a hundred years ago; but the amount of lobster they catch is barely more. Because of enormous increases in the number of lobstermen and number of lobster traps; because of the size and sophistication of today's lobster boats, there are fewer, and smaller, lobsters in the ocean.

Photo by George French, courtesy Maine State Archives.

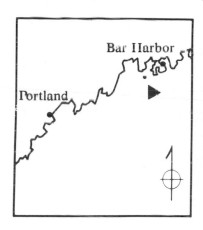

18.

Swan's Island:
King David
To Rockefellers

Swan's Island is 6,000 acres of rather flat land halfway between Isle au Haut and Mount Desert. Almost every acre is rich with tales of fascinating people who've lived on it over the centuries.

But let's begin with the value of the island itself. Thomas Kench, the first white settler in 1776, paid nothing for it. He fled here as a deserter from the Revolutionary Army, and for 14 years existed here as a solitary recluse. More about Kench later. Then in 1791, fabled "King David" Smith landed, fathered 24 children, over 50 grandchildren, bossed the island and lived to be 80. Spectacular and swashbuckler extrordinary, Colonel James Swan, Kench's old army commander, then bought Swan's Island and 24 nearby islands, over 9,000 acres in all. Swan paid two pounds an acre in 1786. The colorful Swan envisioned creating a feudal kingdom here with himself as king. He gave the island his name, but he died in a Paris prison. More on him in a moment, too.

Now leap from early days of American Independence to the 20th century. In 1952 an oceanfront acre of Swan's still fetched only $15, but today the price of a building lot on Mackerel Cove is $50,000. Lawsuits about this land have involved the Rockefellers, who own lots of it. The big change was due to a boat — the Maine State ferry, which carries cars, makes six trips daily on a forty-minute run to the mainland. The ferry service, begun in 1960, sent population and the price of precious land zooming. So today Swan's Island has an airfield, a huge camp ground, paved roads, summer colonies, a school, churches and about 200 resident taxpayers. But Swan's islanders saw the dangers of speculative land development and quickly passed some of the best land-use ordinances in Maine. Result: they have saved their island. Swan's is still a fascinating, lovely jewel in Penobscot Bay.

And now, back to the first white settler on Swan's Island.

Thomas Kench, ex-soldier of the Revolution, hauled his small boat ashore here and turned hermit for 14 years of solitary existence. Kench came from England to the colonies before the Revolution, perhaps a lonely adventurer from the start. He enlisted when Benedict Arnold led that ghastly march on Quebec in the autumn of 1775. Kench paddled up the Kennebec in one of those leaky bateaux built in a hurry from green wood at Pittston; portaged those damnable heavy boats across the Maine wilderness. Like all in that heroic company, Kench became sick, cold, desperately hungry, munching with joy when he ate the carcass of a dog. He survived, only to freeze in a tent during November and December on the Plains of Abraham. He survived a raging epidemic of smallpox which killed men around him. Kench came through it, strong enough to be among the first American soldiers to climb the cliffs, scale the walls and attack Quebec's Citadel. He survived again, one of the few to get back alive to American lines. In defeat, Kench survived that terrible winter of retreat, struggling and straggling back to Maine, through the wilderness, hip deep in snow. He finally reached Boston. Even after that experience, Kench volunteered for more. In 1776 he became a gunner in the artillery company commanded by a very young captain named James Swan.

There something went badly wrong. Maybe Kench, the soldier who'd survived the Arnold march, rebelled against the spit-and-polish of an artillery company headed by a Boston dandy. Kench deserted and fled, heading to the lonely islands off Mount Desert. On a day late in 1776, Kench grounded out his boat on a tiny islet of Swan's Island. He arrived a desperate, angry man, but a survivor.

He was to live the next 14 years alone there; then six more years with "King David" Smith for unwanted company. After 20 years on Swan's, Kench moved off, a changed man. He bought a hundred acres of land at Brooksville, on Cape

Rosier, took up farming, married, sired six children, and when he was past 90 years, Kench died.

For 14 years Kench's only company on the island had been a cow and a few sheep. He kept apart from the fishermen from Mount Desert, 10 miles away, who would occasionally sail into the harbor. He kept apart from the Indians who came down in summer from Old Town in canoes and went about their summer business; the braves hunting seals and fishing from their canoes, the squaws and children digging and drying clams for winter food, making baskets from the island's long sweetgrass. Kench kept his distance from them, too.

The one person Kench could not keep away from was David Smith. Smith and his family arrived 14 years after Kench had found his solitude; and Smith intruded grossly by building a log cabin on the same islet in Burnt Coat Harbor. Smith, like Kench, was a wounded veteran of the Revolutionary War. After the Revolution, Smith had moved from New Hampshire to Deer Isle and married there. In 1791, Smith, his wife and children left Deer Isle, sailed out to the island and settled in, close to the recluse, Kench. Perhaps it was this exposure to the Smith family, especially the children, which turned Kench around from a total "loner" into the new man, a man who five years later would move to the mainland, become a farmer, a husband, a father, and live to be a patriarch of 90 years.

This David Smith is revered today as the true father of Swan's Island. He married three times, fathered at least 24 children, farmed 240 acres, and saw his children's children grow and build homes on the island. He was known then, and is still known as "King David," the man who dominated life on Swan's Island till he died at 80 years.

But the most colorful of Swan's early white men was Colonel James Swan, the officer from whom Kench deserted. Swan was a swashbuckling, ambitious, enthusiastic business man, bon vivant and dreamer. His name lives on in Swan's Island.

Swan, born a Scotsman, left Fifeshire at 11 years and landed in Boston. There he soon became a star among the young bloods. He worked as a teenager in banks, brokerage offices and counting houses. A fellow clerk he liked and admired was Henry Knox, the man who became Secretary of War under George Washington, who built the palatial mansion, "Montpelier," at Thomaston, Maine, and who remained Swan's hero forever.

Swan was a free-thinking, fast-writing, liberal. By the time he was 17, he had published a fiery book titled "A Dissuasion of Great Britain from the Slave Trade," which made him one of the youngest and first abolitionists. He became an early and ardent member of the Sons of Liberty, and helped dump 342 chests of English tea into Boston Harbor. He fought at the Battle of Bunker Hill, was wounded twice, recovered and came back to serve as an artillery captain in the siege of Boston. The rising star, still in his twenties, became Secretary of the Massachusetts Board of War, Adjutant-General of the Commonwealth and a member of the legislature.

Swan also became rich early, and a friend of the famous and powerful. He was lucky enough to inherit an unexpected fortune from a crusty Scotch uncle, a bachelor, who admired the guts of the youngster who had left Fifeshire at age 11 and done so well in the New World. Swan soon parlayed this fortune into a bigger fortune. He used the inherited money to buy cheaply confiscated Tory lands around Boston and Dorchester. He also bought vast tracts of land in Virginia, West Virginia and Kentucky. He bought privateers and made money fast on the cargoes and ships they captured. He speculated wildly, sometimes losing heavily. He lived high on the hog. He kept a grandiose home at the corner of West and Tremont streets in Boston. There he and his wife entertained Lafayette, Rochambeau and George Washington. He drove the most ornate carriage in North America.

This was the man who at 30 years old bought Swan's Island (then called Burnt Coat Island) and 24 nearby islands from the Commonwealth of Massachusetts in 1786. Young Swan and his family began talking about their new holdings as their "island empire." They planned to build a magnificent home on their island, entertain in kingly style — and make money from the 9,000 acres.

Swan, the dreamer, saw lumber mills, flour mills, his own great manor house and many settlements of workers' and farmers' cottages; and himself as lord of all he surveyed in Penobscot Bay.

He offered free land up to 100 acres, to settlers. Many came. He began felling trees for saw mills and started trade with Boston. Above all, he started building a grand manor for himself. Up went a huge structure, complete with colonnades, balconies, porches, ballrooms, a palatial home totally out of place on a rough, barely settled island. He was doomed never to live in it.

Swan, ever a businessman, persuaded his political friends in Massachusetts to exempt his 25 islands from all taxes for twenty years, provided he got 22 Protestant families settled, each in a home at least 22 feet square, and built a church and school.

But Swan, the high flyer, high liver and gambler, hit a streak of bad financial luck. He was suddenly on the verge of bankruptcy. To escape his creditors he fled incognito to France in 1788, only two years after beginning his island empire. Swan even spoke of entering a monastery and starting an entirely new life in France.

But the French Revolution killed that unlikely idea. Swan, the maker of deals, the friend of the great in France and America, the man who had dumped tea in Boston Harbor, been wounded at Bunker Hill, began an exciting new enterprise in Paris. He became the American agent of the revolutionary French government, the man who purchased needed goods for them in America, and then got the goods smuggled through the British blockade. By 1795, Swan, who had fled to escape bankruptcy, was back in the United States, flying very high again. He successfully negotiated settlement of the American debt to France, thereby providing France with dollars to buy needed goods in America. But his creditors were soon on his tail, and Swan fled back to France.

Swan's Island was by now far out of his mind. The great mansion, though still new, was on its way downhill. "King David" Smith, by now the father of a dozen or more children, moved into the abandoned manor and took squatter's possession. He renamed it "King David's Palace." But King David left it for his new 240-acre farm on the northern shore. By 1840 the big house had served as home to a dozen squatters and had become a hovel. Fire swept through it that year and reduced Swan's dream to ashes.

In Paris, the sky was falling on Swan. The French Republic stripped him of his monopoly as its American agent. He was accused of pocketing two million francs, and thrown into jail in Paris. He absolutely refused to pay the two million francs, contending he was innocent. He chose to stay in a debtor's prison 22 years. His wife, in Boston, supplied ample funds. Swan used the money to buy presents for his guards, rich furnishings for his jail quarters and to pay off debts for other prisoners. He spent lavishly to establish an elegant household across the street from the jail. There in absentia, he gave huge dinners for his friends. He kept boxes at the theater and opera, and entertained friends there, again in absentia. Swan asked only one thing — that a chair be set for him at the head of the table, that a seat be kept for him in the boxes at the opera and theater.

In 1830 Louis Phillipe was restored to the throne of France. The king released all debtors, including Swan. Swan left the prison only to do one thing — to embrace his old friend, Lafayette. This he did, and then he returned voluntarily to prison. After 22 years in that prison he felt at home only there; and there he died in 1830.

Swan's Island meanwhile was in a legal mess. Swan's agent, Joseph Price, torn between Swan, creditors, settlers, claims and counterclaims, had given up and left. Daniel Webster was involved as a lawyer trying to unravel Swan's mortgage complications.

The islanders took matters into their own hands. In 1834 the 200 residents formed their own government as a plantation, drew up a tax list, built a school and a road and changed Swan's Island from a mixed-up feudal proprietorship into an orderly, self-governing community of Maine. All that remained of Swan was his name. The island Champlain had christened Brule Cote (Burned Coat) Island in 1603, has been called Swan's Island for almost 200 years.

Fishing, not lumber, not flour mills, became the basis of Swan's Island prosperity. The island led all the New England coast in catching mackerel. In 1879 the Swan's Island fleet landed 15,000 barrels of mackerel, valued at five dollars each. The Swan's Island schooner, Alice, and her fabled skipper, Captain H. B. Joyce, ranked first in mackerel catching. The Alice, with 40 men in her crew, netted 30,000 fish in one spring day off Block Island. In 1881 the Alice cured 5,000 barrels of fish, worth $28,000. Then five years later the mackerel vanished. The Swan's Island fleet fell apart. Even Captain Joyce had to sell his Alice. The male population of the island was thrown out of work, after years of being 100 percent employed in fishing or building fish boats. Slowly the island turned, less successfully, to herring fishing. Later lobstering became the foremost occupation.

Almost 100 years later, aboard Steer Clear, we crept through thick fog along the shore off Swan's Island, trying to find the entrance into Burnt Coat Harbor. This was the same approach Thomas Kench made in late 1776 when — on a clearer day, I hope — the first settler went ashore at Burnt Coat. But in this twentieth century we had the Light and the fog signal on Hockamock Point to guide us. Trouble was we could not hear the fog signal or see the light. We cut the motors to listen hard, and lay wallowing in the slow swell, straining our ears. Not a sound from the big fog horn, though we should be abreast of it according to my dead reckoning. Then we heard the gong at the harbor entrance, its clappers clanging in the slow swell. With relief, I put the engines into gear and crept to that sound. Suddenly the blast of the fog horn blew so loud it made us jump. It was only a hundred yards to port, but the breeze had been carrying the sound inland over the island and up the Bay toward Blue Hill.

Later we heard that fishermen from Burnt Coat Harbor had complained for years to the Coast Guard that they couldn't hear the horn coming in from the sea. They had asked for a noise reflector. They never got it. Now, in 1981, there is no fog signal keeper. The Coast Guard abandoned the lighthouse, despite protests from fishermen, and pulled out Coast Guardsman E-5 Philip Felch, who had kept the light, and his red haired wife and three children. In 1981 there is only an automated beacon.

We crept into the harbor and anchored. Late that night, when the wind blew 50 miles an hour, it proved an uncomfortable, bouncy place. In the gale of wind our anchor dragged. We had to reset it from a bouncing bow at 3 a.m.

Next day, we went ashore. First stop was the town office. It was one small room at the back of the fire station at Burnt Coat Harbor; two desks, three straight chairs, some filing cabinets and a closet.

"Come Election Day, we clean out the closet, take off the door, hang up a red, white and blue curtain, and the closet becomes the Swan's Island voting booth," said Myron Sprague, Jr., first selectman that year, at a salary of $2 a day. Swan's Island officials were mostly young. Sprague was 26 when he was first elected a selectman. The night we talked with him he was 31, the oldest man on the Board, and chairman. David Joyce, 30, and Dexter Lee, 28, were the other two selectmen of the island. The three-man school board was even younger. Gerry Smith was 29, Terence Staples was 27, and Sheldon Carlson, old man of the school board, was a World War II veteran. That summer of '72 Swan's Island had hired its first policeman, Tom Collins, only 21. "We chose an off-islander so he couldn't be accused of playing favorites," said Myron Sprague, Jr. "Tom came from as far away as you'd want to go — Bridgton, Maine."

After dinner that first night the wind picked up and the rain started, signs of a coming squall. We sat in the one-room town office with Sprague while he showed us old town reports. The names of the town officers had not changed much. In the 1952 report, his father, Myron Sprague, was moderator of town meeting, member of the school committee, the budget committee and the planning committee. The Staples name was there, too. Herman W. Staples was town clerk, member of the school committee, budget committee, and the committee for health and sanitation. Loel Staples was a selectman; Milton Staples was road commissioner; Carroll Staples was constable; Norman Staples and Maynard Staples were on other town boards.

The continuity of the same family names in the governance of Swan's Island, generation after generation, holds true with the Joyces, the Burns, the Norwoods, the Holmes and the Kents, as well as the Spragues and the Staples.

Families like these, rooted to the island's soil, have long been and still are the best guardians of Swan's future. Nowadays the old island families reach out sometimes to draw on the

special abilities of newcomers in the summer colony. Take the
time in 1970 when rumors flew that developers planned to put
243 cottages on handkerchief-sized lots. Eugene Norwood was
a 54-year-old lobsterman at the time and head of the planning
committee. He and his committee knew fast action was needed
to protect the island. They knew, too, that words like "zoning"
might put up the hackles of island families, fearful that state
bureaucrats would dictate what they could or could not do with
their property. They knew, too, that whatever local ordinances
the island might write, those ordinances might face court chal-
lenges by smart lawyers from the city.

"We worked like the deuce," Norwood told me, "and drafted
a proposed ordinance regulating subdivision development of
the island, but none of us on the planning board were lawyers.
We were mostly lobstermen. So for expert help we went to a
Boston lawyer and a New York lawyer who summered here.
They soon put what we wanted on paper, and we called a public meeting to explain to our neighbors what we had in mind,
and to scotch some crazy rumors flying around. The neighbors
raised, and we answered, questions for hours. After that meeting we waited a week so everyone had a fair chance to talk it
over. Then we called a special town meeting on March 17,
1971, to vote on the proposed zoning ordinance."

The closet back of the fire station was emptied out to serve,
as always, as the voting booth. The island people passed the
ordinance by a vote of 49 to 12.

The ordinance was later seen by a Rockefeller lawyer, who
wrote from New York to say it was about the finest ordinance
of its kind enacted anywhere in the United States.

The ordinance required that every lot in a subdivision should
have at least two acres, and that lots which bordered on the
shore or any road should have at least 200 feet frontage; that
no building could be closer than 30 feet to the boundary line
of another lot, nor closer than 100 feet to any existing building on an adjacent lot, nor closer than 60 feet from the center
of any road, nor closer than 30 feet to the high tide line. Other
provisions prohibited tents, campers, house trailers, and set
strict standards for sewer systems, water systems, fire hy-
drants, telephone and power lines. The island required details
of all proposed development be first submitted for approval to
the planning board, and that performance guarantees of sub-

stantial amounts be posted before the final plans would be considered.

The ordinance has prevented mass development; but it has also pushed land prices so high that only the well-to-do can now buy property on Swan's Island. Therein lies a predicament, voiced to me by a young fisherman. "I was born here, and I'm 22 now and fishing on my own. I'm in a mood to get married and start my own family here. Of course, we want a place of our own, near the water, where I can get to my boat. But how am I going to get that building lot when someone from away is ready to pay $25,000 or $50,000 for it? Am I going to be frozen out, so I have to move off the island where I was born, where I fish now, where I want to raise my new family?"

The same predicament faces many Maine islanders.

People from away now own more than two-thirds of Swan's Island, and they pay most of the taxes. This change in ownership is a direct result of the frequent car ferry service to the mainland, which started in 1960. Within 10 years of the start of the Maine State Ferry Service, most of the island was owned by people from away. Whoever owns the land and pays the taxes, finally calls the tune.

But no ferry service, no amount of newcomers changed Clyde Torrey. Clyde Torrey was for over 30 years after World War II the most colorful, most eccentric, most loved character on Swan's Island, and surely the island's most photographed man. That fine book about Swan's Island, "Biography of an Island" by Perry D. Westbrook, was dedicated to Clyde Torrey, and he enjoyed autographing copies. Clyde is dead now.

Clyde Torrey was past 75 when I last talked with him a few years back. He had an old, grey, dilapidated farmhouse on the east side of the island, with spectacular views across the open water to the islands of Placentia and Great Gott, on to Mount Desert and Cadillac Mountain. But Clyde seldom lived inside the farmhouse. He preferred to cook and sleep in the abandoned cars beside it, even in winter. Clyde Torrey looked weird, and made that weirdness a point of personal pride. In summer he usually wore old blue overalls, over a series of long-john undershirts. He rolled his pants leg up over his calf to

let the salt air get to a place which pained him, and on his head
he wore a wild-looking Scotch tam o' shanter, gift from God
knows whom. He was a lean man with bad teeth, a good smile
and a dirty stubble of beard, and he played endlessly on his
accordion — ballads, bawdy songs, sea chanties, drinking songs
and square dances.

Clyde looked like a bum, but he was a well-educated, well-
spoken man, who simply preferred his odd and lonely life style.
He grew a few vegetables and potatoes, dug clams and often
shared talk and sometimes a bottle, with summer campers on
Mertie Morrison's nearby campgrounds.

"Way back, Clyde went to school with me," said a classmate
with a long memory. "That was over 60 years ago, when 120
kids went to three schools in the island's three communities of
Atlantic, Minturn and Swan's Island. He drove us crazy, even
then. Clyde would get straight A's without seeming to do a
lick of work."

Clyde played his accordion and stomped out the beat for
hundreds of country dances on the island. He played and called
square dances for years down at the camp grounds in summer.
When Myron Sprague, Jr., went off to the army, Clyde stuck
posters on the island roads which read "Hootenanny for Sonny
Sprague tonight, before he goes into the army. Dancing to the
music of Clyde Torrey!"

During World War II, Torrey himself got a notice from the
draft board on the mainland, saying that he was being called
up. "Struck me as odd," he said, "because I was 45 years old
then. But I got into my skiff before daybreak and rowed clear
over to the mainland. With currents and all I rowed better
than 10 miles. When I got to the draft board I found it was
a government snafu. They didn't want me at 45. So I got into
my skiff and rowed back 10 miles. That was my army career."

Another Swan's Island eccentric, long before Clyde Torrey,
grew the world's finest tuberous begonias here. He was an
able, inventive man from Pennsylvania, who came to Swan's
Island for his health after World War I, and bought himself
a house on Mackerel Cove. To shelter it from cold winds, he
amazed islanders by encasing the entire wooden frame house
with an outer wall of granite blocks, hewn from local quarries.

Then he installed an electricity plant and plumbing, and began growing his tuberous begonias. To fertilize the soil, he gathered huge amounts of rockweed washed up on the shore near his house. Then he sheltered his flower garden from the winds by planting evergreen hedges. When his beds were ready, he eventually planted over 2,500 begonias in each one. The flowers were so spectacular in their dazzling colors they drew worldwide attention. He hired an English gardener to work year-round on them, built a greenhouse and a potting shed. Millionaires in their yachts sailed over from Bar Harbor to see the begonia gardens on Swan's Island and bought plants to take home. Even Lady Astor took his plants home to England. Between 1920 and 1945 this eccentric gardener sold up to 40,000 tuberous begonias a year all across the nation and overseas. His secret was the heavy application of seaweed to the thin soil lying atop island granite.

The gardens and the begonias are long since gone. The greenhouse, the dwelling, the wharf have rotted away. Weeds are the only crop where tens of thousands of dazzling begonias, the finest in the world, once grew.

19.

Mount Desert:
From The French To The Fire

The feet of three and a half million visitors a year are wearing away the topsoil and even the granite of ancient Acadia. Mount Desert is the mecca for millions who come to feast their eyes on its bold beauty and stirring seascapes.

As they stand atop Cadillac Mountain and look to islands offshore and the Atlantic beyond, their feet rest on pink granite 400 million years old. This granite forced its way up through volcanic turbulence as magma, the molten mass of the earth's inner crust. As it cooled it fell back into the tortured gaping holes, and hardened to become the massive granite of Mount Desert. Out of it came Cadillac Mountain, towering 1,532 feet over the sea, highest mountain on the Atlantic coast; and the 17 other mountains beside Cadillac which form the spectacular spine of Mount Desert.

Today a handsome road with hairpin bends and magnificent lookouts for sightseers in cars and buses has opened to millions the beauties of Cadillac.

Europeans came to Mt. Desert 400 years ago; Indians were here 4,000 years before Christ. Archaeologists have discovered artifacts which by the carbon 14 method of dating were left here about 4000 B.C. They are much like "finds" from the ancient Indian grounds in New Mexico.

Three thousand years later, around 1000 A.D., came another Indian civilization called the Red Paint people, because of the red ocher found in their gravesites. Where the came from or where they vanished to is not known. Long after them came the Abnaki Indians about whom we know quite a lot. They did not live year round on Mount Desert, but only summered here.

They came down streams and rivers and across carry points in birch bark canoes from May to October to fish, to plant corn, to paddle to the nearby islands. After the settlers arrived the Indians slowly ceased even their summer visits.

The beauty remains. Some believe this island, 16 miles long and 12 miles wide, is the most dramatically beautiful island in the world.

Mount Desert is the boundary line, in terms of birds and of plants, between the sub-arctic and the temperate zones. Here birds and plants from both climates meet and abound together. Two of America's great naturalists, James Audubon and Louis Agassiz, were so enthralled by Mount Desert that they did much of their great work here.

A Portugese, Estevan Gomez (Stephen Smith) was probably the first European to sail here in 1525 and he ventured up river as far as Bangor. What we call the Penobscot River Gomez christened on his map "Rio de las Gamas" — River of the Deer.

Next came a Frenchman. In 1604 Samuel de Champlain, navigator for Sieur de Monts, sailed to this island and called the region La Cadie; which became L'Acadie; which became today's Acadia National Park. Champlain left the main French camp on St. Croix Island in a 17-ton ketch. With 12 sailors and two Indian guides he came one September day in 1604 on an exploring trip and discovered Mount Desert.

"This island," he wrote 377 years ago, "is very high, and cleft into seven or eight mountains all in a line. The summits are bare and deserted. Nothing but rock. I named it Isle des Monts-deserts."

Champlain made that one short stopover here, then sailed off to explore the rest of the Maine coast naming Isle Au Haut on the way. In his map Champlain drew Mount Desert and the Cranberry Isles with remarkable accuracy. He then left Maine's coast to become the founding father of Quebec.

A French lady, Antoinette de Pons, the beautiful but virtuous Marquise de Guerchville who refused to become mistress of King Henry of Navarre, now enters the Mount Desert story. In 1613 this lady of extreme virtue got the land deed formerly held by Sieurs de Monts. The deed, given her by King Louis XIII, was enlarged to cover all of North America south to the Gulf of Mexico.

Antoinette financed a Jesuit expedition to make Catholic converts of the Indians. The expedition commander was Sieur de la Sausseye. The religious leader on Mount Desert was a Jesuit priest, Pierre Briand, professor of theology at the University of Lyons. The good priest was foolhardy enough to sail in a ship ill-named Jonas. On a bright day in June 1613, the Jonas dropped anchor in a lovely Mount Desert cove. Father Briand and his Jesuit colleague, Father Massé, celebrated mass and named the spot Saint-Sauveur.

Mount Desert so charmed Father Briand that he decided to start his mission on the spot. The ship's company of 25 colonists and 35 sailors moved ashore, pitched tents and left the Jonas at anchor while they set up camp and began searching for Indian souls to save. They spent a happy summer month encamped near Fernald's Point, meeting, befriending and converting local Indians.

Then their luck turned bad.

Down the coast off Blue Hill Bay, a small squadron of English ships were on the prowl with the mission of chasing any French intruders on what England considered English soil. In command of the English was Captain Samuel Argall, a tough sea captain who had helped establish the English colony in Virginia six years earlier. As he cruised Blue Hill Bay he met friendly Indians and invited them aboard. They told him other white men were nearby. Argall suspected they were Frenchmen. He got the Indians to act as his local pilots and together they sailed down the Western Way to Mount Desert. Argall soon saw smoke from the cooking fires of Father Briand's camp. He headed for it, aboard his 14-gun ship Treasurer, with all hands at battle stations. He found the Jonas at anchor and took her skeleton crew by surprise. In a brief fight the Jonas got off one badly aimed shot and Treasurer quickly killed the man who fired off the only shot from Jonas. Argall captured the ship and sent his men ashore to round up Father Briand and all his soul-savers and sailors. The French surrendered without much resistance. Argall tore down their camp, erected a new protestant cross and a plaque inscribed with the name of the King of England; and thereby established the claim to Mount Desert as the soil of England rather than France.

For the next 75 years no new white settlement by either

English or French was attempted on Mount Desert. It was a risky outpost, too close to the feuds between Indian, French and English to tempt settlers.

But the area was nevertheless a bone of contention between the French and English crowns. In the hope that a military man would nail down the English claim to Mount Desert, King James I gave title to an admiral of the English navy, Sir Robert Mansell. The King hoped Mansell would go to Mount Desert to make certain that the flag of England flew unchallenged; but all Sir Robert did was change the name from Mount Desert to Mount Mansell. That bit of egotism failed to take hold. The French name of Mount Desert has stuck.

Sailors of all nations knew Mount Desert well, by sight. It was one of the biggest landmarks of the New World for ships from Europe. In clear weather a ship 60 miles to sea could spot Cadillac Mountain, according to ships' logs. For example, when Governor Winthrop sailed by Mount Desert in June 1630 on his way to settle Massachusetts Bay, he drew the first known sketches of Mount Desert as it looks from 40 miles at sea. Sketches like the one drawn by Winthrop appeared in every edition of "The English Pilot" from 1706 on. The sea traffic past Mount Desert was frequent, but few set foot ashore.

One who did and left his mark, was Antoine Laumet, son of a small-town French lawyer. Few have heard of him by that name, but his alias is a household word — Cadillac.

Laumet emigrated from France to Canada. In 1688 this adventurer obtained a land grant from the French Governor of Canada, of six square miles in Maine, plus the Isle des Monts Deserts, almost abandoned since Captain Argall captured Father Briand and the Jesuit colony in 1613. By the time Laumet got his land grant, he had changed his plebian name to the more aristocratic name of La Mothe, and added the fake title "Sieur de Cadillac," a little town near his birthplace in France. Laumet, now going by the grand name of Antoine La Mothe, Sieur de Cadillac, in 1688 took his bride to Mount Desert. The couple spent only one summer on the island, but Laumet now added the resounding extra title "Seigneur des Monts Deserts." In his own honor he christened the highest mountain of his new domain Cadillac Mountain.

Laumet was a born hustler. After his one summer on

Mount Desert, he upped stakes for Montreal. There he became a fur trader of importance, and soon founded a trading station he called Detroit. Detroit returned the compliment hundreds of years later by naming its most prestigious car after him. To this day the emblem of the Cadillac is Laumet's phony coat of arms, further emblazoned with the coronet of a count — an honor not even Laumet dared invent for himself. The adventurer Laumet kept on the upward move, and ended his career as governor of French Louisiana.

Thus the highest mountain on the Atlantic coast and the most famous American car carry the name of the adventurer who came from a village in Gascony and spent one summer almost 300 years ago on Mount Desert; but his imprint on the history of Maine was by no means over when the Seigneur des Monts Deserts sailed away from Cadillac Mountain.

Close to a hundred years after he left, Laumet's granddaughter arrived from France in the newly independent United States, and filed claim to her grandfather's land on Mount Desert. Her name was Madame Barthelmy de Gregoire. She arrived in Boston from France in 1786, at the age of 41, with a husband and three children. She promptly filed suit with the General Court of Massachusetts (to which Maine belonged till 1820), claiming ownership of her grandfather's lands. She brought with her letters of introduction from Lafayette. Thomas Jefferson, who had close ties to France from his negotiations in Paris for French help during the Revolution, was in the White House. The young United States and France were enjoying a happy honeymoon period. So when this 41-year-old French woman presented her prestigious letters of introduction and her claim, the Court of Massachusetts listened in a kindly mood. They promptly gave her and her family American citizenship; and then gave the lady ownership of all the eastern half of Mount Desert, plus some of the adjoining mainland.

Madame de Gregoire and her family, ownership papers in her purse, sailed to Mount Desert and settled at Hull's Cove. She quickly opened the first Mount Desert real estate office and began selling her land to squatters, at the bargain rate of five dollars for 100 acres. That dribble of income was not enough. In 1792 she went after bigger money and sold most of the eastern half of Mount Desert for $6,000 to Henry Jackson of Boston. He in turn sold to Senator William Bingham of Philadelphia. When Madame de Gregoire died in 1811, Bingham bought the rest of her land.

The Binghams, already one of the wealthiest families in America, established the Bingham Trust which soon had enormous holdings in Maine. To bankroll their land speculations, the Bingham Trust took into partnership the Baring family, bankers in London. Together they embarked on still more land speculation. Their agent in these parts was Colonel John Black. He prospered hugely, as witness the Black Mansion at Ellsworth, a dazzling and extravagant display of classic Georgian architecture which Colonel Black built in 1802. In frontier Maine, the Colonel's house was a rich man's palace. (Today it is open to the public.)

Madame de Gregoire's presence on Mount Desert triggered new French interest in the island. Soon after she came to Hull's Cove, wealthy and energetic Madame Bacler de Leval fled here from the French Revolution, bringing a large retinue of friends and servants. She bought land from Madame de Gregoire with the idea of starting a center of French culture and trade. In the French-named town of LaMoine she built a grand French-style home, "Fontaine Leval," complete even to a long driveway lined with French poplars, grown from seeds she had brought from France. Her enterprise failed, but her retinue left behind descendants with French names who have become distinguished citizens of Mount Desert. One delightful French coincidence is that on land owned in the 1790s by Madame de Gregoire and Madame de Leval, the Monteux School of Music was established in 1964 by the widow of the famed French conductor Pierre Monteux. The school is famous and flourishing today.

Another memorable French connection to Mount Desert is the famous Talleyrand, right-hand man to the Emperor Napoleon. Talleyrand came to Mount Desert with the purpose of buying land for French refugees from the Reign of Terror and the guillotine of the French Revolution. In the end he bought no land here, but his presence gave rise to the story that Talleyrand had been born on Mount Desert — a story with no truth.

Samuel Eliot Morison, a man with deep ties to Mount Desert,

gives a neat explanation for the origin of the story, which he tells in his excellent book "The Story of Mount Desert." He says the myth of Talleyrand's birth on the island started because someone who saw Talleyrand strolling about said, "That fellow looks like the little French bastard who was running around Southwest Harbor thirty years ago."

The General Court of Massachusetts gave the eastern half of Mount Desert Island to Madame de Gregoire, granddaughter of the Sieur de Cadillac. What of the western part of the island? The Court of Massachusetts, still in a generous mood, gave title to that magnificent scenery to the Bernard family. The claims by the de Gregoires and the Bernards had a certain similarity.

In September, 1762, while England still ruled the Massachusetts Bay Colony, Francis Bernard was the royal governor of the Province of Massachusetts. Bernard, who had a wife and ten children to support, cast envious eyes on the vast, empty land to the east. So the governor took a cruise down east in the official sloop Massachusetts, to take a personal look at Mount Desert. While there, Governor Bernard gave official land deeds to the settlers already in place — the Somes and Richard families, the Stanleys, Spurlings, Bunkers and Hadlocks. Then and there he decided to provide well for his own future, and issued deeds to himself for most of the western half of the island.

But there was not to be much future in America for him. The Boston Tea Party and the American Revolution put a sudden end to the dreams of Francis Bernard, the English governor, and he beat a retreat to England. There King George III rewarded him by making him a baronet; but the American revolutionaries confiscated all his lands, and his hopes for a large slice of Mount Desert went down the drain.

However, his son, John Bernard, had not flown the coop to England. The son had stayed in Bath, where he was smart enough to join the winning Revolutionary side. After the War of Independence had been won, John Bernard went before the General Court of Massachusetts and petitioned to get back his father's confiscated lands. The kindly Court gave him title to all the western half of Mount Desert Island as a reward for sticking with the Revolutionaries when his father had fled home to the King. But once John Bernard had title he turned tail. He mortgaged his land at Mount Desert to Thomas Russell of Boston, took the money, caught a boat to England where he made amends to the King and wound up with a civil service job in the West Indies.

Thus, before the 1780s were out, one half of Mount Desert belonged to the son of an English baronet; and the other half belonged to the granddaughter of that French adventurer who called himself Seigneur des Monts Deserts. From one or the other of these, all land titles on the island derived.

The first true white settler on Mount Desert has left his name on one of the loveliest villages here — Somesville, at the head of Somes Sound.

Abraham Somes sailed up Somes Sound in the summer of 1761. He came not as an explorer or as a colonist, but as a man from Gloucester looking to cut a boatload of barrel staves. He also had two ideas in his head which may have leaned him toward settling.

First, he had sailed this way earlier, in 1755; and on that trip had bought Greenings Island from an Indian for a gallon of rum. His shipmate, Ebenezer Sutton, had made an even better deal; he got a deed to the island written on birch bark for only two quarts.

His second idea had more substance to it. Somes had been promised plenty of free land by Governor Bernard if he and his new companion, James Richardson, would leave Gloucester and start a settlement on Mount Desert. They set sail. When Somes and Richardson reached the head of the Sound, both men liked the spot so well that they called it Somesville, and brought up their families the following spring.

James Richardson was the son of an early version of "Lady Chatterley's Lover." His father had been head gardener on the estate of a Scottish nobleman. He and the nobleman's daughter, Lady Jane Montgomery, enjoyed a love affair, got secretly married and eloped to America. James Richardson, pioneer settler of Mount Desert, was their son.

Slowly others followed the Somes and Richardsons. A chart drawn in 1772 by Samuel Holland shows six homes at Bar Harbor and Hull's Cove, four at Somesville, two at Southwest

Harbor, four more on the Cranberry Isles, and one on Bartlett's Island. The population grew a little each year.

There were enough men to hold the first town meeting on March 30, 1776, at the home of Stephen Richardson. There it was agreed all settlers would join forces and build a road, and further agreed that no one would take any hay off the island to sell elsewhere, as all of it was now needed to feed local cattle.

Foreign visitors still came and reported favorably. In 1792 a Frenchman, Bancel de Confoulens, made a trip to Mount Desert to buy land for other French emigrants.

"I saw very well-kept houses," he wrote, "and settlers honest, affable and generous, living as well as people in Boston and Philadelphia. They cultivate enough land to provide themselves with potatoes, corn, barley and vegetables, but spend most of their time cutting wood into shooks and barrel staves which they sell at a good profit. Each family has a small boat from which they catch cod and cure it and exchange it with the merchants for flour, sugar, soap, molasses, oil and rum . . . On the day of my arrival there were five ships in Frenchmans Bay, one of which sailed for London, one for Santo Domingo, and three for Boston."

Four years later, in 1796, Alexander Baring of London took a rather fancy cruise to Mount Desert on a vessel belonging to the Binghams. Women, children and servants were aboard. Baring was here representing the London bank of his name which had lent money to Senator William Bingham to buy land here and elsewhere. To cement the two families, in love as well as money, Alexander Baring married the senator's daughter, and his younger brother married the senator's younger daughter. Baring, who had earlier visited New York and Pennsylvania frontiers, reported that "the settlers in Eastern Maine are vastly superior in character to the pioneers in western New York and Pennsylvania."

By 1837 so many settlers were prospering here that Capt. Joseph Smith, U.S.N., reported to the Secretary of the

Treasury stating that "there were 600 ships in Mount Desert Harbor." By 1860 all the best farmland was under cultivation. By 1870 all the first growth timber had been cut for ships and homes or sent away as barrel staves in cash trades.

A bridge to the mainland, built in 1836, speeded the influx. A group of enterprising islanders formed the Mount Desert Bridge Corporation, which built, owned and operated the bridge from 1836 right up to 1917, when the county took it over.

Thomas Cole, painter, can be credited or blamed for starting the transformation of Mount Desert into a famous summer resort. Cole came across the bridge on September 4, 1844, just eight years after it had been built, bringing his brushes, his paints, his canvases, and his romantic eye with him. Cole was the founder and centerpiece of those romantic landscape artists known as the Hudson River School. He led them all in his passion for the picturesque and the sentimental, and he exploited the fashionable urge of the wealthy to spend summers enjoying the "Good Simple Life of Nature." Having painted every view possible of the Hudson, Cole now began to paint Mount Desert.

With his declamatory oils and his purple prose, he sold the wealthy, not only his paintings, but also his admiration for the joys of Mount Desert's simple life. He did for Mount Desert what artists and writers soon after him would do for the Isles of Shoals (as told in an early chapter), and what artists would do in the 1920s for Monhegan Island.

Cole popularized Mount Desert. His paintings persuaded Charles Tracy, a wealthy New York lawyer, to bring his large family here for a vacation. One of the Tracy girls grew up to become Mrs. J. Pierpont Morgan, and soon the great banker was here with his great steam yacht Corsair.

"The Rustication Rush" was on in full flood. On an August day in 1855 Charles Tracy estimated he could see 200 yachts under sail from Sargent Mountain. President Chester A. Arthur sailed in with the North Atlantic Squadron of the U.S. Navy; but the Russians had beaten him to it. In 1878 the auxiliary cruiser, Cimbria of the Imperial Russian Navy, spent six long and reproductive months at Southwest Harbor. She had 700 sailors on board. Most nights 100 of them had shore leave. It is said today there is considerable Russian blood on the island.

By 1887 there were 17 hotels in Bar Harbor, four of them run by the four Higgins brothers, and seven of those hotels could each accommodate 500 guests; there were five more hotels at Northeast Harbor, six at Southwest Harbor, three at Somesville and two at Seal Harbor.

The Rockefellers, the Stotesburys, the Vanderbilts, the millionaires, the Episcopalian bishops and the college presidents (notably Charles W. Eliot of Harvard) came to Mount Desert in droves. Some built cottages with bedrooms for 40 servants. The Atwater Kents built a cottage with a garage for 15 cars. During Prohibition Mrs. Stotesbury had 600 guests in for her dances where they drank $6000 worth of bootleg liquor of an evening.

Early in the 20th century these millionaire "rusticators" so wanted to preserve the feeling of being simple country folk that they banned all automobiles from the island. Long after cars were common on the mainland Mount Desert was still horse-drawn. In 1913 a patient died because a horse-drawn doctor could not reach him in time, and the great automobile war was over. Cars by the thousands came to Mount Desert. So did the visitors. The influx was hugely accelerated by boats and overnight sleeper trains from Boston and New York to Hancock Point. Three times daily Maine Central ferries carried train passengers from the Hancock Terminal to Mount Desert. Tourists who were less than millionaires now swarmed to Mount Desert.

The wealthy summer colony feared they would soon lose their rusticating haven. To protect "their island" from developers they took up collections among themselves to buy thousands of acres. When they had 15,000 acres they did not know quite what to do with it. The federal government finally agreed to accept all 15,000 acres in 1916, and Acadia National Park was born — the first National Park east of the Mississippi.

Today the Park has expanded to 30,000 acres, with about half of that total on Isle au Haut and Schoodic Point. The beautiful land has been beautifully protected. Walks, bridle trails, mountain climbs, swimming holes, camping areas have been handsomely installed, but now the Park faces the danger of over-use, with visitors and campers topping three million a year. Engineers have built a splendid road with many wonderful lookout points to the very top of Cadillac Mountain. The view across the Maine Coast for 50 miles east and west and out across all the islands of Penobscot and Frenchmans Bay is spectacular beyond description.

The French adventurer Laumet who named the mountain after the little French town near where he was born would be astounded at the crowds atop the mountain which carries his name but which he never climbed.

The Great Fire of October 1947 was the death blow to the great estates. So great was the glamor of Bar Harbor as American's haven for the very rich that the fire made headlines around the world. In Paris the story took a new twist. The newspaper "Le Figaro" reported the peasants of Mount Desert had staged an uprising and put the torch to the feudal castles of the rich.

The Great Fire

On the 30th anniversary of the fire I went back to Bar Harbor to talk with people who had lived through it. Their words and their memories of that ghastly catastrophe tell the story more vividly than any re-hash. Therefore, let me extract from the newspaper piece I wrote for the Maine Sunday Telegram of October 23, 1977.

They ranged from George Abbott, who had been police chief, at the center of the action; to Charlotte Stuart, who handled the town switchboard; Albion Emery who ran a pumper; Inez Henckler, who gave birth to a son; Cora Harris, a hystologist at the Jackson Laboratory, who still winced at the recalled smell of 90,000 suffocated mice; Fred Salisbury, who saw the great Satterlee estate which he supervised mostly burned to the ground; Jimmy Cough who as a 14-year-old schoolboy filled oil tank trucks with water.

They can smell the great fire still. They blink their eyes, and say they can still see, and will never forget, the fire blazing down the hills and leaping a thousand feet at a jump to come ever closer to their homes, their town and their bodies.

The great fire peaked in its devastation and terror on October 23, 1947. It began October 17 and was declared officially out November 14. It burned 17,188 acres on Mount Desert Island; destroyed 237 homes. More than 2,000 women and children were evacuated by truck convoys; and 400 more were taken off by small boats, while gale force winds between 50 and 70 miles an hour fanned the furnace on shore.

George C. Abbott was chief of police then, age 43. Thirty years later at 73, he was still a vast, out-size man with crew-cut hair and a presence that in full uniform could strike fear into any thief.

Abbott and his wife live in a spacious and handsome senior citizens housing project.

"Funny thing," he says, brown eyes laughing, "this apartment of ours is smack on the site where the Belmont and Malvern hotels burned to the ground that night. All 500 rooms. Flame came down the mountain and both huge wooden hotels took fire, and blazed together back to back. Now, on their land stands this senior citizens' housing.

"I had a force of eight full-time police and thirty reserves. For 11 days and nights they were on duty . . . We got great help from 250 National Guard, and wardens from Sea and Shore Fisheries and the Hancock County Sheriff's Department and State Police.

"There was never any looting. Every hotel burned to the ground. Scores of houses of millionaires burned, with contents to match their purses. Almost 240 houses afire. And not one case of looting. It's a wonderful tribute to the people . . . But one reason may be that I had the Governor ban the sale of all hard liquor, beer and ale anywhere on the island."

Mrs. Abbott chimes in. "I was with the 2,500 women and children being evacuated that terrible Thursday afternoon and night. We were packed first on the athletic field. Hauled there by Army trucks. Then the gale of wind shifted. They moved us all down to the Municipal Pier, because for a while it seemed the only escape would be by water."

The official Fire Department report states: "Soon after three o'clock in the afternoon the wind began to veer from southwest to west and with increasing velocity swung into the northwest . . . the Coast Guard clocked the wind between 63 and 70 miles an hour at 4 p.m. that afternoon."

No matter the velocity, it's a wind anyone on Mount Desert Island that day will never forget. It is remarkable that many people were not burned to death; for the fire, stirred to an inferno by the gales, descended on the outskirts of the town of Bar Harbor, jumping hundreds of yards at a time, sweeping all before it. One fireman reported he looked up, and it looked as though two gigantic doors had opened and towering columns of roaring flames shot down on his position.

Mrs. Abbott, huddled with her smallest son and the thousands waiting to be evacuated says, "From 5:30 until 7:30 that evening we saw a wall of flame coming at us. Cottages and hotels on Eden Street and West Street blazed and exploded. The gale fanned the furnace. Behind us on the pier the gale whipped up waves like mountains around the lobster boats trying to take people off."

Police Chief Abbott remembers that tense, packed crowd of women and children. "Their men were off, fighting the fire. Some had been gone for days. Women and kids stood and some saw their houses burning . . . I had Father Edward Fitzpatrick with me, the only clergyman left in town. He did wonders with the women and children, comforting and calming them. We got 'em loaded onto 150 trucks."

Bulldozers cleared burning rubble on the roads so convoys could escape through the fires. They took the evacuees to City Hall in Ellsworth, where families sought out each other, and the Red Cross volunteers provided food and shelter.

Amazingly, there were only three deaths. Helen Cormier, 15, was killed in a traffic accident in the evacuation. One man who had been fighting the fire hard took a breather on the wharf and died of a heart attack. An elderly man, about to be evacuated by truck, held his cat in his arms. The terrified cat jumped out and ran away; and the man ran after his pet into the danger area and was burned to death. About 400 women and children went off by boats.

Cora Harris and Lester Bunker were working at the famous Jackson Laboratory. "Most of the men were out fighting the fire. The women workers were in the lab feeding the animals. We left about 3:30 p.m., Thursday, October 23, not knowing the fire was changing direction and would soon be headed this way. By the time we reached home, the fire whistles were blowing seven frantic blasts. That meant evacuation. Dr.

Katharine Hummel and I were picked up by the National Guard, put in trucks and evacuated to Ellsworth. I couldn't get a pass to get back on the island till Monday. Nobody could move past all the road blocks without special passes. When I saw our labs, I wept . . . And the smell; I can never forget that awful smell . . . About 90,000 of our mice died. Suffocation. It looked as if all the scientific work was lost. I wept. But Dr. Little, the director, swore "We'll begin again right now."

Inside 10 days Dr. Little had received responses from architects to his request for new plans. "And telegrams poured in from other labs around the world offering to help us get rebuilt." Jackson Lab is famous for genetic research.

Cora Harris, who specializes in making hystology slides, looks around the new lab buildings.

"I began work here in 1942. When the fire came in 1947, there were 30 of us. And 90,000 mice. We saved 400 mice. And all the people. Now we have 450 people working here and 700,000 genetic mice. So we rose."

Cora Harris and Luther Bunker smile at one benefit from the fire. "Our lab had been plagued by Harvard bedbugs, which came with mice sent from Cambridge. Since the fire — no bedbugs."

Charlotte Stuart works in a Bar Harbor gift shop, "But on that night of October 22-23, 1947, I was one of two telephone operators on duty. At three that afternoon my sister and her husband, Hugh Kelley, lost their dairy, the first in-town business to burn.

"I called home to reach my eight-year-old daughter. She'd guided some people to safety, and taken herself and them to my mother's camp. I didn't see or hear from my child till late the next day . . . I got a call they needed me at the telephone exchange and went to work. It was a hot, humid day. I wore a silk dress and sandals, as though it were August instead of October. Then up came that awful gale — cold and strong and by night I was wearing winter boots."

The old telephone exchange was in the upper floors of a Main street building. "We had a manual board. Lines kept burning out all over the island. But all night long we kept one circuit open to Southwest Harbor. And Southwest had one circuit to Ellsworth. We kept that one communication line to the mainland open all night.

"Lillian Ingalls worked all night with me. No electricity. We worked by candles. My home didn't burn, but I saw all the houses across the street burning. I remember one weird call from the milk man who worked for my brother-in-law's dairy.

" 'Should I deliver the milk I've got?' he asked. I told him he might as well. He did, on Friday morning.

Inez Henckler gave birth to a son in the Bar Harbor Hospital while the great fire still burned.

"Most patients had been evacuated," she said. "It was pretty dark and only candles when we got there. We came in from Southwest Harbor. My time came suddenly. National Guardsmen and police stopped us all along the road, but helped when they knew our emergency. I remember the unbelievable, eerie sight of the sky and the burned buildings and rubble. I saw fires out my window. And the smell. I'll never forget that smell. But Dr. Weymouth and the nurses delivered Don okay."

Other fire-babies include a pair of twins — Paul and Peter Hodgkins of Lamoine, born October 22. Paul is the golf pro at Rockland Country Club. Peter works for the telephone company. And Carl 'Whitey' Griffin, another baby born in the fire, is a cook at Tripp's Restaurant across the street.

Fred Salisbury was superintendent at the big waterfront estate of Herbert Satterlee at Great Head.

"The fire burned our own home, and six others on the estate to the ground. My wife had just put up 400 quarts of preserves. She lost 'em all. And we'd fresh painted the house, and just hung $80 worth of new curtains. It all went. We lost six other estate houses and all furnishings. I evacuated my family to Lamoine. Saw flame 1,000 feet up, over our heads as we drove. The Army wouldn't let me back. The city manager of Ellsworth would not give me a pass to get back. Finally a county agent got me one. Took four days for me to get back to the estate. The fire was underground then. No flame to see. But before your eyes big trees would fall over — burned from underground. Kept burning until mid-November."

Fire Chief Sleeper's own report, written with Capt. John

Heath, makes stirring reading on this 30th anniversary of the terrible fire they fought.

"The catastrophic spread and intensity of the conflagration is indicated by the fire's sudden enormous expansion from approximately 1,900 acres at 4 p.m. to 16,000 acres by midnight on October 23 . . . Right here it must be stated that the courage of the Bar Harbor people cannot be excelled anywhere in the world. When it became apparent that for 2,500 of them the best means of escape would be by water, they were transferred to the Pier. With the bay whipped into mountainous waves by the gale wind, with their town being apparently obliterated at their back, with no certainty that any of them would get out alive, they calmly waited rescue without any sign of panic . . ." he wrote.

"The morning of October 24 dawned beautifully clear and quiet, as though nature was seeking to make up for the terrible things she had done to us the night before," wrote Sleeper. He ended his official report with these words: "Of the thousands of people who either fought the fire or escaped from it, all of them have interesting, and in most cases, thrilling stories. One thing they all cannot but be impressed with, and that is with the utter helplessness mere man can possess when confronted by the full fury of nature on the loose. It is an experience they will never forget."

In Bar Harbor they are remembering still.

20.

Heritage:
Safeguarding The Islands

This book has been a celebration of the Maine islands and the Maine island people and this island heritage beyond price which is given to us. Now we need to ask: What of their future? Will these staunch and beautiful islands be spoiled or safeguarded? What, if anything, should be done to protect them? And protect them from what?

The Maine coast is endowed with close to 3,000 islands. They range in size from rocks only big enough for a basking seal to granite ledges with room for a lighthouse, and on to islands of thousands of acres and hundreds of inhabitants. But no matter their size every one is important to some living human, bird, animal or plant. These are the outposts of America from which our nation really began.

As such, they are a national heritage of history, beauty, struggle and courage in which the whole nation has a stake. The islands are also a very special preserve — a kind of wilderness in the sea — of the natural world of sea birds, sea life, plants, trees and animals whose territorial rights to these islands deserves respect.

A new awareness of the special qualities of Maine islands has, thank heaven, become widespread and urgent in the past 20 years or so. The State of Maine, which long ignored or despised these islands, is now developing a plan to safeguard almost 1,300 of them which belong to it. The Maine Coast Heritage Trust, a private, nonprofit organization begun in 1970, is performing enormously valuable service to island landowners in helping them to safeguard the future of the islands they love so well. In its first ten years, this organization has helped protect under law the future of 76 entire islands and portions of 66 other islands. The Maine chapter of The Nature Conservancy, in its 25-year history, has played a leading role in safeguarding the future of 68 other islands. The good work done by these organizations is possible only because of the eagerness of island owners to insure and safeguard the future of their loved land.

Yet there is a tension, an inevitable conflict, which only goodwill and common sense can resolve, between the desires to protect the islands and the desires of ever more people to get to them and enjoy them. There is something inherently wrong, even absurd, about a battery of "No Trespassing" "Keep Out" and "Private Property" signs along the shore of a Maine island. But they are going up on more islands every year. Infuriating as such signs are to a boatsman seeking to stretch his legs or swim from an island beach, there is, unhappily, good reason for some hostility by island owners. Too many islands are grossly abused. It is sickening for an island owner to see rubbish left by picnickers; annoying to have his peace destroyed by a noisy flotilla of invading boats; and it is downright terrifying to think careless strangers may have begun a fire on a tinderbox, defenseless island. Many island homes have been vandalized and robbed. Some islands have recently been used as drop-points in million-dollar drug smuggling. Islands, which are the fragile habitats of seabirds, have been so disturbed that the birds no longer nest upon them; rare lady slippers and wild orchids which once filled an island meadow in glory have been rooted out by thoughtless and uninvited visitors. Such are the penalties to islands caused by easy access by modern boats.

Yet these islands cannot and should not become over-protected, private preserves, wrapped, so to speak, in cotton-wool. Precious and fragile as island ecology may be, the islands are also tough.

These islands were born as mountains a million years ago, created in the tortured explosions of a boiling earth. They were transformed from mountains to islands after the last Ice Age, some 10,000 years ago, after the meltdown and movement of ice sheets a mile thick and weighing many million tons an acre gouged out the land and the sea poured in. These islands were once home to races of people who have vanished without a trace. But the islands survived.

These islands have survived Indians who summered on them centuries before Christ; they endured English and European fishing crews 400 years ago, and the first settlers in a New World who clawed a toehold on their shores: they have survived wars and revolutions, fires and a million violent storms. Thousands of nesting cormorants and herons and gulls have destroyed trees and vegetation on some islands. Lumbering operations have stripped others of trees; and they have recovered. Sheep have gnawed the grasses to extinction on other islands. Granite by the millions of tons has been blasted out of island guts. But the islands have survived.

None of these perils, however, matched today's perils: popularity and easy access. Islands which once were hard to come to are now in easy reach to tens of thousands. For centuries most mainland people despised or ignored the Maine islands. Now the islands are magical meccas. Islands which not long ago were the unwanted stepchildren of Maine are today's prize possessions. Islands which 20 years ago were used only by lobstermen for storing traps are today sold for hundreds of thousands of dollars.

Let the record tell the story.

No sooner had Maine separated from Massachusetts on March 15, 1820, than both states moved to rid themselves of the islands they owned but did not want. The Massachusetts government, by Resolves of Jan. 30 and June 13, 1823, instructed George Coffin and the state treasurer to sell all islands inside Maine which still belonged to Massachusetts. They got rid of 68 islands.

Then Maine acted. The newly independent legislature ordered James Irish, the first state land agent, "to sell all the islands and parts of islands belonging to the state in such manner as to him may seem fit." But he found few takers. After 10 years, by 1830, only 21 islands had been conveyed from state ownership to private hands. In the next 46 years, between 1830 and 1876, only 20 more state-owned islands cou' ' find buyers; and so the state made another try to be rid the pesky islands. On Feb. 11, 1876, the governor of M;

signed a new law by which "The Land Agent is hereby authorized and required to sell all islands on the coast belonging to the state at public auction."

Incredible bargains in islands were offered by land agent Edwin C. Burleigh at the public auctions held in Rockland in November and December, 1876. He sold 66 islands, mostly in Penobscot Bay, at prices from 25 cents to $450. The record shows 34 islands sold for five dollars or less; ten islands sold for between five and fifty dollars; and only four islands fetched over $50.

Bargains like that will never be seen again; yet they merit a place in this book on the islands. Here is a sample from the record of that memorable auction:

ISLANDS	Estimated Acres	Where Situated	Amount
Barred islands	10.00	Northwest of Beach Island	9.50
Barred "	3.00	Southwest of Little Deer Island	3.00
Barred "	4.00	West of Deer Isle	13.50
Bill's island	2.00	South of Deer Isle	4.00
Black "	9.00	West of Mt. Desert Island	10.00
B "	3.00	North of Mt. Desert Island	7.50
Burnt "	2.00	Southwest of Calf Island	2.50
Block "	2.00	Southwest of Calf Island	2.50
Burnt "	3.50	East of Stave Island	5.00
Compass "	10.00	Southwest of Little Spruce Head	13.50
Conary "	90.00	In Eggamoggin Reach	85.00
Crow islands	7.00	East of Little Deer Isle	16.00
Crow island	7.00	East of Swan's Island	16.00
Crow "	3.00	West of Grindstone Neck	1.90
John's "	2.00	In Deer Isle Thoroughfare	3.50
Lassell's "	148.00	In Penobscot Bay	440.00
Lazygut islands	10.00	East of Deer Isle	21.00
Little Mark island	1.00	In Deer Isle Thoroughfare	1.50
Lime "	1.00	North of Kimball's Island	1.05
Mouse "	6.00	East of Lassell's Island	4.00
Mahoney "	5.00	South of Naskeag Point	14.00
Matinic Green island	10.00	South of Matinic Island	35.00
No Man's Land "	2.00	Northeast of McGlathery's Island	2.50
No Man's Land "	15.00	Northeast of Matinicus Island	31.00
Ned's "	5.00	South of Grindstone Neck	5.25
Outer Bar "	6.00	In Indian Harbor	3.75
Potato "	2.00	In Deer Isle Thoroughfare	7.50
Peggy's "	2.00	In Deer Isle Thoroughfare	1.00
Robinson's Rock	2.00	In Penobscot Bay	3.00
Ram island	1.00	Northwest of Merchant's Island	1.00

The state sold 66 islands, and realized the sum of $1,109.15 from the entire sale.

But the unhappy land agent still had unwanted islands on his hands. The next year, 1877, he was ordered to hold still another auction. He managed to sell seven islands off Washington County and realized a total of $251 for all seven.

Then suddenly the island market changed. Four years later, summer people were demanding to buy islands, and pestering the land agent. His report for 1882 complains: "There are numerous applications now on file in the Land Office for islands on our coast, and as the land agent has no personal knowledge of their value and since their value does not appear to warrant the expense of a personal inspection, no action has been taken."

Seven years later, swamped with unanswered inquiries, the land agent registered yet another complaint. His report of 1889 contains this snide comment on island lovers: "The repeated calls for information about titles to islands is somewhat perplexing. Inquirers evidently think there is somewhere a schedule of all the islands on the coast and that they can easily learn whether the State has title or not." There was no such list. An attempt was made to compile one in 1892. "I have prepared a new list of all islands that have been conveyed by the state," wrote the land agent. "The general opinion is that islands not on this list are the property of the State, although there are many instances of pretended owners basing claims on the statement that their families have claimed them for many years." (Those words were prophetic; the same problem was to plague the state again in the 1970s.)

In 1913, the state legislature got another attack of "island-itis," and passed yet another island law. But this one was a total and complete reversal of all previous policy, which for 90 years had been to get rid of the pesky islands. The law of 1913 suddenly proclaimed that "Title to all islands not held in private ownership shall remain in the State of Maine and shall be reserved for public use."

The brave words produced a fine "Report on Island Land Titles," by Melvin H. Simmons, the best bureaucratic and most readable document ever written on this topic. But the law did very little more; the state took no significant action to show it really gave a hoot about the islands it owned or the public enjoyment of them. Nor did most of the Maine population. A few close-in islands in Casco Bay were crowded with resort hotels and cottages; some, like Isle au Haut and Monhegan had a small, intensely loyal summer colony. But on most islands, the resident population was decreasing. Each new generation moved in greater numbers to the mainland for jobs, the conveniences, the good life and a better chance at marriage or wealth. All through the 1930s, 1940s and 1950s, islands were for sale dirt cheap. A few dozen wise, lucky and sometimes famous and wealthy families bought island paradises for the price of a car today. When the federal government, which had taken islands by eminent domain to make them into military posts, offered to return these islands as gifts to the state, town or city, they had no takers — even though many of these islands now had paved roads, water and power supplies and fine brick homes, all built at taxpayers' expense.

In the 1960s change began and by the 1970s, islands were in high demand fetching premium prices, mostly from out-of-state buyers. A little island which sold for $3,500 in 1950 would fetch $35,000 by 1960 and upward of $200,000 by 1981.

Seeing prices rise like rockets, the state once again began to wonder which of the precious islands belonged to it. In 1972, the State Planning Office researched the titles of ownership to islands in Penobscot Bay, as a test sample. They found quite a lot of title claims had little or no basis in law, which was a surprise to the state and a shock to some presumed owners. As a result, a new state law of 1973 required owners of islands with fewer than four residential buildings on them to file claims of ownership with the local registrar of deeds by Dec. 21, 1974.

The first result was chaos. So a year later the Coastal Island Registry was established within the Department of Conservation, and the law was amended and clarified.

The result is that today, really for the first time in history, Maine state government has an authenticated list of all the islands and who owns them and pays taxes on them.

The Coastal Island Registry shows that some 1,700 islands are privately owned, and that 1,299 unregistered islands and ledges belong to the State of Maine.

No sudden bonanza of island real estate was dropped into the State's lap. The biggest of the unregistered, or state-owned, islands proved to be a 12-acre island, and the smallest a rock large enough for one man to stand upon without his dog. But the knowledge that the state owned 1,299 islands forced Maine to develop and publish an official, written plan of how the state hopes to use and to protect the islands and ledges which belong to it.

These islands are a mixed bag. The state owns 820 bare ledge islands, which average only one-third of an acre. Certainly they are small, and bare, but many of the 820 are valuable seabird habitats. Several of Maine's largest cormorant rookeries are on bare ledge islands. The perky black guillemots, which are a favored prey of gulls, find safety on these bare ledges, build nests and raise young in their rocky crevices. The ledges offer safe sanctuary also to the rare razor-billed auk.

Next most numerous state-owned islands are 72 saltmarsh islands, mostly in estuaries and tidal river channels. They too are small, averaging two-thirds of an acre. But they are important producers of vegetation needed by wildlife and vegetation which reduces toxic chemical oxygen in estuary waters. Beaver, otter, muskrat, ducks, herons and teal feed or nest on these saltmarsh islands.

Those spits and gravelly bars which often emerge only at low water are called "islands of unconsolidated marine sediment." The State of Maine owns 51 of these. No vegetation grows on them, though they sometimes make good spots for clamming. However these gravel spits and bars are favorite nesting spots for common terns, arctic terns and roseate terns.

Another category of state-owned islands includes the small islands, averaging just over an acre, called "shrub vegetation" islands. The state owns 214 of these. Often in generations past, island farmers would graze sheep on them. The incessant gnawing by those sharp-toothed sheep, prisoners on a little islet, came close to killing all tree and grass growth. Now these islands are recovering and may soon again produce shrubs and trees. Goldenrod, raspberries, wild strawberries, primroses, wild asters, blueberries and even gooseberries are already profuse on many of them. These islands are preferred nesting places for herring and black back gulls and eider ducks. Where tall grasses grow, laughing gulls often nest, filling the islet with their strange cries. On the "shrub vegetation" islands which were not used to graze sheep, enough peaty soil is still left so that Leach's storm petrels and Atlantic

puffins burrow down to nest and raise their young below
ground.

Finally, among the state-owned islands, are 142 islands with
trees and good soil, which average close to two acres, and
these are the most attractive to human use. The biggest and
best are Harbor Island, 11 acres, off Isle au Haut; Crow Island,
10 acres, in Eastern Penobscot Bay; and Hay Island, 9 acres,
at Vinalhaven. These forested islands are favorites of the
great blue herons, snowy egrets and glossy ibises, all of whom
are at the northern end of their breeding range.

Maine is now developing a straightforward, sensible plan for
the future protection and management of these 1,299 widely
different types of state-owned islands. The state plans to give
stewardship of most to the most appropriate and qualified
agency. For example, the Bureau of Parks and Recreation may
take over the care and management of those islands most suitable for human recreation. Some inshore islands may be given
to the stewardship of a nearby town on the mainland to use
for the benefit of its citizens. The islands further off shore
may become a series of modest state parks for cruising boats.
The Department of Marine Resources may be given authority
over those scores of ledges and estuary islands critical to the
well-being of marine life; the federal Wildlife Bureau may be
offered those remote ledges which are precious breeding and
nesting grounds for migrant seabirds; and certain other islands may be put under the guardianship of organizations such
as The Nature Conservancy or the Maine Audubon Society or
the Maine Coast Heritage Trust. The rest will remain the responsibility of the state's Bureau of Public Lands.

In 1981, this plan is mostly a paper proposal. Whether it
will work depends on the ability of one state agency to persuade other agencies to take on responsibility for islands in
their field of expertise. If those agencies are short of money
or people, they may duck. If this happens, then the future of
these 1,299 state-owned islands could be grim. There is no
existing office in Maine state government capable of safeguarding and managing 1,299 islands. Because there is no "island
lobby" with political clout in Augusta, the whole program could
fall through the cracks, and the state will again ignore its islands, as it has done for most of its 160 years.

What of the other 1,500 or so islands and ledges which are privately owned? How may they fare in the future? Two forces on the side of the angels are at work. One is private money. The other is the growing ecology movement. Fortunately the two often go hand-in-hand, at least on many privately-owned Maine islands. From this happy combination, the Maine Coast Heritage Trust and the Maine Chapter of The Nature Conservancy and the Maine Audubon Society draw most of their stature and effectiveness.

These organizations have become quiet but competent experts in such legal matters as "easements" and tax write-offs. Each has easy entree to rich island owners. For example, Thomas D. Cabot, of Boston, and David Rockefeller, of New York City, were largely instrumental in starting the Maine Coast Heritage Trust. Together, they own more island property in Maine than they care to admit publicly. They have safeguarded and protected the future of their islands by full use of easements and write-offs; they are therefore in good positions to influence other wealthy, concerned island owners to protect their loved land in similar fashion — and at the same time get a tax advantage. The Maine Chapter of The Nature Conservancy and the Maine Audubon Society have sponsors similar in clout and wealth to the Cabots and the Rockefellers.

In layman's language, the easements and restrictions recommended by these organizations are enough to prevent any future undesirable commercial development of island property, even generations hence. Land with such restrictions on it may often earn a lower tax assessment, or a lower inheritance tax, than land without restrictions. Frequently these organizations arrange for a third non-profit or governmental agency to take either title or responsibility for enforcing the restrictions.

In 11 years, since it was founded in 1970, the Maine Coast Heritage Trust has helped landowners arrange over 190 conservation easements for over 90 islands or parts of islands from Biddeford to Jonesport, and for headlands, beaches and saltmarshes on the mainland coast. More than 15,000 acres so far have been thus protected.

The Maine chapter of The Nature Conservancy, since it was founded by Rachel Carson and seven others in 1956, has been successful in safeguarding the future of more than 60 Maine islands.

Encouraging as these accomplishments are, the fact remains that over 1,000 privately-owned islands have no formal safeguards for their future, except perhaps money. Good-sized islands which might have a potential for truly commercial development now have values of $400,000 to a million dollars. Most families which own such islands are already very wealthy, and have spent scores of summers on them, with their parents or their children and grandchildren. They are inclined to fight tooth and nail to prevent any gross change in their beloved island. They, of course, are the future "clients" which the Maine Coast Heritage Trust, the Nature Conservancy and other similar organizations are seeking.

Important major islands, such as Monhegan, Isle au Haut and Swan's Island, have safeguarded themselves through island ordinances. Others have fought hard and successfully when radical change threatened. One such instance told in the early chapter on the Isles of Shoals, merits recapping here.

In 1973, Olympic Oil Refineries, largely owned by the late Aristotle Onassis, announced plans to build an offshore docking station between the Isles of Shoals and the mainland. Supertankers would unload crude oil near the Isles of Shoals into underwater pipelines to supply a 400,000 barrel-a-day appetite of a new refinery to be built on the mainland. Quickly a dozen organizations formed to fight the proposal. It died a swift death at the Durham town meeting three months later, when local people voted 1,254 to 144 against the required rezoning.

When King Resources proposed a supertanker oil terminal at Long Island in Casco Bay, the organized protests from Casco Bay islanders roused all Maine. The terminal was not built.

When the Pittston Company launched its proposal to bring supertankers into Eastport, coastal opposition was extremely vigorous; now, almost a decade later, no tanker has come and no refinery has been built.

Yet, a new threat is imminent: exploration for underwater oil and gas off the New England coast. Dangers to the islands may come from the ocean bottom as well as from helicopters, hotels, hydrofoils and ferries.

But the greatest danger to the islands is one which no laws, ordinances or organizations can prevent.

This is the erosion of island families, year-round island residents, and the very special sense of values, caution, kindness, mutual support, courage ad confidence that island living breeds in them.

There is a rare and wonderful inner strength, inner kindness and inner serenity found only among men and women who have lived close to the bone of man and nature on the islands of Maine.

On most islands out of commuter range, the year-rounders are dwindling down to a precious few. Maine and the nation — indeed, the world — will lose an irreplaceable breed when they all are gone. The islands need to flower with something stronger and closer to the sea and the soil than even the best of summer people.

Perhaps some future swing in human values or economics will again make it feasible for a new wave of resilient men and women to live and love, to farm and fish, to raise children and bury their dead on some of the lovely but only half-used islands of Maine.

BIBLIOGRAPHY

I have used and enjoyed many books in the preparation of this book on Islands of Maine. Below are some I suggest to anyone interested in further reading.

Chapter 1. The Beginning: Ice Age to Indians

Discovering Maine's Archaeological Heritage by David Sanger, (Maine Historic Preservation Commission). Discovery of North America by Cummings, Skelton and Gurnu (American Heritage, 1971). Antiquities of the Indians of the Kennebec Valley (Maine Historic Preservation Commission and Maine State Museum, 1980).

Chapter 2. The Treasure Hunters and Explorers

The European Discovery of America, The Northern Voyages A.D. 500 — 1600 by Samuel Eliot Morison (Oxford University Press, 1971). Ramusio's "Divers Voyages", (Hakluyt's Translation, 1582). Verrazano's Letter to the King, 1582. The Viking Explorers by Frederick J. Pohl (Thomas Y. Crowell, 1966). Atlantic Crossings before Columbus by Fred Y. Pohl (W. W. Norton). Voyages of the Northmen to America, editor Edmund F. Slafter (Prince Society, Boston 1877). David Ingram's Accounts (from Magazine of American History, March, 1883). Sailor's Narratives of Voyages Along the New England Coast, 1524-1624 by George Parker Winship (Houghton Mifflin Co., 1905). Leif Erickssen by E. Grey (Oxford University Press). Hakluyt's principal Navigations, Voyages & Discoveries, c 1587. The Voyages of Giovanni de Verrazzano: by Lawrence C. Wroth (Yale University Press, 1970).

Chapter 3. Fish: The Silver Mines of Maine

James Rosier's "True Relation of Capt. George Weymouth's Voyage" (London, George Bishop, 1605). Captain John Smith, "The Description of New England", (London H. Lownes, 1616). "Beginnings of Colonial Maine", by Henry S. Burrage, (Portland, 1914). Tallman Lecture Series, Bowdoin College, 1976, by Spencer Appollonio. New England Canaan by Thomas Morton, (London, 1632). Voyages of Samuel de Champlain (1604-1618).

Chapter 4. Men and Boats

Thomas Prince's Chronological History of New England, 1736, (Massachusetts Historical Society). History of the State of Maine, by William D. Williamson - 2 volumes, 1832 (Glazier, Masters Co. of Hallowell, reprinted by Cumberland Press, Freeport). Samuel Purchas' Pilgrimmage. The Maritime History of New England by Samuel Eliot Morison (Houghton Mifflin, 1921). Whimzies, or a New Cast of Characters, by Richard Braithwaite, (London, 1631). Elizabethan Ships, by Gregory Robinson (London, Longman's 1956). Frobisher's Second Voyage, (London, 1577). The Maritime History of Maine by William Hutchinson

Rowe (W. W. Norton, 1948). Colonial Vessels by William A. Baker (Barre Publishing Co. 1962).

Chapter 5. Sir Ferdinando Gorges

A Brief Relation of the Discovery and Plantation of New England, by Sir Ferdinando Gorges, (London, 1622; reprinted by Prince Society, Boston, 1890). Captain Smith's Description of New England. Gorges of Plymouth Fort by Richard A. Preston (University of Toronto, 1953). Sir Ferdinando Gorges by Henry Morrill Fuller (Newcomen Society, 1952). The Real Founders of New England by Charles Knowles, Boston, (F. W. Faxon Co., 1929).

Chapter 6. Popham, 1607

Memorial Volume of the Popham Celebration by Edward Ballard (Bailey & Noyes, 1863). Popham Colony by Edward E. Bourne (B. Thurston, 1864). Popham Colony by James Davies (University Press, 1880). The Sagadahoc Colony by Henry O. Thayer (Research Reprints, 1980). Historie of Travaille into Virginia Britannia by William Strachey (London, Hakluyt Society, 1849). Beginnings of Colonial Maine by Henry S. Burrage (Marks Printing, 1914).

Chapter 7. Isles of Shoals

A Stern and Lovely Place by Susan Foxon (University of New Hampshire, 1977). Among the Isles of Shoals by Celia Thaxter (Houghton, Mifflin, 1897). Isles of Shoals in Lore and Legend by Lyman V. Rutledge (Star Island Corporation, 1971). Ninety Years at the Isles of Shoals by Oscar Laighton (Star Island Corporation, 1971). The Story of the Isles of Shoals by Louis C. Cornish (Beacon Press, 1936). Murder at Smuttynose and Other Murders by Edmund Pearson (Doubleday, Page, 1926). Brief History of the Isles of Shoals by Rev. E. Victor Bigelow. Isle of Shoals by Peter E. Randall (KJ Printing, Augusta, Maine, 1981).

Chapters 8 & 9. Casco Bay Islands

The Calendered Isles: A Romance of Casco Bay by Harrison Jewell Holt (1910). The Isles of Casco Bay in Fact and Fiction by Herbert G. Jones (1946). Casco Bay Yarns, William Haynes (1916). Buried Treasure of Casco Bay by Ben F. Kennedy (Vantage Press, 1913). The Romance of Casco Bay by Edward R. Snow (Dodd, Mead, 1975). Chronicles of Casco Bay by Daniel C. Colesworthy (Sanborn and Carter, 1850).

Chapters 10 & 11. Lighthouses and Keepers

Lighthouses of the Maine Coast by Robert Thayer Sterling (Stephen Daye Press, 1935). Lighthouses of Casco Bay by Peter Down Bachelder (Breakwater Press, 1976). The Lighthouses of New England. 1716-1973 by Edward Rowe Snow (Dodd-Mead, 1973).

Chapter 12. Damariscove Island

Collection of 34 Articles by Rev. O. Thayer, 1914-15, (Maine State Library).

Chapter 13. Monhegan

Monhegan, The Cradle of New England by Ida Sedgewick Proper (Southworth Press, 1930). The Fortunate Island of Monhegan by Charles Francis Jenney 1922. (Vol. 31 American Antiquarian Society). Monhegan Island by W. W. Ellsworth (Hartford, 1912). History of Monhegan by Herbert M. Sylvester (Stanhope Press, 1904).

Chapter 14. The Fox Islands-North Haven and Vinalhaven

History of Vinal Haven by Albra Josephine Vinal (Ellsworth, 1898). The Geology of the Fox Islands by George Otis Smith (1896). Days of Uncle Dave's Fish House by Ivan E. Calderwood (Rockland, Maine Courier-Gazette, 1969). Vinalhaven by the Centennial Committee (Press of the Star Job Print, 1900). Fish Scales and Stone Chips by Sidney L. Winslow (Machigonne Press, 1952).

Chapter 15. Granite

Tombstones and Paving Blocks by Roger L. Grindle (Courier-Gazette, 1977). The Granites of Maine by Thomas N. Dale, (Government Printing Office, 1907). History of the Granite Industry by A. W. Brayley (National Granite Industry Association, 1913).

Chapter 16. Isle au Haut

Sailing Days on the Penobscot by George Wesson (Marine Research Society, 1932. Here on the Island by Charles Pratt (Harper & Row, 1974).

Chapter 17. Lobstering

The Lobster at Home in Maine Waters by W. H. Bishop (Scribner's Magazine, 1881). Fish and Men in the Maine Islands by W. H. Bishop (Reprinted from Scribner's Magazine by L. Berliawsky, Camden, Maine). Fisheries Industries of the U. S. Edited by George B. Goode (U. S. Government Printing Office, 1887).

Chapter 18. Swan's Island

History of Swan's Island by H. W. Small (Ellsworth, 1897). Swan's Island by Perry D. Westbrook (T. Yoseloff, 1958).

Chapter 19. Mount Desert

The Story of Mt. Desert Island by Samuel Eliot Morison (Little, Brown 1960). The Story of Bar Harbor by Richard W. Hale Jr. (Ives, Washburn, 1949). Mount Desert, A History, by George A. Street (Houghton, Mifflin, 1926). Pioneers of France in New England by Francis Parkman (Little, Brown, 1865). The Jesuit Relations, edited by Charles H. Levermore (New England Society of Brooklyn, 1912).

Chapter 20. Heritage: Safeguarding the Islands

Island Land titles by M. H. Simmons, Maine Forest Commissioner, Biennial Report 1914, Maine Legislature. Unregistered Islands by Maine State Bureau of Land Resources, 1976. Newsletters and Annual Reports of the Maine Chapter of the Nature Conservancy. Reports and newsletters of Maine Coast Heritage Trust.

General Reading and Reference

Maine Islands by Dorothy Simpson (Lippincott, 1960). Islands of Maine by John B. Moore (Oxford University Press, 1933). Seacoast Maine by Martin Dibner (Doubleday, 1973). Ranging the Maine Coast by Alfred Loomis (W. W. Norton & Co. 1939). Along the Maine Coast by Dorothy Mitchell (McGraw-Hill, 1947). The Maine Coast by the Maine Development Commission 1944. The Coast of Maine by Louise D. Rich (Crowell, 1962). Enjoying Maine by Bill Caldwell (Gannett, 1977). Maine Magic by Bill Caldwell (Gannett 1979).

INDEX